IS THE COLD WAR OVER?

A New Look At Communist Imperialism

by

Dr. Anthony Trawick Bouscaren
Professor of Political Science
Le Moyne College

THE CAPITOL HILL PRESS

IS THE COLD WAR OVER?

A New Look at Communist Imperialism

Copyright © 1973 by Anthony T. Bouscaren

Library of Congress Catalog Card Number: 73-85062

ISBN: 0-88221-005-X

First Printing October 1973

Printed in the United States of America

The Capitol Hill Press
———a division of———

Prospect House, Inc.
7777 Leesburg Pike
Falls Church, VA 22043

IS THE
COLD WAR
OVER?

Other books by Dr. Bouscaren:

Soviet Expansion and the West, 1950
Imperial Communism, 1953
America Faces World Communism, 1954
A Guide to Anti-Communist Action, 1958
Security Aspects of Immigration Work, 1959
Soviet Foreign Policy: A Pattern of Persistence, 1962
La Politica exterior sovietica, 1963
International Migrations Since 1945, 1963
A Textbook on Communism, 1965
The Last of the Mandarins: Diem of Vietnam, 1965
The Case for Free China, 1967
Tshombe, 1967
Left of Liberal, 1969, 1972
European Economic Community Migrations, 1969

Contributions to:

Background to European Governments, 1951
The Great Pretense, 1956
Modern Ideologies, 1961
Education for Survival, 1961
Outside Looking In: Critiques of American Institutions, 1971

TABLE OF CONTENTS

INTRODUCTION

The 1970's, we are told, will finally usher in the era of negotiation. We will sit down and talk with the newly "matured" Communist powers, and compromise our differences. This new alignment in the world is proclaimed with all the breathlessness of a new-found, unique revelation. But those with a knowledge of history may perhaps be forgiven an uneasy stirring of *deja-vu*. Haven't we heard this somewhere before?

In the 1920's some Kremlinologists told us that the Bolsheviks had reformed and were only interested in "socialism in one country." They argued that the Soviets had abandoned the idea of exporting Communism abroad. In the '30's certain sages informed us that the Stalin purge trials were justified, and that the 1936 Constitution was democratic. They claimed that Communists the world over were good allies to have in the anti-Fascist crusade. The Hitler-Stalin Pact pulled the rug out from under such prophets, but many returned during the period 1941–1945 to talk about "our gallant Soviet ally" which supposedly had no claims on eastern and central Europe.

When President Roosevelt returned from Yalta in 1945, few top American officials doubted the peaceful intentions of the Kremlin. "We really believed in our hearts that this was the dawn of the new day," wrote Harry Hopkins. "We were absolutely certain that we had won the first great victory of peace."

In 1947 Henry Wallace broke with the Truman Administration because he believed that Washington was about to stop being kind to Moscow, and the next year he and an army of "intellectuals" launched the great Progressive Crusade to save the world from American imperialism.

The Moscow-inspired invasion of South Korea brought most Americans back to reality, but the end of the war led to a return to wishful thinking. A well-known newspaperman, C. L. Sulzberger, wrote a book that was typical of the times, *The Big Thaw*. Its thesis was that the Soviet iceberg was mellowing, and that "there was a certain finality" to Communist rule in eastern and central Europe. Unfortunately the book was published shortly before Hungary (1956).

Then we were assured there were no Soviet missiles in Cuba. Khrushchev was not that sort of person. But it turned out that Soviet Foreign Minister Andrei Gromyko had lied to President Kennedy, who discovered, the painful way, about Moscow policy.

I have no desire to be pessimistic about the USSR, although I tend to subscribe to the views of Andrei Amalrik who suggests in *Will the Soviet Union Survive Until 1984?* that it won't. But, I do have a very keen interest in looking at the Soviet record in a factual and realistic way, and that is the reason for this book.

Two of my earlier books about Soviet foreign policy, *Imperial Communism,* (1953), and *Soviet Foreign Policy: A Pattern of Persistence,* (1962), did not get very high marks in the *New York Times* book review section, because the reviewers believed that I was too severe with Moscow. They suggested that things were changing both within the USSR and in reference to its relations with the world—for the better.

American public opinion about the Soviet Union has almost invariably erred on the side of exaggerated hopes, followed inevitably by feelings of equally unwarranted depression. The history of American-Soviet relations is full of Spirits which had to be laid to rest: the Spirit of Geneva and the Spirit of Camp David, the Spirit of Paris and the Spirit of Vienna. Looking back on more than a quarter of a century of American-Soviet relations, the great riddle is not what Soviet policy is, but rather why American policy-makers seem to have such difficulty in understanding it. It simply is not true that we know very little about the Soviet Union. On the contrary, a solid body of knowledge has been amassed over the years.

President Nixon and the Soviet leaders have now vowed that, in the nuclear age, there can be no alternative to peaceful coexistence. But difficulties appear when you consider the different meanings which Nixon and the Soviets attach to the same phrase. To America, peaceful coexistence means that the world situation will remain *"grosso modo,"* as it is now, for an unlimited number of years. But the Soviet interpretation is that peaceful coexistence does not preclude a decisive shift in the global balance in favor of the Soviet Union. Nor does it exclude so-called wars of national liberation, or the containment of

China or the squeezing of the United States out of Europe, the Middle East, and other parts of the world. In fact, confidence in such a global shift underlies official Soviet writings and policy statements. Soviet leaders believe that with America in the process of "decommitment," history is moving in their direction.

Some observers in the West argue that Soviet ideological pronouncements which talk about the impending demise of the Western political system are not to be taken seriously. This familiar argument insists that with growing embourgeoisement, Soviet foreign policy will be less and less affected by ideological impulses. The talk of world domination may remain, whether from force of habit or as window-dressing, for the old-line party faithful. But the new-fangled pragmatists in the Kremlin have begun to accept the fact that there are limits to the realization of their political ambitions.

Unfortunately (1) there is no symmetry between West and East, that is, American decommitment is proceeding much faster than any supposed Soviet ideological cooling, and (2) American neo-isolationism may give fresh impetus to the activists in Moscow who want to make use of opportunities which offer themselves as the result of American retreat.

The neo-isolationist school of thought maintains that it is not Soviet policies but rather American "imperialism" that has been responsible for most of the conflict over the last quarter of the century. On the extreme wing of this school is the New Left historian Gabriel Kolko's thesis which claims that since America has to import columbium, beryllium, titanium and certain other rare metals (crucial components in heavy industry), it is bound to pursue an imperialist policy. It is an interesting theory and it has great possibilities. For by the same token it can be argued that Sweden and Switzerland are even more imperialistic. There is no industrial nation in the world which has all the necessary raw materials as natural resources; all modern economies have to import at least some of them from distant parts.

In the field of history, the neo-isolationists have rewritten the history of the Cold War not in the light of any new facts or perspectives but against the background of American domestic politics: Because President Johnson was forced to escalate the Vietnam war in the 1960's, it had to be shown that President Truman, too, had been wrong to pursue anti-communist policies in the 1940's. Such rewriting of history for political reasons is not uncommon in the annals of historiography; it usually generates a great deal of heat but little, if any, light.

Some neo-isolationists have gone even further back in their research. Richard Barnet has persuaded himself that the war against Hitler, too, was unjust and ineffective for no nation "can enforce virtue, moderation or justice in another country." Making war on Germany, says Barnet, did not save the Jews: "Indeed the mass exterminations did not begin until the war was on." Again an interesting argument, albeit not an original one; the neo-Nazi school of history in Germany has made precisely the same claim for many years. However, the Allies made war on Hitler not to "enforce virtue" on Germany, but because Hitler began to export his own "New Order." As for the Jews, there is every reason to believe that Hitler would have exterminated European Jewry anyway, even if his invasions had been unopposed. If, on the other hand, Britain, France and the other Western powers had decided to stop Hitler in 1935 and 1936, six million Jews and millions of others as well might have been saved. But this, of course, was impossible during those years, because appeasement and isolationism had even more influential spokesmen than they have today.

The interested student may benefit from Robert Maddox's new book, *The New Left and the Origins of the Cold War,* which takes revisionist historians to task for outright fraud and misrepresentation. Maddox is thoroughly scholarly and restrained in his approach, which makes his carefully documented indictment all the more convincing.

The moderate wing of present day neo-isolationism does not go that far in its arguments. While it regards a *Pax Americana* as a calamity, it believes that a *Pax Sovietica* would be a disaster. However, such a danger is considered quite unreal, for as Senator William Fulbright says, "Russia can now properly be regarded as a conservative power in international relations." To prove this point, the advocates of this thesis try to show that the Soviet leadership faces grave internal difficulties, that liberalization is taking place in Eastern Europe, and that the Soviet Union cannot possibly want to extend its sphere of influence any further because this would be against its own best interests. Ronald Steel, one of the most eloquent spokesmen of this school, wrote several years ago that a Communist Poland does not offer much more military safety for the Soviet Union than a neutral Poland. Unfortunately he has not succeeded so far in convincing the Soviet leaders. Steel also wrote in 1967 that the Soviet bloc had ceased to exist and that the Communist party of Czechoslovakia was equal in authority to the Communist party of the Soviet Union. It is a matter of regret that Mr. Steel's predictions were not born out by subsequent events.

If it were true that Soviet intentions are merely to receive "official" sanction for existing borders in Eastern Europe, to expand trade, and to pave the way to balanced force reductions, there would be little cause for concern in the West. But the Soviets may want more: to become the dominant power in Europe. Russia, in contrast to China, has pursued an expansive policy for the last 200 years, and it is too early to say with any certainty that a radical change of heart has taken place of late. I am not referring necessarily to military invasion, but domination by the threat of force, political pressure and diplomacy. Conditions now seem to favor such ambitions since American domestic pressure for a reduction of U.S. forces in Europe is likely to grow.

It is often said that the conflict between the Soviet Union and the United States is mainly one of "different philosophical approaches," but this is an unsatisfactory definition of the real state of affairs. The conflict is not a matter of disputations on the merits of dialectical materialism vs. peaceful economic competition. The two super-powers are not debating philosophers; they remind one of two duelists who find to their consternation that they have let themselves in for a contest with shotguns at three-yards distance and so have now formally decided to adopt something akin to the Queensbury rules. But it is still an open-end struggle in which one or the other may be knocked out. In this struggle, one that may go on for many years, America will be at a disadvantage. As Henry Kissinger wrote in *Nuclear Weapons and Foreign Policy* (1957), "this contest has many of the attributes of a competition between a professional and an amateur, in which even a mediocre professional will usually defeat an excellent amateur." This is not because the amateur lacks intelligence or ability, but for him, in contrast to the professional, foreign policy is a series of problems to be worked out until one has achieved a theoretically "elegant" solution. To the professional it is a matter of life and death.

Adherence to Communist ideology also gives the Soviets an apparent strategic advantage. Ideology gives them a ready-made long-range plan, in which each provocation has its place in the final goal, which is supposed to be inevitable. The American policy-makers, even if they have an over-all concept, cannot react with matching speed and force, because unlike the Soviet leaders, they face serious domestic constraints. The fact that American leaders cannot enact their every decision with brutal swiftness is one of the fundamental distinctions between a totalitarian and a free society. Nonetheless, it causes short-term disadvantages, which must be compensated by superior knowledge and imaginative strategy which is consistent with the preservation of freedom.

The Soviet record, together with those of other Communist states, does not inspire confidence in their peaceful intentions. No matter how much we want peace there will be no peace if the other side persists in conflict. There will be no permanent peace in Indo-China just because we pull out and sign a document.

It is time to get a historical perspective about the Communist World, and especially the USSR, which is its most important representative. We cannot treat each Communist challenge in isolation, for these challenges tend to follow a pattern, even if one is Soviet, one is Russian, one is Vietnamese, or another is Cuban. Communism claims to transcend national boundaries, and to a degree the claim is justified. The problem that exists is not a national problem—not Russia, China or any other country—but rather Communism, especially the 13 million adherents who rule the USSR, and who retain the loyalty of most Communists except the Chinese.

The emphasis of this book then is on realism. The essentials of the Soviet and Communist record since 1917 are presented in a factual way, so that we may better understand what we are up against and accurately answer the question, Is the Cold War Over?

ANTHONY TRAWICK BOUSCAREN
Fayetteville, New York
February 20, 1973

Nearly twenty years after Stalin's death, the political philosophy of the Soviet Union remains virtually unchanged .... ideology is just as important in Moscow today as it was in 1934, when I first stepped on Russian soil.

For the United States, the ideological element of Soviet policy is of vital importance. It means that there can be no harmonious relations with Moscow .... the leaders in the Kremlin still regard every government of a non-Communist state as in a transition phase on the way to achieving Soviet status.

Charles E. Bohlen,
Witness of History

Chapter 1

IDEOLOGY AND PROTRACTED CONFLICT

The Bolsheviks have come a long way since those dark days, only half a century ago, when all they possessed was a rented room in Zurich. Today, Communists control one-third of the world's population and one-fourth of its land area. There are 50 million Communists in the world: 20 million in China, 14 million in the U.S.S.R., 10 million in the eastern European states, and most of the remainder in Yugoslavia, Cuba, Italy, and France.

But while there are 50 million Communists, as yet, "Communism" does not exist. All they have now is what they call "socialism," an admittedly imperfect society. The chief obstacle to the successful transition from the imperfect society of socialism to the perfect society of Communism is the United States. Khrushchev said that peaceful coexistence in the world depended on whether or not the United States resisted. The U. S. must be buried if the Communists were to achieve Communism. What are the prospects for reaching this goal, and what success have the Communists had so far?

The strength and influence of the international Communist movement cannot be accurately measured by noting the number of Communists in a given country, or even by the total vote cast for a Communist party—which in countries like France and Italy is about five times the number of Communist party members. One has to analyze the importance of a given country in the Soviet scheme of things, the extent of Soviet-bloc support, and most importantly, the number of prominent non-Communists and non-Communist organizations which support the Communist line in that country.

Some idea of Communist successes in recent years can be gleaned from a comparison of the international situation in 1938 and the situation today. In 1938, Stalin described the international situation as one of capitalist encirclement of the socialist camp. But in 1956, at the 20th Congress of the Communist Party of the Soviet Union, Khrushchev described the situation as socialist encirclement of the capitalist camp. What did Khrushchev mean? One only has to look at the map of 1938 and the maps of 1956 and today to understand what has happened. The socialist camp has been steadily expanding while the Free World has been steadily shrinking. When World War III was started with the Communist uprising in Greece in December, 1944, Communists controlled 170 million persons and 8 million square miles of territory. Today Communists control 1,168,350,000 persons and 14 million square miles of territory. What is the key to this success?

In 1959 a team of scholars at the Foreign Policy Research Institute of the University of Pennsylvania assembled a book called *Protracted Conflict* which remains one of the most important contributions to a clear-eyed view of global Communist policy. This book analyzes the Communist doctrine of *"protracted conflict"* which is being waged against us today. The Chinese Communist leader Mao Tse-tung, in one famous passage, distills the essence of this doctrine into 17 words:

> The enemy advances, we retreat; enemy halts, we harass; enemy tires, we attack; enemy retreats, we pursue.

An important factor in Mao's writings is his conviction that both time and wisdom are on the side of the Communists, and that, inescapably, the forces of the Free World, lacking a conceptual framework of the conflict, will succumb to the enveloping tide of revolutionary Communism.

The Communist strategy of protracted conflict seeks to avoid a general, direct, decisive encounter with the enemy unless and until overwhelming physical superiority sufficient to ensure the enemy's complete destruction—and this alone—has been acquired. To avoid this encounter, the fullest possible reliance must be placed on indirect, irregular, unconventional strategies. The indirect approach is the standard strategy for military forces as well as revolutionary movements confronted by a more powerful enemy. As long as the Free World possesses superiority, a premature frontal military encounter must be avoided, even at the cost of temporary setbacks.

The advantage possessed by the Communists is derived from their broader strategic vision—their ability to view the conflict in all of its dimensions. It is derived also from an intimate knowledge of the enemy: his disposition of forces, strategic doctrine, and last, but not least, his psychological makeup.

The problem confronting the Communists is how to extend their sway without provoking the West into direct and formidable retaliatory action. The strategy of the indirect approach relies on proxies for the accomplishment of certain missions. It permits the Communists to execute their strategy of protracted conflict, leaving the Soviet Union free to disown the legal responsibility for their actions. It also enables the Western nations to back away from a firm position without appearing to capitulate to Communist initiatives.

Success in pursuit of the protracted conflict strategy is predicated upon keeping the enemy in a defensive and reactive frame of mind and thus preventing him from seizing the initiative. This is primarily a matter of psychological conditioning. The Communists seek to exploit the enemy's ideological preconceptions, and harden those assumptions (whether consciously held or not), which inhibit his ability to counter their challenges. A prize example is the Communist conception of a bipolar world, divided into the "war zone" and the "peace zone." Communism defines the rules and the area of the protracted conflict; the West is made to accept them. Through a process of conditioning, the Western powers can be induced to respect the boundaries of the "peace zone" (which is the Communist World), while implicitly taking it for granted that the battle will be waged solely in the area not yet dominated by Communist power, i.e., the "war zone."

Since World War III began three decades ago, the Communists have marked out the non-Communist territory as the "war zone" and have succeeded in confining the war to this part of the world. Much of the Free World has unconsciously accepted the Communist rule of international conduct; under its dispensation the West must tolerate Communist forays into the non-Communist "war zone" and abstain from launching counterthrusts into the Communist "peace zone." The Communists, in short, have been allowed to define the territorial limits of the protracted conflict.

Thus the Communists are likely to win World War III because they know they are in it. That the United States is not conscious of having been involved in a mortal struggle these past three decades, does not make the appalling defeats thus far any less real. On the contrary, the measure of success of Communist protracted-conflict principles is that the Communists have gained control of regions heretofore firmly held by the Western powers without provoking a counterattack by the Free World.

The Communists, ever since they embarked upon their march to power, have operated from an inferior position in terms of raw power. At the outset, they could not begin to match the military and economic power of their opponents. They were inferior in many respects—but not in their determination to win a power monopoly, nor in their skill in exploiting the irresolution of those whom they proposed to conquer.

The Communists are striving to overawe the people of the West with their supposed strategic capabilities. They are attempting to paralyze the decision-makers of the Western nations. To this purpose, they will increasingly exploit a variety of communications channels to produce conditioned guilt complexes, schizoid attitudes toward the Communist threat, and an excessively defensive mentality and diverse social neuroses among Western elites. Meanwhile, they will continue to mask the serious internal weakness of the Soviet Empire while working steadily to divide the West and drain it of its strength.

During the Greek War, 1947–1949, the Communists succeeded in restricting hostilities to the "war zone," that is to say, to the Free World side of the boundary running between Greece, on the one side, and Albania, Yugoslavia, and Bulgaria, on the other. Similarly, during the Korean war, the Chinese Communists, by their own admission would never have invaded Korea had they not been all but certain that the United States would respect their privileged sanctuary across the Yalu River into southeast

Manchuria. During the Indochina conflict the Allied forces never sent troops into North Vietnam, and most of Laos and Cambodia were long privileged sanctuaries for the Communist Vietminh. And ever since the 1962 Kennedy-Khrushchev Agreement on Cuba, that country has served as a privileged sanctuary for Communism.

So it has been in every battle of World War III. The Communist enemy can cross the 50-yard line into our side, but we cannot cross into his territory. In diplomacy, we have been mouse-trapped into accepting agendas favorable to the Communist side. Thus, the 1960 Paris Summit Conference had on the agenda, not the situation in East Berlin and East Germany where free elections have yet to be held, but rather the status of West Berlin. Most remarkable about Communist expansionism is that it has taken place against the wishes of the peoples involved, and most of it occurred during that period when the United States possessed a monopoly of nuclear weapons.

One reason for this success has been the consistency of Communist policy. It remains today essentially what it was before the first concession was made. The Communists, then, are motivated primarily by ideology, not by ordinarily accepted understandings of national interest. Once the ideological essence of Communist foreign policies is recognized and firmly grasped, one can easily understand that no amount of flexibility, Summitry, East-West trade, cultural exchange or mutual understanding is going to dissuade Leonid Brezhnev or Mao Tse-tung from carrying out their programs.

The beginning of wisdom in studying Communism, the Soviet Union, and the international Communist movement is to recognize their ideological essence. Communism is pre-eminently a disease of the mind. That is why it has made so many inroads among the so-called intellectual elements of society; it appeals to their anti-religious and anti-capitalistic prejudices, and plays upon their frustrations and inner hatreds. Perhaps Communism also fills two divergent psychic needs—providing a "scientific" explanation of historical development for the mind and a cause to which one can attach oneself for the emotions.

For months prior to Khrushchev's first visit to this country in late 1959, a growing chorus of Summit fans, pacifists, flexibility advocates, corn growers, autograph collectors, and a host of politically confused men and women had been demanding a

Summit confrontation. Advocates of the meeting said that Khrushchev might have a modification or change of heart occasioned by the things he would see and the people he would speak to in this country. Only a few realists demurred. On the eve of Khrushchev's arrival in Washington, Henry Kissinger made the following trenchant observations about U. S.-Soviet relations in the *New York Times Magazine* (Sept. 6, 1959):

> The cold war is not the result of a misunderstanding between our leaders and those of the Soviet Union. It is the product of a conscious Soviet policy which includes the suppression of freedom in Europe, the Soviet refusal to accept schemes for the control of arms, Communist pressure on all peripheral areas of which Laos is only the most recent example, the unprovoked threat in Berlin. If Mr. Khrushchev compares his position now with what it was last November when he first threatened Berlin, he may well conclude that bellicosity has its rewards. . . .

The slogan which the leftists forever repeat is "Let's talk to the Russians." But as Salvador Madariaga points out in his book, *The Blowing Up of the Parthenon*, we are not in a position to talk to the Russians at all, we can only talk to the communist bosses, which is quite a different affair. The slogan, "Let's talk to the Russians," is therefore meant to cash in on all the diffuse, sentimental sympathy for Old Mother Russia and the Volga Boatmen and the Russian ballet and our Russian comrades in arms who defended Stalingrad. But the persons with whom we are dealing are actually not the Russians, Ukrainians, Georgians, or others, but the tiny minority who hold these people in an immense concentration camp called the Soviet Empire.

Soviet intentions have been openly proclaimed from Lenin's day to the present time and were again clearly spelled out in the resolutions of the 20th Party Congress in 1956.* Recently the Moscow magazine, *Kommunist,* referred to the implacable struggle leading to the inevitable end of capitalism and the total triumph of Communism. At the end of 1960, representatives of 81 Communist parties met in Moscow and they issued a procla-

---

*See Khrushchev's *Mein Kampf,* edited by Harrison Salisbury, Belmont Books, 1961.

mation which reads in part: "Our time is a time of struggle . . . a time of socialistic revolution . . . a time of transition of more peoples to the socialistic position, of the triumph of Socialism and Communism on a worldwide scale."

In his famous speech of January, 1961, Khrushchev called for "national liberation wars" against the Western powers. And addressing the 23rd Party Congress, March, 1966, Brezhnev declared:

> It goes without saying that there can be no peaceful coexistence where matters concern internal processes of the class and national liberation struggle in the capitalist countries or in colonies. Peaceful coexistence is not applicable to the relations between oppressors and oppressed.

The widespread belief that the Soviet Union has become increasingly less revolutionary might be less prevalent if more people took the trouble to make a continuing-in-depth study of Soviet publications and pronouncements. With the exception of occasional statements by Brezhnev and Kosygin, articles and speeches by Soviet leaders, military and political, are almost uniformly ignored by the Western press. This is a great pity, because a careful scrutiny of the Soviet press is essential to a clear understanding of their theories, their policies, and their tactical and strategic objectives.

If the Gallup organization were to poll several hundred university graduates, the chances are that it would not find one who had ever read an article by Boris Ponomarev, and that no more than a handful would even be able to identify him. But Ponomarev is one of the most powerful men in the world Communist movement. He was a member of the Comintern's Executive Committee from 1926 to 1943. He has been in charge of Communist Parties in all non-Communist countries since 1955. And he is Chairman of the Foreign Affairs Commission of the Soviet of Nationalities. Given his importance in the Communist hierarchy, it is clear that when Ponomarev writes a major article for *Kommunist* (which is the house organ of the Central Committee of the Soviet Communist Party), what he has to say must be taken seriously by anyone who would understand Communist intentions.

Ponomarev's article (*Kommunist,* Oct. 21, 1971) makes it clear that the Communists still seek world-wide revolution and that they feel the present world situation is developing rapidly in their favor. ". . . the Communists," says Ponomarev, "always remain the party of the socialist revolution, a party which never tolerates the capitalist order and is always ready to head the struggle for the total political power of the working class and for the establishment of the dictatorship of the proletariat in one or another form."

For the guidance of the world Communist parties, he sets out the criteria by which a true combat party may be judged. These criteria include:

> "faithfulness to the [Soviet] theory of scientific communism; pursuance of a 'course toward the revolutionary liquidation of the capitalist system'; mastery of 'all forms and methods of the class struggle,' including the ability to perform fast tactical switches; an ability to convince the masses 'of the need for revolutionary changes,' and to mobilize them for specific economic and political demands; a policy leading in fact to the unification of various left currents, including workers, anti-monopolists, democratic and anti-military movements; and, last but not least, a 'systematically internationalist approach' and 'coordination of action with other revolutionary units' . . ."

Ponomarev unquestionably speaks with the authority of the Soviet leadership behind him. As if to underline this fact, he was recently elevated to the rank of candidate member of the Politburo. Congress and the American people might do well to ponder the implications of this article, written by the man who is directly in charge of Communist subversive activities throughout the Free World.

STRATEGY AND TACTICS

The basis of Soviet foreign policy is the philosophy of Marxism-Leninism. The realization of Marxist-Leninist theory is to be accomplished by the extension of "proletarian dicta-torships" throughout the globe as the necessary prerequisite to the transition from Socialism to Communism, and the "withering away" of the state. In the Communist view:

> . . . whatever the form in which the transition from capitalism to socialism is effected, that transition can come about only through revolution. However varied the forms of a new, peoples' state power in the period of Socialist construction, their essence will be the same—dictatorship of the proletariat, which represents genuine democracy . . . The revisionists . . . seek to rob Marxism-Leninism of its revolutionary spirit, to undermine the faith which the working class and all working people have in the Socialist cause, to disarm and disorganize them in their struggle against imperialism.[1]

> The Party holds that the dictatorship of the working class will cease to be necessary before the state withers away. The state as an organization embracing the entire people will survive until the complete victory of Communism.[2]

The success of the Bolshevik revolution in Russia and the establishment of Socialism in that country are but initial steps toward the world revolution and the establishment of Socialism throughout the world:

> As a result of the devoted labor of the Soviet people and the theoretical and practical activities of the Communist Party of the Soviet Union, there exists in the world a Socialist society that is a reality and a science of Socialist reconstruction that has been tested in practice. The highroad to Socialism has been paved. Many peoples are already marching along it, and it will be taken sooner or later by all peoples.[3]

> Our epoch, whose main content is the transition from Capitalism to Socialism, is an epoch of struggle between the two opposing social systems, an epoch of Socialist and national liberation revolutions, of the breakdown of imperialism and the abolition of the colonial system, an epoch of the transition

---

1. Harrison Salisbury, *Khruschev's Mein Kampf*, Program of Soviet Communist Party (New York, Belmont Books, 1961), p. 69.
2. Ibid., p. 135.
3. Salisbury, *Khruschev's Mein Kampf*, p. 44.

of more and more people to the Socialist path; of the triumph of Socialism and Communism on a world-wide scale.[4]

There can be little doubt, then, that Communist foreign policy has as its objective the extension of Socialism throughout the world in order to make possible the establishment of Communism and the withering away of the state. Communist satellite states and Communists everywhere also have the same objective. However, Marxism-Leninism teaches that the tactics to be employed to realize these objectives must be flexible; they must be changed depending on whether the revolutionary tide is ebbing or flowing:

> The strictest loyalty to the ideas of Communism must be combined with the ability to make all the necessary practical compromises, to "tack," to make agreements, zigzags, retreats and so on, in order to accelerate the coming into power . . .[5]

> Strategy deals with the main forces of the revolution and their reserves. It changes with the passing of the revolution from one stage to another, but remains essentially unchanged throughout a given stage . . . Tactics are the determination of the line of conduct of the proletariat in the comparatively short period of the flow and ebb of the movement, of the rise or decline of the revolution, the fight to carry out this line by means of replacing old forms of struggle and organization by new ones . . . by combining these forms, etc. . . . While the object of strategy is to win the war . . . tactics concern themselves with less important objects, for they aim not at winning the war as a whole, but at winning a particular engagement, or a particular battle . . . Tactics are a part of strategy, subordinate to it and serving it.[6]

Soviet foreign policy and the actions of leading Communists everywhere can be divided into identifiable tactical periods, al-

4. Ibid., p. 29.
5. Lenin, V.I., *Address to Eighth Party Congress* (Moscow, Foreign Languages Publishing House, 1919).
6. Stalin, J., *Foundations of Leninism* (Moscow, Foreign Languages Publishing House, 1924).

most all of which were either zigs or zags, advances or retreats ("two steps forward, one step back"). When the leaders of the international Communist movement have believed that there existed a flow of the revolutionary tide, they have moved forward, often with a joint military-subversive offensive. When they have thought that the tide was ebbing, they have retrenched, proclaimed their peaceful intentions, and sought to create united fronts with Socialists and "progressives" against fascism, capitalism, "war", etc.

The first of these tactical periods in the history of the international Communist movement is commonly known as "War Communism," beginning in November, 1917, and lasting until the spring of 1921. During this period Lenin and his associates began by hoping and planning for world revolution in the aftermath of the First World War, and ended by recognizing that the world was not yet ripe for Socialism, and that the security of the Soviet base of operations must be established prior to the launching of successful worldwide revolutionary activities.

The second tactical period extended from 1921 to mid-1924 and consisted of united front operations aimed at penetrating mass organizations.

The third period lasted from June, 1924, to 1928, and was characterized by "Bolshevization" of Communist parties; it took an anti-Socialist and anti-reformist line.

The fourth period was 1929–1934, during which time the international Communist movement sought to take advantage of a worldwide depression to stir up revolutionary activity.

The fifth period was 1935–1939, a classic united front period. In these years the Communists temporarily shed their revolutionary garb, and induced socialists and progressives to make common cause with them under the banner of anti-fascism.

The sixth period was 1939–1941, when Stalin joined with Hitler against the West. Soviet Forces invaded Poland, Finland, the Baltic states, and Rumania.

The seventh tactical period, 1941–1945, was thrust upon the Soviets by the German invasion. This period may be divided into two cycles: the defesive, 1941–1943, and the offensive, 1943–1945. During the defensive cycle the propaganda emphasis was on "save the U.S.S.R."; whereas during the offensive cycle there was stress on "our gallant Soviet ally," with the purpose of extracting major military and political concessions from the West in the name of "allied unity." In the offensive cycle not only did the U.S.S.R. gain control of eastern and central Europe, but it also gained dominance in Manchuria and North Korea.

The eighth period, 1945–1948, was based on a frank recognition that the United States (and to a lesser degree, Britain) was the major enemy. This was an era of Communist offensives: in Europe the Soviets sponsored hot-war operations in Greece (1947–1949), subversion in Czechoslovakia (1948), the Berlin Blockade (1948), and cold war in western Europe. In the Far East the war was hot in China, and the Communists carried out guerrilla warfare operations in southeast Asia.

The ninth period, 1948–1953, was a combination of the "peace" campaign in Europe and in the United States, and Communist invasion of Korea.

The tenth period, 1954–1962, was characterized by inducements to the West to make peace ("end the cold war") combined with threats, based on Soviet "Sputnik" diplomacy, and support of "national liberation" movements in Asia, Africa, and Latin America. It culminated with the Cuban missile crisis of 1962.

The eleventh period, 1963 to the present, has featured the Moscow-Peking split, problems with Czechoslovakia and Rumania (the former resolved by Soviet invasion), Soviet-engendered tensions in the Middle East, and continuation of "national liberation wars" in southeast Asia. Brezhnev, taking over from Khrushchev in 1964, told party leaders on November 6 of that year that the U.S.S.R. would support, by arms if necessary, "national liberation wars."

Through all these periods, as our detailed discussion will show, Communist leaders have relied on Marxist-Leninist ideology as their guideline to action. Though conditions and realities have changed, and details of interpretation have differed, the pattern of ideological motivation which emerges should be clear to objective observers.

Chapter 2

WAR COMMUNISM 1917–1921

The leaders of the Bolshevik wing of the Russian Social Democrat party (later the Communists), led by Lenin, were brought back into Russia from exile in Switzerland in the spring of 1917 with the cooperation of German authorities:

> ... Lenin and a number of his associates, in returning to Russia in the spring of 1917 through Germany, operated on the basis of some sort of agreement with the German authorities. There is even some evidence of political understanding, in the sense that hints were thrown out by the German intelligence agents that Germany would be willing, if the Bolsheviki were successful in Russia, to terminate the war. ... The Germans, anxious to see the war on the eastern front brought to an end, had every reason to subsidize the Russian faction which was most deeply committed to the achievement of an early peace...[1]

1. George Kennan, *Soviet-American Relations, 1917–1920*, Vol. 1. (Princeton, Princeton University Press, 1956), p. 455.

The Bolsheviks succeeded in overthrowing the Provisional Republican government of Alexander Kerensky in November (October of the old calendar), 1917. The November revolution, according to Josef Stalin:

> . . . has ushered in a new era, the era of proletarian revolutions in the countries of imperialism . . . of colonial revolutions which are being conducted in the oppressed countries of the world in alliance with the proletariat and under the leadership of the proletariat.[2]

"Peace" had been one of the major political slogans on which the Bolshevik faction had made its way to power. The promise to take Russia out of the war represented a political commitment of long standing on the part of the Soviet leaders, dating from the Zimmerwald Conference of European socialists in 1915. This was a basic tenet of Bolshevik policy. It was founded, of course, on the traditional left-socialist attitude of hostility toward "imperialist" wars. In addition, the Bolshevik leaders were not unmindful of the fact that only by a termination of the war effort could the army be successfully destroyed as a possible focal point of armed resistance, and the support of the peasant-soldier masses for the new regime assured.

Preliminary German-Soviet truce negotiations began on November 27, 1917, after military operations had come to an end. At the same time Lenin, and his foreign minister, Trotsky, appealed to the proletariat of the warring countries to rise up and act against their own governments.

Naturally, Britain, France, and the United States did not want Russia to leave the alliance and make a peace settlement with Germany, for this would permit the Germans to liquidate the eastern front and concentrate their efforts on a breakthrough on the western front. The Western allies hoped against a Bolshevik-German agreement; indeed some Western leaders felt the Bolshevik regime would soon be succeeded by another pro-Western government which would continue the war effort against Germany.

2. Stalin, J., *Problems of Leninism* (Moscow, Foreign Languages Publishing House, 1940), p. 198.

Meantime, the Bolsheviks were beginning to discover that they had very little bargaining power with the Germans, and that unless they accepted the German terms, they would be faced by almost certain military defeat and German occupation. Trotsky opposed accepting the Germans' terms, whereas Lenin, the realist, felt that there was no alternative acceptable to the Bolsheviks.

Lenin completely mistrusted the Western allies, and believed that although the proposed terms were unfortunate, they would give the Bolshevik regime a breathing spell. During the time the treaty gave them, revolutionary activity could be carried on in Germany and elsewhere in Europe. Actually the final German terms, coming after much Bolshevik procrastination, were not nearly as stringent as they might have been.*

The treaty of Brest-Litovsk was signed March 3, 1918, on the Soviet side by Chicherin, who had replaced the intransigent Trotsky.

The Fourth Congress of Soviets, which ratified the Brest-Litovsk Treat on March 15, 1918, also sent a message to the United States which made clear the continued Bolshevik adherence to the doctrine of world revolution, by distinguishing between the United States government and its "toiling and exploited classes":

The Congress expresses its appreciation to the American people, and in the first instance to the toiling and exploited classes of the United States of North America, for the expression by President Wilson, through the Congress of Soviets, of sympathy for the Russian people in these days when the Soviet Socialist Republic of Russia is undergoing heavy trials.

The Russian Socialist Soviet Federated Republic avails itself of this communication from President Wilson to express to all those peoples perishing and suffering under the horrors of the imperialist war its warm sympathy and its firm confidence that the happy time is not far distant when the toiling masses of all bourgeois countries will throw off the yoke of capitalism and will establish a socialist order of society, which alone is

---

*Byelorussia, the Ukraine and the Baltic areas were taken over by Germahy, but the Bolshevik regime survived and later re-took Byelorussia and the Ukraine.

capable of assuring a firm and just peace as well as the
cultural and material well being of all the toilers.[3]

Fearful of having Allied arms and equipment located in Archangel, Murmansk, Odessa, and Vladivostok fall into German
hands, the Allies sent expeditionary forces to these ports after the
Brest-Litovsk treaty was signed. It was feared that these arms,
originally destined for a Russia still at war, might be turned over
to the Germans by the Bolsheviks. Beyond this, some of these
Allied forces, for a time, played a small role in helping Russian
counter-revolutionary armies (called "White") fight the Bolsheviks. Even after the war with Germany ended in November,
1918, the Allies continued a limited policy of intervention in the
Soviet Union which included a blockade of Soviet territory as
well as the furnishing of supplies and munitions to White governments. There was still hope in some Allied circles that the
Bolshevik regime was transitory, and that it would be replaced by
a pro-Ally government.

The Bolsheviks, for their part, not only sought United States,
British, and French diplomatic recognition and support, but also,
particularly as World War I came to an end, peace treaties with
these countries which would end forever the nightmare of an
active, full-blown Western policy of aid to the White armies.
William Henry Chamberlain wrote:

> The inability of the Allies either to make war effectively on
> Soviet Russia or to come to an amicable agreement with it
> can only be understood if one takes into account the political
> and social conditions which prevailed in Europe immediately
> after the end of the War. The statesmen in Paris were sitting
> on a thin crust of solid ground, beneath which volcanic forces
> of social upheaval were seething. Two of the most pronounced
> psychological characteristics of the time were immense war-
> weariness, in the victorious as well as in the defeated coun-
> tries, and acute labor unrest. So there was one absolutely con-
> vincing reason why the Allied powers could not fulfill the
> hopes of the White Russians and intervene with large numbers
> of troops: no reliable troops were available. It was the general
> opinion of leading statesmen and soldiers alike that the at-

---

3. As quoted in Kennan, *Soviet-American Relations, 1917–1920*, p. 512.

tempt to send large numbers of soldiers to Russia would most probably end in mutiny.

> . . . But probably the decisive factor in bringing about a continuation of the policy of limited intervention was the fear, by no means unreasonable or ungrounded in 1919, that Bolshevism in one form or another might spread to other European countries. The Bolshevik leaders had made no secret of their belief in the speedy coming of an international socialist revolution, as a sequel to the World War, or their intention and desire to promote it by every means in their power . . .[4]

Certain peripheral aspects of the civil war need to be noted in passing, as they affected Soviet relations with the Western Powers and Japan. The Bolsheviks quite consistently sought to dissuade the Allies from intervening in Russia on behalf of the Whites. The Allies, on the other hand, had inaugurated a limited military intervention in the summer of 1918. The Allies at first were more concerned with fighting Germany; afterwards, they pursued vacillating policies toward the Soviets, culminating in the withdrawal of interventionist forces from Russia in 1920.

But this picture soon changed due to the actions of a small force of Czechoslovaks, former war prisoners and deserters from the Austro-Hungarian Army, and citizens of a state which still existed only in the imagination of its nationalist leaders. This Czechoslovakian force made possible the temporary overthrow of the Soviets in vast Siberia, in the Middle Volga region, and in part of the Ural regions.

The Allies, and especially the French, had tried to induce the Soviets to send the Czechs to the western front to help in the battle against the Germans. As a result of misunderstandings, and Communist revolutionary activity among the Czechs by the Bolsheviks, bad feelings developed. The Bolsheviks cared little what happened on the western front, although formally they were committed to returning the Czechs to the West. Indeed, Trotsky agreed in May, 1918, to facilitate the transportation of most of the Czechs to Archangel, whence they would be taken by ship to France. By this date a sizable number of Czechs had already

---

4. William Henry Chamberlin, *The Russian Revolution* (New York, Macmillan, 1935), p. 152.

proceeded as far as Cheliabinsk, a Ural railroad junction, on their way to Vladivostok, and ultimately to France. In Cheliabinsk a series of incidents took place after the local Soviet had arrested some Czech soldiers. Fighting broke out between the Bolsheviks and the Czechs. On May 23rd, 1918, the Moscow government instructed the Soviets to take "swift measures for the detention, disarming and dissolution of all trains and detachments of the Czechoslovak Corps."

Two days later Trotsky sent out an even sharper order which began as follows:

> All Soviets on the railroad line are instructed, under heavy responsibility, to disarm the Czechoslovaks. Every Czech who is found armed on the railroad is to be shot on the spot.[5]

Open warfare now broke out at various points on the Trans-Siberian line where Czech forces were in transit. Almost everywhere the Czechs took the measure of the Bolsheviks and gradually obtained control of the Trans-Siberian railroad.

By August, the struggle in the Far East had acquired an international character, mostly due to the Japanese interest. On August 3, Japanese and British forces landed in Vladivostok, to be followed by much smaller American and French contingents. President Wilson had finally yielded to the Allied pressure for intervention. But it was too late. At the time when intervention in behalf of the Whites might have been decisive, only the French Government, and especially the military, understood the consequences of a Bolshevik victory. The Japanese interest, dictated solely by Japanese interests in establishing a beachhead in Siberia, was too late to affect the situation, unless supported by the other Allies. Then, too, the various White factions in Siberia constantly quarreled with each other, and with the Czechs. From the autumn of 1918 the Czechs ceased to play an active part in the Russian civil war. They were disappointed by the failure of the Allies to intervene on a large scale and were increasingly disinclined to shed their blood in a Russian civil war which was becoming increasingly severe as the Red Army grew in organized strength.

5. As quoted in Chamberlin, *The Russian Revolution*, p. 7.

The Czechs had struck the Soviets a hard blow just when they were weakest and had made possible the esablishment of anti-Bolshevik rule over a huge territory. But they did not succeed in creating in the place of the Soviets the democratic regime with which most of them sympathized. The threat to Soviet interests in the Far East was finally ended in 1922 when Japanese forces evacuated Siberia:

> Japan's evacuation of Russian territory was a major Russian success, but it was also obvious that the victory was due in large part to the strong support of the United States. Skvirsky, the unofficial Far Eastern Republic's envoy to the United States, visited the State Department immediately after Japan's withdrawal and expressed his gratitude for America's aid. "The Russian people," he said, "appreciate the large part which the friendly interests of the United States have had in bringing the evacuation about.[6]

By the spring of 1920 the British had pretty well given up in the area, although the French actively continued a policy of aid to anti-Bolshevik forces not only in south Russia but also in Poland. But after fighting bravely against great odds, White Russian General Wrangel's forces, now assisted only by the French, were finally defeated in November, 1920, in the Crimea.

Prior to discussion of Soviet policy toward Poland (and to a lesser degree toward the Baltic states), some attention must be paid to Soviet attitudes and actions relating to Germany and Hungary. Germany in particular was the pivotal force in deciding whether Lenin's great dream of liquidating the World War by means of a world revolution could be realized:

> The principal link in the chain of revolution is the German link and the success of the World revolution depends more on Germany than upon any other country.[7]

The attempt to create a German revolution began with a naval

6. David Dallin, *The Rise of Russia in Asia* (New Haven, Conn., Yale University Press, 1949), p. 176.
7. Lenin, "Report of October 22, 1918," *Collected Works* (Moscow, Foreign Languages Publishing House, 1940) Vol. 23, p. 235.

mutiny in Kiel on October 30, 1918, but it was not sustained, in spite of everything that Soviet Ambassador to Germany Joffe could do in the way of financial support to the 'Spartakus Bund' (later Communists). Furthermore, the German Communists were overanxious and unwilling to make even temporary compromises with actual and potential leftist allies. Against the wishes of the Communist leaders Liebknecht and Luxembourg, extremists led the party into revolt in January, 1919, leading to suppression of the insurrection and the killing of the Communist leaders. A Soviet Republic was proclaimed in Munich on April 7 and lasted for a month's time; it failed not only because of lack of popular support, but because of internal disputes between the Communists and their anarchist and pacifist supporters.

Lenin severely criticized the German Marxists for their failure to create a united party comparable to the Bolsheviks in Russia:

> A successful proletarian revolution in Germany would immediately and very easily have shattered the shell of imperialism . . . it would have brought about the victory of world socialism for certain . . .[8]

Practically speaking, Lenin and his associates believed that the best means of actually making contact with fellow revolutionaries in Germany and western Europe was via Poland, and to a lesser degree, the Baltic states. Certain German Socialists were invited to Moscow by the Soviets, who tried to solicit their support for a Soviet invasion of Poland which would have as its ultimate objective the conquest of western Europe.

War between Poland and Russia broke out in April, 1920, after the two countries failed to reach an agreement on boundary questions. After initial successes, the Poles were driven back and a Soviet victory appeared imminent. The Bolsheviks convinced themselves that Poland was seething with revolutionary ferment and that only a little pressure from the Red Army was needed in order to make possible the emergence of a Polish Soviet Republic. This belief was strengthened by news which came from a number of countries of the refusal of working-class organizations to ship munitions to Poland.

8. Lenin, V.I., *Selected Works* (New York, International Publishers, 1943), Vol. 7, p. 365.

However, events showed that Poland possessed unsuspected reserves of resistance to Bolshevism. There was strong nationalist feeling among all classes of the people, including the workers. The peasants, who constituted the majority of the Polish population, generally followed the leadership of the priests and the middle-class intellectuals. And when the Red Army troops were actually within sight of the suburbs of Warsaw, they were profoundly discouraged to find Polish workers coming out, not with red flags to greet them but with rifles to fight them.

The Polish armies not only held at the gates of Warsaw, but soon executed a counter-offensive which drove Russian troops completely out of Poland. Peace negotiations were conducted in neutral Riga late in 1920; the Soviets wanted peace as quickly as possible, in order to be able to concentrate their forces against the last of the Whites, Baron Wrangel. So the terms of the preliminary peace treaty and armistice concluded at Riga on October 2, 1920, were quite favorable to Poland.

In March, 1919, the founding Congress of the Third International met in Moscow. Ever since 1914, Lenin had been determined to create a new organization in place of the ineffective Second International. When the Congress convened, the picture did not look bright for the revolutionaries. Bolshevik territory was cut off by fighting armies from the industrial countries of Europe; Kolchak's offensive was approaching the Volga; Luxembourg and Liebknecht were dead; revolution had been suppressed in Finland and was collapsing in Latvia; and the Hungarian Soviet Republic had not yet been proclaimed. The "delegates," with two exceptions, were either tools of Soviet Russia or European Communists who happened to be in Moscow. The two exceptions were the German Eberlein and the Austrian Steinhardt, both of whom had made their way through the lines of the civil war. Despite these difficulties the Congress decided that the new International should directly and immediately assist the cause of revolution in Central Europe. The international Socialist Conference which had been held in Berne in February, 1919, and which tried to recreate the prewar Second International was, of course, denounced and repudiated. The Communist International, or Comintern, issued a manifesto to the "Proletarians of the whole world," which praised the Soviet form of government and the dictatorship of the proletariat, stressed the need to support colonial peoples, and urged a fierce struggle against non-Communist labor movements. The new International was soon

joined by the Communist parties of central and eastern Europe
and by the Swedish left-Socialists, the Norwegian Labor party
and the Italian Socialist party.

The dream of a world, or at least of a European, revolution
was the bright image that helped to sustain the morale of the
Communists in the difficult years of 1919 and 1920. How high
their hopes rose in this connection is evident from some ut-
terances of Gregory Zinoviev, President of the Comintern:

> The movement advances at such dizzy speed that it may be
> said with confidence: Within a year we will already begin to
> forget that there we will already begin to forget that there was
> a struggle for communism in Europe, because within a year all
> Europe will be Communist.[9]

During the Russian invasion of Poland in 1920, and after the
collapse of Soviet governments in Hungary and Bavaria, the
Second Congress of the Communist International met in
Moscow, from July 21 to August 6. The meeting was filled with a
spirit of exalted revolutionary optimism. The spirit of the
Congress is reflected in the following excerpt from one of its resolutions:

> The world proletariat is on the eve of decisive battles. The
> epoch in which we live is the epoch of direct civil war. The de-
> cisive hour approaches. In almost all the countries in which
> there is a significant labor movement the working class is on
> the eve of a series of embittered struggles, weapons in hand.

The Second Congress laid down the principles of organization
for Communist parties; they were formulated in the Twenty-One
Conditions, which all Communist parties were thenceforth bound
to accept. Of these the following were the most important:

> All parties joining the Comintern must resolutely fight against
> reformism, centre tendencies and pacifism, remove from their

---

9. As quoted in Chamberlin, *The Russian Revolution,* p. 378.

membership all persons holding any such views, and break off all friendly relations with such groups.

Communists must form nuclei within their countries' trade unions in order to capture these from within. . . .

Communists must make propaganda within their countries' armed forces, when necessary by secret and illegal means.

Communists must make special efforts to win peasant support.

Communists must support the emancipation of oppressed nationalities and colonial peoples. They must develop among their own workers fraternal feelings towards the workers of colonies or of oppressed nationalities subject to their own nation. They must agitate among their own armed forces against oppression of colonial peoples.

In countries where a communist party is permitted by the laws to function legally, it must nevertheless maintain, parallel with its legal organisation, a "clandestine organisation capable at the decisive moment of fulfilling its duty towards the revolution."

In countries with a parliamentary system, communist parliamentary groups must be completely subordinated to the party's central committee, which must give them exact directives as to how to behave in parliament.

Communist parties must support unreservedly all soviet republics in their struggles with counter-revolution, urge workers to refuse to transport arms or equipment destined for the enemies of a soviet republic, and pursue propaganda by legal or illegal means among all troops sent to fight against a soviet republic.

Communist parties . . . must proceed to "periodic purges of their organisations, in order to remove interested and petty bourgeois elements."

All decisions of Congresses of Comintern were to be binding on all parties belonging to it.

Special stress was laid on the need to exploit anti-Western feeling in colonial areas. Lenin's theory was that imperialism represented the final stage of capitalist development. So he naturally turned his attention to the non-white races who were politically and economically dependent on the Western empires: "If the fortress of capitalism could not be taken by direct frontal attack, by means of workers' uprisings in the European countries, perhaps it could be reduced by a sapping process, by tearing off the colonies which supplied raw materials."

This stress on the potential revolutionary significance of the East had an interesting aftermath. In September, 1920, almost two thousand Easterners including 235 Turks, 192 Persians, 157 Armenians, 14 Hindus, 8 Chinese and representatives of most Asiatic nationalities of Soviet Russia gathered in Baku, on the Caspian Sea, for the "First Congress of Peoples of the East." Three revolutionary agitators, Zinoviev, Radek and Bela Kun, organized the Congress. Zinoviev said the following:

> . . . a new page in the history of humanity has opened; the sun of communism will shine not only on the proletarians of Europe, but on the working peasantry of the whole world.

> The real revolution will blaze up only when the 800 million people who live in Asia unite with us, when the African continent unites, when we see that hundreds of millions of people are in movement. Now we must kindle a real holy war against the British and French capitalists. . . . We must say that the hour has struck when the workers of the whole world are able to arouse tens and hundreds of millions of peasants, to create a Red Army in the East. . . .

> Long live the Red East, which, together with the workers of Europe, will create a new culture under the banner of communism.[10]

As a follow-up to the Baku Conference, Bolshevik forces which had been fighting Russian General Denikin's White (anti-Communist) army spilled over into the Persian province of Ghilan, where a form of Soviet government was established in

---

10. As quoted in Chamberlin, *The Russian Revolution*, p. 392.

mid-1920, and lasted until October, 1921. This action ran counter to Soviet protestations to Persia of their desire for peace, and Soviet renunciation of Tsarist expansionist aims in the Middle East. After Georgia was forcibly Sovietized in 1921, some Caucasian Communists proposed a march on Teheran; it required strenuous diplomatic representations on the part of the Soviet ambassador to Persia to thwart this premature action.

The Third World Congress of the Comintern convened in Moscow in mid-1921. Under Lenin's guidance, it recognized that the revolutionary wave had subsided, that a "relative stabilization" of capitalism had developed, that the Communists were a tiny minority within Western labor, and that their immediate job was not revolution but winning the masses. According to historian Franz Borkenau:

> The new line found shape in the tactics of the United Front . . . in the beginning of 1921. . . . The basic idea was simply to approach the social-democratic workers with the suggestion to fight in common for the everyday demands such as higher wages and lower taxes. The underlying assumption was that, in a period of emerging structural unemployment and of continuing economic stress, these demands were not likely to be granted, and that the struggle for them would disrupt the fetters of legal democratic action and lead the socialist workers jointly with the communists into revolution.[11]

To conclude, it can be said that the first tactical period in Soviet foreign policy (and therefore of the international Communist movement) began on a note of optimism but concluded on a note of pessimism with the meeting of the Third World Congress which ushered in a new tactical period—that of the United Front.

11. Franz Borkenau, *European Communism* (New York, Harper, 1953), p. 53.

Chapter 3

RETRENCHMENT AND REVOLUTION 1921–1934

The doctrine of the ebb and flow of the revolutionary tide was reiterated by Stalin in 1925 in order to make it clear that the "retreat" which began in 1921 was only temporary:

> The epoch of the world revolution . . . may occupy years, or even decades. In the course of this period there may occur, nay, must occur, ebbs and flows in the revolutionary tide. . . . Since the October victory we have been living in the third . . . stage of the revolution, during which our objective is the overthrow of the international bourgeoisie . . . We shall witness a succession of ebbs and flows in the revolutionary tide. For the time being the international revolutionary movement is in the declining phase; but . . . this decline will yield . . . to an upward surge which may end in the victory of the world proletariat. If, however, it should not end in victory, another decline will set it, to be followed, in its turn, by yet another revolutionary surge. Our defeatists maintain that the present ebb in the revolutionary tide marks the end of the revolution. They are mistaken now just as heretofore . . . the

revolution does not develop along a straight continuous and upwardly aspiring line but along a zigzag path . . . an ebb and flow in the tide . . .[1]

During the twenties, the revolution seemed to be in retreat in Russia, and in Europe the remnant of the revolutionary fervor soon fizzled out. The unsuccessful attempts of 1923 in Germany and Bulgaria were mere undistinguished epilogues. Thereafter the European Communist parties, and the Comintern itself, were increasingly dominated by the Russian party, and the internal dissensions in the Russian party were reflected in the main European parties.

The Third World Congress of the Comintern, meeting in Moscow in the summer of 1921 under Lenin's guidance, recognized that the revolutionary wave had subsided, that the Communists were a small minority within the ranks of Western labor, and that their immediate objective was not to make a revolution but to win the masses. The Third Congress denounced left-wing extremism and urged closer contact between the Communist parties and the masses.

Because some of his followers were very unhappy that the world revolution must await a more auspicious moment, Lenin found it necessary to declare, on several occasions, that revolutionaries must know when to retreat as well as when to attack:

> When it was necessary—according to the objective situation in Russia as well as the whole world—to advance, to attack the enemy with supreme boldness, rapidity, decisiveness, we did so attack. . . . And when, in the spring of 1921, it appeared that the advance guard of the revolution was threatened by the danger of becoming isolated from the mass of the people . . . then we resolved unanimously and firmly to retreat. . . . Proletarian revolutions will not be able to fulfill their tasks without combining the skill in . . . attack with the skill in retreating in revolutionary order.[2]

By the end of 1923 it truly appeared that hopes for revolution

1. J. Stalin, *Leninism* (New York, International Publishers, 1928), p. 220.
2. As quoted in Nathan Leites, *The Operational Code of the Politburo* (New York, McGraw-Hill, 1951), p. 82.

in Europe had been crushed. Communism in Italy had been destroyed by Mussolini, and the Communists could not prevail on Socialists in the other countries to actually join them in revolutions. Comintern-inspired uprisings in Germany and Bulgaria in 1923 failed, because the Communists found themselves alone and isolated, even though they had been invited by Socialists in Saxony and Thuringia to enter those state governments. The purpose for which the Comintern had been created had manifestly not been achieved.

On the diplomatic level, the Soviet Union and Germany signed a treaty at Rapallo, in May, 1922, which had the effect of ending the isolation of both states. In Moscow it was regarded as a foundation on which to build further, an outlook which was in fact implemented by the 1926 Berlin Treaty, and the even more famous Hitler-Stalin pact of August 23, 1939. At the same time, the Soviet Union, through the Comintern, tried to stir up waves of revolutions in Germany.

During the 1920's, Stalin and his associates were strongly opposed to the Versailles peace system and its enforcer, the League of Nations. As a supporter of revisionism and an enemy of the League, Stalin hoped not only for German withdrawal from the Western peace system, but also continued to believe that Germany was the country most likely to follow Russia's revolutionary example. As late as 1924, even with the failures of the previous year well in mind, Stalin could say:

> Of all European countries Germany is the one most pregnant with revolution; a revolutionary victory in Germany is a victory all over Europe. If the revolutionary shake-up of Europe is to begin anywhere it will begin in Germany. Only Germany can take the initiative in this respect, and a victory of revolution in Germany is a full guarantee of victory of the international revolution.[3]

At the Fifth Congress of the Comintern, held in June, 1924, a new panacea was announced for the international Communist movement. The united front strategy was abandoned, and a left-wing development set in. Communist parties were ordered

3. As quoted in David Dallin, *Russia and Postwar Europe* (New Haven, Yale University Press, 1943), p. 62.

"bolshevized," meaning that they must be organized on the model of the Communist party of the U.S.S.R., and they were instructed to take an aggressive, more revolutionary line in which they would divorce themselves from Socialist leaders, while striving to win over the Socialist rank and file to insurrectionary activity. This new "hard" line was associated with Comintern leader Zinoviev.

But the new line did not work any better than the old one. Attempts to transform the French party along Bolshevik lines fractured that party's leadership, and the German leaders rebelled against taking so many orders from Russians. The result was that Stalin revamped the Comintern, undermining Zinoviev's influence, and causing a greater dependence of foreign parties on the Comintern and the U.S.S.R.

The influence of Manuilsky (later Comintern boss) gradually replaced that of Zinoviev in the Comintern, and Stalinist puppets like Ernst Thaelmann of Germany began to take over the leadership of Communist parties outside the U.S.S.R. The only country where the more radical approach temporarily paid off was Britain. In May, 1926, Laborites and Communists launched a general strike, and an Anglo-Russian Committee was created, ostensibly to facilitate cooperation between labor movements, but actually to propagandize British labor forces and to work against "imperialist" elements in Britain.

THE SIXTH WORLD CONGRESS

In 1928 the Communist International was again called into congress. It convened at a time when the usurpation of power by Stalin (from Trotsky, Zinoviev and Bukharin) was virtually complete. The purpose of the Congress was to prepare the proletariat for the war which the Bolsheviks thought the impending economic crisis must soon generate. Its Manifesto stated that:

> . . . the capitalist states 'with England at their head' were preparing war against the Soviet Union. The Congress decided that a 'third period' had begun. The first had been the revolutionary period up to 1923, the second the period of stabilisation of capitalism since 1924. This third period was marked by growing contradictions of imperialism and by a sharpening of the class struggle.

The Congress issued three different documents: the *Program* of the Communist International, the *Resolutions* on Communist activities on colonial and dependent areas, and *The Struggle against Imperialist War and the Tasks of the Communists.*

The *Program* of the Communist International was based on the premise that imperialism "inevitably" will give rise to wars which will shake the world, and lead "inexorably" to the world proletarian revolution. It also assumed that the struggle between the bourgeoisie and proletariat was taking on an international (rather than a purely national or internal) character.

The *Program's* analysis claimed that local crisis and wars were giving way to world crises and wars. The workers and oppressed peoples were teaming up against the capitalists. This development had been enhanced by the proletariat's seizure of state power and its newly won capability of conducting the struggle on an "enormous and really world scale." "The working class of the world now has its own state—the one and only fatherland of the international proletariat." The power of world capitalism was being corroded because of conflicts between imperialist states, the rising of the masses in the colonial countries, and the action of the revolutionary proletariat in the imperialist states. The international revolution was developing under the hegemony exercised "by the leading force in the world revolutionary movement, the proletarian dictatorship in the U.S.S.R." Before the revolution could succeed, however there would have to be a long transition period, replete with general crises, proletarian civil wars, national wars, and colonial rebellions.

According to the *Program* it was historically "inevitable" that the proletariat would come to power by a variety of ways and at different speeds in various areas, depending on its degree of economic and political development. The world dictatorship of the proletariat "comes only as the final result of the revolutionary process." This *Program,* then, constitutes a restatement, within a different context, of the idea that wars are a part of the world revolution and that peace will not come to the world until the Communists have established a world dictatorship.

The *Resolutions* of the Sixth World Congress dealing with *The Struggle against Imperialist War and the Tasks of the Communists* are based on the Comintern *Program.* They outline the strategy and tactics which Communist parties in non-Communist states should adopt during war. "Just" wars are those conducted by Communists against anti-Communists. Unjust wars are those conducted by "imperialist" states against the U.S.S.R. Naturally Communist parties must support the first type of war, and oppose and sabotage the second type:

> The question is not, who is the aggressor, who is waging an unjust war, but, who represents reaction, the counter-revolution and exploitation; who is on the imperialist side, and against the national proletarian revolution?

The *Resolutions* pose a strange riddle: it is stated specifically that "the overthrow of capitalism is impossible without force, without armed uprising and proletarian wars against the bourgeoisie." But we are also told that the Communists:

> . . . in the interests of the masses of the workers and of all the toilers who bear the brunt of the sacrifice entailed by war, wage a persistent fight against imperialist war and strive to prevent imperialist war by proletarian revolution.

The overthrow of the bourgeoisie, therefore, requires war, and yet the Communists, who are committed to that overthrow, are opposing war. Actually the solution to the puzzle is not difficult to find. Dr. Stefan Possony Director of the Stanford University's Hoover Institute on War, Peace & Revolution explains it thus:

> According to the Communists, war is inevitable. War will come regardless of any pacifist propaganda which the Communists make. . . . Imperialist wars can be prevented only through the elimination of the bourgeoisie in the most important countries, but such an event is most improbable before the outbreak of hostilities.
>
> Hence the Soviets devised a strategy of eating their cake and having it too. A resolute opposition to war would provide the Communists with gradually increasing support and give them a chance to stimulate pacifist sentiments. . . . By posing as champions of peace, the Communists would derive strength

from those elements who, in the course of the war, lose their patriotic fervor and become inclined to terminate the war at whatever price. Thus, the fight against war is seen as the best cover and lever to build up a revolutionary organization. By fighting for defeat and immediate 'peace' or surrender, the Communists exploit war to create revolutionary situations and to launch revolutionary attacks.[4]

The Sixth World Congress *Program* warns against premature revolutions, and stresses the premise that there should be no action until the revolutionary situation is ripe:

When the revolutionary tide is rising, when the ruling classes are disorganized, the masses are in a state of revolutionary ferment, the intermediary strata are inclining towards the proletariat and, the masses are ready for action and for sacrifice, the Party of the proletariat is confronted with the task of leading the masses to a direct attack upon the bourgeois State. This it does by carrying on propaganda in favor of increasingly radical transitional slogans ... and by organizing mass action, upon which all branches of Party agitation and propaganda, including parliamentary activity, must be concentrated. This mass action includes: a combination of strikes and demonstrations and armed demonstration; and finally, the general strike conjointly with armed insurrection against the State power of the bourgeoisie. The latter form of struggle, which is the supreme form, must be conducted according to the rules of war; it presupposes a plan of campaign, offensive fighting operations, and unbounded devotion and heroism on the part of the proletariat. An absolutely essential condition precedent for this form of action is the organization of the broad masses into militant units ... and intensified revolutionary work in the army and navy.

The *Program* denounces Socialists as reformers whose actions put them in the camp of the bourgeois enemy; they are also denounced because of their inability to rise above nationalistic loyalties:

4. Stefan Possony, *A Century of Conflict* (Chicago, Regnery, 1953), p. 147.

Unlike the Social Democratic, Second International, each
section of which submits to the discipline of 'its own' national
bourgeoisie and of its own 'fatherland', the sections of the
Communist International submit to only one discipline, . . .
which guarantees victory in the struggle of the world's
workers for world proletarian dictatorship.

Unlike the Second International, which splits the trade
unions, fights against colonial peoples, and practices unity
with the bourgeoisie, the Communist International is an organization that guards proletarian unity in all countries and the
unity of the toilers of all races and all peoples in their struggle
against the yoke of imperialism.

Despite the bloody terror of the bourgeoisie, the Communists
fight with courage and devotion on all sectors of the international class front, in the firm conviction that the victory of the
proletariat is inevitable and cannot be averted.

The Communists disdain to conceal their views and aims.
They openly declare that their aims can be attained only by
the forcible overthrow of all existing social conditions. Let the
ruling class tremble at a Communist revolution. The proletarians have nothing to lose but their chains. They have a
world to win. Workers of all countries, unite.

The Sixth Congress maintained that Social Democrats and
Fascists were really allies of the bourgeoisie: the former tried to
demoralize workers from within and the latter to destroy them
from without. In the following years, until roughly 1935, Communists in Europe looked upon Socialists as "social-fascists",
and opposed them both on the political and trade union level.

In the years 1927–1932, European Communism suffered even
greater setbacks than in the dismal period 1923–1927. In Poland
the Communists supported Pilsudski on the premise that he was
another Kerensky, only to be bested by him. In Italy and
Hungary Communists were sternly repressed and their influence
in Austria, Czechoslovakia, and Rumania remained limited.
Directed by the Comintern, German Communists directed their
attacks against the Social Democrats while Nazism grew:

The true significance of events in Germany was lost to the communists. This was that the misery of the economic depression was driving the masses not to the communists but to the Nazis. The latter not only appealed to the despairing middle class . . . but also enlisted many thousands of unemployed workers, for whom the trade unions had been unable to do anything, and who listened eagerly to the Nazi denunciations of the social-democratic bosses and Judaeo-Marxist agents of Moscow.[5]

In April, 1931, the German Communist Party (K.P.D.) ordered its followers to vote in favor of the Nazi-inspired referendum which sought to overthrow the Social Democratic government of Prussia. Hitler became Chancellor in January, 1933, without incident.

At the same time that Communist parties abroad (working under the direction of the Comintern) took a leftward course, formal Soviet diplomacy concluded a number of non-aggression pacts designed to impress foreign states with the U.S.S.R.'s peaceful intentions. Indeed the Soviet Union was a signatory of the Kellogg-Briand pact of 1928 which "outlawed war." The U.S.S.R. also established diplomatic relations with many states, and resumed normal diplomatic relations with Britain, which had been broken off by the British in 1927 in protest against Soviet interference in the internal affairs of Britain. In 1933 the Soviets signed a protocol with Nazi Germany based on the Non-aggression Treaty of 1926 and the Conciliation Protocol of 1929, which included the following text:

The people of the Soviet Union will undoubtedly endorse the reentry into force of the Berlin treaty . . . in spite of their attitude to Fascism the people of (the) U.S.S.R. wish to live in peace with Germany . . . and have no desire to make any change or revisions in Soviet policy with regard to Germany.[6]

Consonant with his policy of further strengthening the

5. Hugh Seton-Watson, *From Lenin to Malenkov* (New York, Praeger, 1953), p. 109.
6. As quoted in Max Beloff, *The Foreign Policy of Soviet Russia* (London, Oxford University Press, 1949), Vol. 1, p. 25.

U.S.S.R. and the Comintern prior to embarking on vigorous revolutionary activities abroad, Stalin described Soviet foreign policy as a "peace policy," maintained in spite of "provocative acts" by Western powers:

> Our policy is a policy of peace and of increasing commercial intercourse with all countries. The result of this policy is an improvement in our relations with a number of countries . . . Another result is the U.S.S.R.'s adherence to the Kellogg Pact. . . . And lastly, a result of this policy is the fact that we have succeeded in maintaining peace, in not allowing the enemy to draw us into conflicts, in spite of a number of provocative acts and adventuristic attacks on the part of the warmongers.[7]

Soviet policy toward the Western powers, and particularly the League of Nations, although one of continuing suspicion and basic hostility, nevertheless continued to be based on formal contacts (which in the case of the League constituted a change in outlook). The First Congress of the Communist International had denounced the League as "the Holy Alliance of the bourgeoisie for the suppression of the proletarian revolution," and the Manifesto of the Sixth Congress stated in 1928:

> The League of Nations, the product of Versailles, the most shameless robber treaty of the last decade, cloaks the war-like work of its members by working out projects for disarmament.

In 1931, at the insistence of Germany and Italy (with lukewarm support from Britain and against the wishes of France), the U.S.S.R., though not yet a member of the League, was invited to attend a European conference on economic matters. *Pravda* analyzed the Soviet acceptance of the invitation:

> The Genevan Pan-Europeans will have to reveal to the great

7. From *Pravda*, June 29, 1930.

masses of the people, with what methods and by what means, at what price and at whose expense, they propose to restore the health of European capitalism which is suffering from the results of the world crisis. The Soviet Union does not fear such a discussion and will not flinch from it. It has in any case plenty of things in general to discuss with the Genevan 'doctors'. By taking part in the work of the European-Commission, the Soviet Union will wreck the plans of the leaders of the Commission . . .[8]

Furthermore, the U.S.S.R. sought to further its own ends by taking part in the work of the Disarmament Commission of the League from 1927 on. But Soviet pleas for disarmament were

. . . met with scepticism in most foreign quarters, if only because of the contradiction between this policy, and the unrepudiated Soviet doctrine of the necessary armament of the Proletarian Dictatorship—the Soviet State itself. According to the 1928 programme of the Communist International, real peace would only be obtained by the armed peoples of a belligerent state turning their arms against their own ruling classes, turning imperialist war into civil war.[9]

SOVIET POLICY TOWARD ASIA 1921–1933

Thus far we have taken into consideration primarily Soviet and Communist attitudes and actions for Europe. Let us now survey the developments in the Far East from 1921–1933.

Reporting to the Tenth Congress of the Russian Communist Party on the *Immediate Tasks of the Party in Connection with the National Problem* (March 10, 1921), Stalin pointed out that, as a result of colonial expansion, the old national states of the West "ceased to be national states" and hence had become more vulnerable to revolutionary attack. He asserted that part of the power of the imperialist states was based on the colonies. Colonial competition between the imperialist powers produces contradictions which "give rise to war." Stalin went on to say:

8. As quoted in Beloff, *The Foreign Policy of Soviet Russia*, p. 44.
9. Beloff, *The Foreign Policy of Soviet Russia*, p. 46.

> The abolition of national oppression in Europe is inconceivable without the emancipation of the colonial peoples of Asia and Africa from the oppression of imperialism. . . . The former is bound up with the latter.

The last thing that Lenin wrote stressed the importance of Asia to global revolution:

> In the last analysis, the outcome of the struggle will be determined by the fact that Russia, India, China, etc., constitute the overwhelming majority of the population of the globe. And it is precisely this majority of the population that, during the past few years, has been drawn into the struggle of its emancipation with extraordinary rapidity, so that in this respect there cannot be the slightest shadow of doubt what the final outcome of the world struggle will be. In this sense, the final victory of socialism is fully and absolutely assured.[10]

During 1923, an agreement was made between the U.S.S.R. and the Chinese government, by which the Kuomintang (the ruling party in China) hoped to gain from Russia political and military advice and assistance, and the Soviets hoped to penetrate the Chinese government and its dominant political party. After the failure of the Communist uprising in Germany in November, 1923, the Fifth Congress of the Communist International (1924) decided to shift the revolutionary offensive against the East. The new road to world victory led through Asia.

After Lenin's death, Stalin delivered his lectures on the *Foundations of Leninism* at the University of Sverdlov, thus establishing his claim to the theoretical and ideological leadership of world Communism. He stressed his belief that Germany was no longer the center of the revolutionary movement, and that Western imperialists were more vulnerable in Asia than in Europe:

> The chain of the imperialist front must, as a rule, give way where the links are weaker and, at all events, not necessarily

10. Lenin, *Selected Works* (New York, International Publishers, 1943), Vol. 9, p. 400.

where capitalism is more developed. . . . A coalition between the proletarian revolution in Europe and the colonial revolution in the East in a united front of revolution against the world front of imperialism is inevitable.[11]

In 1927 Stalin developed the idea that colonial revolutions take place in three stages:

1) attack of the national united front against foreign imperialism;

2) development of the bourgeois-democratic revolution to the point where the agrarian movement takes over from the bourgeoisie;

3) Soviet revolution.

In his *Marxism and the National and Colonial Question,* Stalin pointed the way to Communist penetration of the Chinese government, taking advantage of the 1923 alliance:

1) Communists within the Kuomintang must exploit their positions of infiltration 'to secure the resignation or expulsion of the Rights from the Kuomintang.'

2) Reliable [i.e., Communist] elements must be placed in the central committee of the Kuomintang in order to change its structure.

3) Infiltration must be enlarged to effect capture of the Kuomintang, thus bringing it under Communist domination.

He compared America and Europe to the front, and the colonies of Africa and Asia as the vulnerable rear of the enemy:

If Europe and America may be called the front, the scene of

11. Stalin, *Problems of Leninism,* p. 21.

the main engagements between socialism and imperialism, the non-sovereign nations and the colonies, with their raw materials, fuel, food, and vast store of human material, should be regarded as the rear, the reserve of imperialism. In order to win a war one must not only triumph at the front but also revolutionize the enemy's rear, his reserves. Hence the victory of the world proletarian revolution may be regarded as assured only if the proletariat is able to combine its own revolutionary struggle with the movement for emancipation of the toiling masses of the non-sovereign nations and the colonies against the power of the imperialists and for a dictatorship of the proletariat.

The Sixth World Congress, July 15–September 1, 1928, informed the comrades all over the world that Communist parties and their allies in the West should agitate for independence of the colonies of Asia and Africa, at the same time that revolution was underway in the colonies:

Colonial revolutions and movements for national liberation play an extremely important part in the struggle against imperialism and in the struggle for the conquest of power by the working class. . . . The establishment of a fraternal fighting alliance with the masses of the toilers in the colonies constitutes one of the principal tasks which the world industrial proletariat must fulfill as the leader in the struggle against imperialism.

By 1927 the uneasy alliance between the Communists and the Kuomintang, which was the fruit of the 1923 agreement between Sun Yat-sen and Soviet Ambassador Joffe, came to an end. Meantime Sun had died, and was succeeded by Chiang Kai-shek, who recognized that Soviet advisers Borodin and Bluecher were subverting Nationalist China for Communism. Therefore, there was a rupture in diplomatic relations between the U.S.S.R. and China in 1927.

But this ending of diplomatic ties did not mean the end of Soviet interference in Chinese affairs. An agreement signed in 1924 had permitted the Soviets to maintain consulates in Manchuria and to continue what had been Imperial Russia's control over the

Manchurian railways. But by 1929 the Chinese government felt strong enough to challenge Russian influence in Manchuria. So it took over the consulates, charging that Soviet representatives were engaged in subversion and regained control of the railways for China. Thereupon Soviet military pressure forced the local Manchurian authorities to restore all Soviet privileges in the region. However, Communist dominance of Manchuria was ended in 1931 with the Japanese invasion.

At the end of 1932 the U.S.S.R. and China resumed diplomatic relations, and the following announcement was published by both countries:

> The elements most disturbing to the peace of the world have now joined hands and Japan stands squarely against these forces. The question for the Powers is whether to allow the forces of destruction to rule in the Orient or the forces of consolidation. The restoration of Sino-Soviet relations poses this issue squarely: beside it the future of Manchuria is comparatively insignificant.[12]

SOVIET AND COMMUNIST POLICIES
1933–1935

As late as December 31, 1933, the Communist organ *Bolshevik* expressed hope that Hitler notwithstanding, Communism would triumph in Germany:

> In Germany the proletarian revolution is nearer to realization than in any other country; and the victory of the proletarian revolution in Germany means victory of proletarian revolution throughout Europe, since capitalist Europe cannot exist if it loses its heart. . . . He who does not understand the German question does not understand the development of proletarian revolution in Europe.[13]

Meantime the U.S.S.R. and Nazi Germany kept on good terms economically and diplomatically. Molotov declared on January 28, 1935:

12. Beloff, *The Foreign Policy of Soviet Russia*, p. 87.
13. As quoted in Dallin, *Russia and Postwar Europe*, p. 52.

It is impossible to close our eyes to the changes that have
taken place in Soviet-German relations with the coming to
power of National Socialism. As for ourselves, we can say
that we have not had and do not have any other wish than to
continue further good relations with Germany.[14]

However, the Nazi government, embittered because of the
Franco-Soviet alliance of 1934, became increasingly anti-Communist and anti-Soviet, to the point that the U.S.S.R. began to
consider courses of action alternative to a pro-German policy.
The German threat to Russia being a distinct possibility, the Soviets, in their own interests, suddenly became supporters of the
League of Nations and of collective security. Not only France,
but also Britain, were sounded out to see what price they might
be willing to pay for a potential anti-Nazi ally in the East.

A major diplomatic and psychological victory for the Soviets
came during 1933 with U. S. recognition of the U.S.S.R. This
gave the Soviets a respectability which they had not previously
had in the Western Hemisphere, and facilitated future
collaboration between Communists and American anti-Fascists.

It was not until the assumption of office by President
Roosevelt in March 1933, that the favorable current of opinion in
the United States itself could be translated into action. This
action was the fruit of the efforts of William C. Bullitt (who became the first U. S. ambassador to Soviet Russia) and Col.
Raymond Robins who had visited the Soviet Union with the
American Red Cross in the 1920's. Both these men had been advocates of Soviet-American friendship since the days when the
Bolsheviks first came to power in Russia. President Roosevelt ex-
changed letters with USSR President Kalinin in October, 1933,
and Soviet Emissary Maxim Litvinov then came to Washington
and clinched the exchange of ambassadors. In addition there was
a mutual pledge to abstain from hostile propaganda, and from
interference in the internal affairs of the United States by the Soviet Union.

In the Far East, the Soviets also followed their self-interest by
concluding an agreement with the Japanese puppet state of Man-

14. As quoted in Beloff, *Foreign Policy of Soviet Russia*, p. 44.

chukuo in 1935 according to which the Soviets sold the Manchurian railways to the Japanese.

The stage was now set for the era of the Popular Front, which was launched by the Seventh World Congress of the Communist International in 1935.

Chapter 4

THE UNITED FRONT 1935–1939

During 1934 the Soviet Union had concluded defensive agreements with France and Czechoslovakia in response to the German threat. The new course in Soviet foreign policy required a new line for the Comintern. This was provided at the Seventh Congress which met in Moscow in July–August, 1935. It proclaimed the tactic of the Popular Front, designed to lure Socialists and anti-fascists generally into a united front against Fascism, which would serve Soviet security interests. Judged by its propaganda appeal, the Popular Front was the most successful tactic ever adopted by the Comintern in peacetime.

Actually the impetus of the Popular Front stratagem was provided by events in France during 1934. Rightwing opposition to continuing cabinet instability provided French Communists with the Fascist bogeyman, against whom they could forge a coalition of Communists, Socialists, and Radical Socialists. The true situation, however, was summarized by Franz Borkenau:

It is important to realize . . . that the fascist danger in France, whether or not Moscow believed in it, was in fact largely imaginary.

The whole policy of the Popular Front, as the bloc of Communists, Socialists and Radicals was coming to be called, was directed against an imaginary danger.[1]

It is widely believed that Moscow ordered the French Communists to change their tactics so as to strengthen the Franco-Soviet alliance, that Stalin really became a convinced anti-fascist. But Borkenau writes:

> ... it seems a certainty, from what followed, that Stalin wanted to avoid a Nazi attack upon Russia at any price—presumably because he feared a Russian defeat—and that he was therefore constantly playing with two balls, with the West and with the Axis. The alliance with France was never to Stalin an ultimate.[2]

The Soviet Union analyzed the world situation in 1935 as follows: we are too weak for war at this time, and there is no truly exploitable revolutionary situation which we can move into. The Axis Powers might threaten the security of the Soviet state, and Chiang Kai-shek might destroy the Chinese-Communist movement militarily. Therefore, while maintaining contact with the Axis, we should improve our relations with France and the League of Nations and develop, if necessary, a temporary anti-fascist strategy which may facilitate our penetration of Socialist and liberal groups in Western society. Taking advantage of our new diplomatic ties with the United States, we should encourage sympathetic attitudes there toward the Soviet Union; Stalin once opined:

> Victory will be won by the side which is allied to the United States.[3]

1. Franz Borkenau, *European Communism*, p. 115.
2. Borkenau, *European Communism*, p. 117.
3. Yves Delbars, *Le Vrai Stalin* (Paris, 1950), p. 432.

According to Stefan Possony, the long term Communist strategy was revolutionary:

> At the same time, revolutionary work was not abandoned. The problem was ... to gain allies among nations whose government and social structure the Communists were determined to destroy and to gain some measure of control over these allies; and, on the other hand, to continue preparations for revolution both against the coveted allies and the fascist countries, where police-state controls copied from the soviet system made subversive work very difficult.[4]

As a solution to this problem, the Communists wanted strong allies who were at the same time either pro-Communist or at least not actively anti-Communist. The solution was to reassure the proletariat of these countries that they were fighting a "national liberation war" against "fascism" on the side of the Soviet Union. This meant that they were fighting a "just" war. Communists were told that they should strive to transform wars for national independence into genuine "people's wars," on the model of the Chinese Communists. The whole people must be armed in order that "the war may be waged in a Jacobin, in a revolutionary manner."[5]

Dimitrov, then Secretary General of the Comintern and subsequently Prime Minister of Bulgaria, explained that the movement toward the people's war, among other things, should aim at the disarming and disbanding of anti-Communist organizations and at purging anti-Communists from the state bureaucracy, army, and police. The Soviet Union must induce France and the West in general to look to it as the main source of strength in the potential anti-fascist crusade, and be prepared to make concessions to it accordingly. At the same time Communist parties in the West must abandon their stilted and stereotyped forms of political activity and find a "common language" with the people in order to end

---

4. Possony, *A Century of Conflict*, p. 207.
5. D. C. Manuilsky, *The Work of the Seventh Congress of the Communist International* (New York, Workers Library, 1936), p. 25.

> ... the isolation of the revolutionary vanguard from the
> masses of the proletariat and all other toilers, as well as over-
> coming the fatal isolation of the working class itself from its
> natural allies in the struggle against the bourgeoisie, against
> fascism.[6]

Fear of fascism was thus selected by the Seventh Congress as
the best bait by which the "united front" of all "anti-fascists"
could be formed under Communist leadership. Dimitrov called
for the strengthening of "transmission belts" between party and
people, particularly trade unions, women's organizations, anti-
fascist and anti-imperialist "fronts." He also urged penetration
of mass organizations which were not yet under Communist control.

These new tactics would achieve their greatest success if Communists were admitted into "united front" governments. But
Communist maneuvering within such governments could succeed
only if liberals could be made to believe that they were working
with honest leftist and progressive coalitions, working within
constitutional frameworks, and uniting all anti-reactionary and
anti-fascist forces. Dimitrov quoted Lenin to the effect that great
attention should be paid to "searching out forms of transition for
the proletarian revolution." He added that the united front
government would prove to be one of the most important transitional forms from bourgeois democracy to Communist dictatorship.

Yet Dimitrov left no doubt that a united front government
could not of itself bring about the desired dictatorship of the
proletariat. Therefore, in addition to setting up and participating
in coalition governments, it is necessary for Communists to
"prepare for the socialist revolution." Dimitrov reminded the
party faithful that "Soviet power and only Soviet power can
bring salvation."

Communists, therefore, were to cast aside the cloak of revolution and pose as progressives and liberals anxious to join
together with others of good will in the fight against fascism.
Mao Tse-tung, in his book *China's New Democracy,* declared
that the united front strategy

6. Manuilsky, *Seventh Congress*, p. 92.

enveloped the Communist pill in the sweetest sugar coating ever given it, and redoubled the effectiveness of the dose at the same time.

Dimitrov, in turn, utilized the slogan of "The Trojan Horse."

Infiltration tactics within united fronts were to be patterned after the . . . ancient tale of the capture of Troy. Troy was inaccessible to the armies attacking her, thanks to her impregnable walls. And the attacking army, after suffering many sacrifices, was unable to achieve victory until with the aid of the famous Trojan horse it managed to penetrate to the very heart of the enemy's camp. We revolutionary workers, it appears to me, should not shy away from using the same tactics with regard to our fascist foe, who is defending himself against the people with the help of a living wall of his cutthroats.[7]

The first important success of the Popular Front was in France. Already in 1934 Communist leader Maurice Thorez had declared:

The united front is not a maneuver. . . . We do not seek petty maneuvers, nor openings for taking advantage of discussions about trifles, for creating divergences between the Socialist leaders. . . . We, the Communist party, are ready to renounce all criticism of the Socialist party during our joint action. . . . Neither from the lips of any of our propagandists, nor from the pen of any of our editors in *Humanité* . . . or in any other of our papers will there be found the smallest attack upon the organization and leaders of the Socialist party, while they are faithful to the agreement they will have concluded with us. We want action at any price.[8]

The Socialists succumbed at the very first onslaught:

7. As quoted in "Strategy and Tactics of World Communism", Transcript of Hearings before the House Committee on Foreign Affairs, 1949, p. 316.
8. As quoted in Borkenau, *European Communism*, p. 125.

In the party there remained Leon Blum as the mouthpiece of
wisdom, and no man on earth was less fit to resist the lure of
the new tactics than this suave, inhibited, deeply serious, and
honest but essentially guileless man. . . . "Unity," he says, ·
with disarming naiveté, "would be the best guarantee against
a victory of facism . . ."[9]

Shortly thereafter, a small incident threw light upon the child-
like naiveté of French Socialist Leader Blum in accepting the
unity pact with the Communists:

On August 12 *Populaire* published a telegram of three
Russian Mensheviks living in forced residence near Kazan on
the Volga, and expressing their enthusiasm about the pact.
Blum added in a leader of the same day: 'I do not think the
tactics of the united action could receive a more powerful and
touching justification.' It did not occur to the eminent expert
in French civil law that people living under the OGPU in com-
pulsory domicile do not usually send telegrams about their
political opinions to non-Communist papers abroad. . . .[10]

Shortly thereafter, Communist leader Jacques Duclos invited
the Radical Socialist party to join the coalition:

In the Popular Front there is room for the masses and even for
the organizations of the radical party. . . . We, who are convinced that one day the popular masses of France will in
practice reach the solution of the Soviets, we who want to
make an end of the rule of Capital, we stretch our hand to
those who do not want a victory of fascism . . .[11]

By mid-1936 some French Socialists were beginning to cool off
in their pro-Communism, because they could see that the Communists were trying to capture the labor unions from them, and
because innate Socialist pacifism shied away from the logical im-

9. Ibid., p. 125.
10. Ibid., p. 127.
11. Ibid., p. 131.

plications of the Franco-Soviet pact. Meantime, Communist leaders, the most important of whom was to desert his regiment in 1940, declared:

> If war should break out despite all our efforts, we shall not become deserters, we shall take our share in the war . . . we shall take the rifle given to us, we shall work for the victory of the Red Army, of the Soviet Union, of the triumph of the revolution.[12]

This same Communist leader, Maurice Thorez, on May 15, made crystal clear where Communist loyalties lay:

> The Soviet Union is the most precious possession of the international proletariat. Therefore, the Soviet Union must be defended by all available means . . . In the case of a counter-revolutionary war against the socialist fatherland, we shall support the Red Army of the Soviet Union with all our force and we shall fight for the defeat of any power at war with the Soviet Union, . . . But if . . . for whatever reason an imperialist country in such a war fights on the side of the Soviet Union, the war is no longer imperialist. For it would be ι ιonstrous to regard as imperialist the camp of the land of socialism, the country of the working class.[13]

On April 26, 1936, the Popular Front electoral coalition in France won the election and proceeded to form a government. However, in accordance with the directives of the Comintern's Dimitrov, the Communists decided to keep out of it. In this way they could sabotage the new cabinet, exert pressure on it, curry popularity by attacking it, while still taking credit for its popular measures. In any case they had an indirect representative inside the cabinet in the person of Pierre Cot, who was supporting them through thick and thin.

The end of the Popular Front came in June, 1937, with the resignation of the Blum government, but Communist penetration

12. Ibid., p. 142.
13. Ibid., p. 167.

of French society continued within the framework of anti-fascism.

Emergence of the Popular Front tactics in France led to the flowering of the Communist movement in Spain. It was under the inspiration of the French model that the Spanish Communists joined with the Socialists in the Asturias uprising of 1934. Although crushed by the Spanish Republican government, the Marxist united front was revived in the January, 1936 election, and as a result Spain found itself with a Popular Front government. This Popular Front was more revolutionary than that of France, and the political Right in Spain was also stronger than the Right in France. In mid-July, 1936 the Right rebelled, and the Communists, along with their Soviet sponsors, played increasingly important roles.

The French Communists shouted for French intervention in Spain on the side of the Popular Front Republican government and they were in deadly earnest. But it was not to be. The French government, instead, insisted on a policy of non-intervention which drove the first serious wedge into the ranks of the Popular Front. This action in France confronted Stalin sharply with a dilemma: should he act himself or must he look on with folded hands while the Spanish Republic was destroyed? The latter policy would deal a terrible blow to Russian prestige, would presumably bring down the French Popular Front and with it a collapse of Russia's policy in the League of Nations. Stalin might thereby face precisely that danger of a four-power pact (Britain, Germany, France, and Italy) which he wished to avoid.

Therefore Stalin decided that to uphold Communist prestige among the European left and Russian prestige among the great powers, Russian intervention in Spain was necessary. The failure to compel France to pluck the Spanish chestnuts out of the fire for Russia forced the Russian politburo to decide, on August 28th, to intervene on the side of the Spanish Republican Government.

Not only did the Soviet Union intervene with aircraft, staff officers, technical instructors, and OGPU agents, but the international Communist movement directed from Moscow mobilized about 40,000 volunteers who constituted the International Brigades.

Without the International Brigades, Madrid would probably have been captured by Franco in November, 1936. And the government would have been no less lost without the trickle of Russian tanks and aircraft the Spanish republicans were receiving down to the middle of 1938.

This Soviet help come with many strings attached. As a condition of sending men and material, Moscow insisted upon the inclusion of two Communist members—Vincente Uribe and Jesus Hernandez—in the government of Largo Caballero, the Socialist leader, and the participation of other Communists in the autonomous government of Catalonia. On September 14, 1936, according to W. G. Krivitsky, the Moscow Politburo passed the fateful decision to create a Spanish section of the OGPU . . . and to subordinate all Communist work in Spain to this section:

> Already in December the terror was sweeping Madrid, Barcelona and Valencia. The OGPU had its own special prisons. Its units carried out assassinations and kidnappings. It filled hidden dungeons and made flying raids. It functioned, of course, independently of the Loyalist government. . . . It was a power before which even some of the highest officers in Caballero's government trembled. The Soviet Union seemed to have a grip on Loyalist Spain, as if it were already a Soviet possession.[14]

The political commissars accompanying the International Brigades were without exception OGPU agents, and so were a large majority of the political commissars with the Spanish units, appointed by Alvarez del Vayo, their supreme chief.

While Soviet control over the Loyalist regime became firm, Communist forces systematically swept aside non-Communist elements within the original Popular Front . . . the Communists set out to destroy all other parties, availing themselves of the slogans 'order' and 'discipline' as a sheen on their totalitarian regime. As in France, the slogan 'unity' served to disintegrate both the Socialist and the Radical parties, each in its own way.

Soviet and Communist control of the Negrin government, which took over from Cabellero early in 1937, was total, and it remained this way until the final defeat in the spring of 1939. Meantime Spain served as a training ground for leading Eu-

---

14. W. G. Krivitsky, *I Was Stalin's Agent* (London, 1940), p. 121.

ropean Communists—France's Marty, Germany's Dahlem, Italy's Longo, Czechoslovakia's Gottwald, and others.

> Communist policies in Spain cost many innocent lives and proved a dismal and contemptible failure. Yet the Spanish civil war yielded to the Soviet Union four important assets: the rejuvenation of the western Communist parties through the International Brigades; a considerable increase in the capabilities of the Communist espionage apparatus; the testing of Russian weapons in competition with foreign munitions, as well as the training of Russian officers and staffs in actual combat; and the gold treasure of Spain which the Soviet Union took into custody but forgot to return to its rightful owner.[15]

Although Stalin failed in Spain, he gained much for the Communist movements in the United States, France and Britain, due to his anti-fascist stance. This was to benefit him after the German invasion in 1941.

In Britain and Scandinavia, though the Popular Front anti-fascist slogans made an impression on liberal and socialist intellectuals, the Socialist parties refused to make common cause with the Communists, and no Popular Fronts were formed. In Italy and Germany all anti-fascist groups were helpless.

In the Balkans the Popular Front period brought only an insignificant increase of strength to the Communists. In Yugoslavia and Bulgaria, Communists won the sympathy and support of many intellectuals because of their anti-fascist strategy. The association of Communism with Russia and France, the two foreign states most popular among Serbs, assisted the Communist cause in Yugoslavia.

In Czechoslovakia, the idea of anti-fascist unity between Communists and other leftists was popular among the Czechs, although not so among the Slovaks. Communism in Greece gained ground, but in Poland, Hungary, and Rumania, it found no takers.

The Popular Front was successful only where a genuine and

15. Possony, *A Century of Conflict*, p. 219.

effective demand for unity of democratic forces already
existed, and where national resistance to the fascist powers
was a real issue. The Communists did not create the demand
but yielded to it. Having thereby won much popularity for
themselves, they tried to exploit the Popular Front for their
party aims, and failed. . . . The Popular Front would have
been more successful if the Communists . . . had been mainly
concerned to ensure the triumph of the democratic forces in
countries threatened internally or externally by fascism . . .
but . . . Moscow's real aim was to strengthen the position of
Soviet Russia. Alliance with the Western Powers was one
possible course: another was alliance with Nazi Germany.
When the first did not produce results, the second was
adopted. . . . The experience gained during the Popular Front
years, especially in Spain, proved valuable in 1944-1948,
when the opportunity came to do what the Soviet leaders had
come to understand by the notion of 'spreading world revolution'—to export the ready-made Stalinist regime by force of
arms.[16]

The real vintage harvested by the Communists during the
Popular Front period thus lay in the field of mass influence and
organization. Compared to these gains the results in the field of
foreign policy, so much over-stressed by most observers, were ne-
gligible, and sometimes negative. Even during the latter phase of
the Popular Front period the Communists, under Manuilsky's
guidance, continued to stress mass appeal rather than obvious
maneuvering in the field of great politics. This was because
Stalin's pretended aim—an Anglo-Franco-Soviet bloc—was not
his real aim, which was to win over Berlin, not London. In the
great choice between mass appeal and political effectiveness,
which had to be made between 1937-1938, the Communists
chose mass appeal. That is what makes the decisive difference
between those years and the later period of the war and post-war,
when the Communists consciously and ruthlessly subordinated
their mass appeal to the immediate needs of Moscow's foreign
policy.

In France, the Communists showed their true intentions as
early as March, 1938, when Blum again took over the reins of
government. By this time Blum recognized the need for at least

16. Seton-Watson, *From Lenin to Malenkov*, p. 190.

some rearmament, and made a desperate effort toward increasing aircraft production. The Communists reacted by leading a strike, on March 24, among the Citroën workers. The Blum government resigned on April 7, 1938. All of these activities in France took place *after* Hitler had marched into Vienna. About this time Stalin began to move again toward a pro-German orientation, although the tendency did not become manifest until the spring of 1938.

The Comintern issued a manifesto on Nov. 7, 1938, which presaged the primarily anti-French and anti-British line which formed the basis of the Hitler-Stalin pact:

> The second imperialist war has already begun in fact, a war of plunder, a war for a new partition of the world . . . Never previously had the popular masses in the capitalist countries felt as strongly, as in these days of fascist brigandage, their indissoluble ties with the great country of socialism. . . . The imperialist cliques of England and France have signed a counter-revolutionary alliance with German and Italian fascism. . . . The condition for a successful struggle for peace is the replacement of the governments of betrayal and shame in the countries threatened by fascism by governments willing to react against the fascist aggressors.

The concluding sentence of the above quotation ties this manifesto to the anti-fascist policy previously followed by the Comintern. But the real meaning is quite different:

> Behind the attacks upon the Chamberlain and Daladier governments there lurks an attack upon Britain and France as such. They are described as imperialist countries. . . . Two theses—that the war is exclusively imperialist and that it is a sham in every respect except in its anti-Soviet implications—will form the basis of the policy of betrayal of their countries adopted by the British and French Communists in 1939. It is only logical that the manifesto does not repeat the previous emphatic appeals to French patriotism. The only loyalties now expected from the workers are those to the Soviet Union. Six months before the first formal pact negotiations were

opened between Berlin and Moscow, Comintern policy had already substantially accomplished the turn.[17]

Let us now consider the impact of the Popular Front strategy in America and Asia.

Comintern Chairman Dimitrov told the delegates to the Seventh Comintern Congress in 1935:

> It is perfectly obvious that the interests of the American proletariat demand that all its forces dissociate themselves from the capitalist parties without delay. It must at the proper time find ways and suitable forms of preventing fascism from winning over the broad discontented masses of the toilers. And here it must be said that under American conditions the creation of a mass party of toilers, a "Workers' and Farmers' Party," might serve as such a suitable form. Such a party would be a specific form of the mass people's front in America. . . . Such a party, of course, will be neither Socialist nor Communist. But it must be an anti-fascist party . . .

In his interview with Roy Howard in 1936, Stalin denied any connection between the Soviet Union and the Communist party, U.S.A.:

> *Howard:* Did not Browder and Darcy, American Communists, appearing before the Seventh Congress of the Communist International in Moscow last summer appeal for the overthrow by force of the American government?
>
> *Stalin:* I admit that I do not recall the speeches of comrades Browder and Darcy. I do not even recall of what they spoke. It is possible that they said something of this nature. But it was not the Soviet people who created the American Communist party. It was created by Americans . . . It would be absolutely wrong to hold the Soviet government responsible for activities of the American Communists.

17. Borkenau, *European Communism*, p. 217.

At the same time, Stalin disclaimed any hostile intentions toward the United States, and introduced the "peaceful co-existence" thesis which was designed to lull the United States into a false sense of security. But behind this facade of a Soviet policy of "hands off" and "coexistence," the Comintern ordered U. S. Communists "to go to the masses" which in Communist parlance means wide infiltration. As Louis Budenz, who was formerly editor of the Communist newspaper *Daily Worker* and an active Communist at this time describes the strategy:

> The second big infiltration drive dates from 1936, when the Communists first indirectly and then directly supported the Roosevelt administration. Conditions now became even more favorable for easy penetration, as open Communists began to hob-nob with leading political figures and the whole situation was softened up for wider entry into the newspapers, radio, and eventually television and all other fields of opinion-making.[18]

The Soviet-directed penetration of the United States government during the days of the Popular Front was directed by the Harold Ware espionage apparatus. Whittaker Chambers, who later broke with Communism and testified against his former Comrades, summarizes the situation:

> I can imagine no better way to convey the secret power of the Communist party in the domestic politics of the United States government from 1933–1943, and later, than to list the members of the leading committee of the Ware group . . .:

> NATHAN WITT (Secretary of the National Labor Relations Board, 1937–1940). . . . LEE PRESSMAN (General Counsel of the C.I.O., 1936–1948). . . . JOHN J. ABT (Special Assistant to the Attorney General of the United States in charge of the Trial Section, 1937). . . . CHARLES KRAMER (Staff member, LaFollette Subcommittee of the Senate on Civil Liberties). . . . HENRY H. COLLINS, JR.

18. Louis Budenz, *Techniques of Communism* (Chicago, Regnery, 1953), p. 163.

(Department of Labor, 1938). . . . VICTOR PERLO (Brookings Institution, 1937–1940).[19]

With respect to Latin America and Asia, Dimitrov outlined the following program to the 1935 Comintern Congress:

In Brazil the Communist party, having laid a correct foundation for the development of the united anti-imperialist front by the establishment of the National Liberation Alliance, has to make every effort to extend further this front by drawing into it first and foremost the many millions of the peasantry, leading up to the formation of units of a people's revolutionary army, completely devoted to the revolution, and to the establishment of the rule of the National Liberation Alliance.

In India the Communists have to support, extend and participate in all anti-imperialist mass activities, not excluding those which are under national reformist leadership. While maintaining their political and organizational independence, they must carry on active work inside the organizations which take part in the Indian National Congress . . . for the purpose of further developing the national liberation movement of the Indian peoples against British imperialism.

In China, where the people's movement has already led to the formation of Soviet districts over a considerable territory of the country and to the organization of a powerful Red Army. . . . Only the Chinese Soviets can act as a unifying center in the struggle against the enslavement and partition of China by the imperialists. . . . We therefore approve . . . the creation of a most extensive anti-imperialist united front against Japanese imperialism and its Chinese agents, jointly with all those organized forces existing on the territory of China which are ready to wage a real struggle for the salvation of their country and their people . . . we send our warmest fraternal greetings, in the name of the revolutionary proletariat of the whole world to all the Soviets of China, to the Chinese revolutionary people. We send our ardent fraternal greetings to the heroic Red Army of China. . . . And we assure the Chinese people of our firm resolve to support its struggle for its com-

19. Whittaker Chambers, *Witness* (New York, Random House, 1952), p. 343.

plete liberation from all imperialist robbers and their Chinese henchmen.

The Popular Front policy achieved substantial success in China. Soon after the Seventh Comintern Congress, at which the Popular Front policy had been forcibly defended by Wang Ming, now the party's delegate to Moscow, on August 1, 1935, the Chinese Communist party launched an appeal for a united front of Communists and Kuomintang against the invaders. At the same time Mao Tse-tung told his comrades in 1937:

> The war between China and Japan is an excellent opportunity for the development of our party. Our determined policy is 70 percent expansion, 20 percent dealing with the Kuomintang, and 10 percent fighting Japan. . . . The first stage is to compromise with the Kuomintang, with the view of maintaining our existence. The second stage is to fight for a balance of power vis à vis the Kuomintang to achieve equilibrium. The third stage is to infiltrate deeply into central China, to establish bases there, in order to launch counter-offensives against the Kuomintang, with the view of taking away from the Kuomintang its leading position.[20]

The purpose of the united front was thus to use the Japanese threat as an excuse for forming a coalition with the Kuomintang, from within which coalition the Communists would as the first order of business penetrate and conquer the Kuomintang, and secondly, defeat the Japanese. Chiang Kai-shek agreed to the united front only after being kidnapped and threatened by the Communists on December 12, 1936.

In the Far East, outside China, Communist influence began to increase. Young Indian intellectuals were attracted by the antifascist slogans of the Popular Front. In Japan a Japan Masses party was formed in February 1937, with a Popular Front tendency, and undoubtedly influenced by Communist tactics. In Indonesia a small illegal Communist party was organized in 1935, and two years later a broader leftist party, the Indonesian

20. As quoted in "Strategy and Tactics of World Communism," Supplement III, House Committee on Foreign Affairs, 1949, p. 24.

People's Movement, led by Socialists, followed the Popular Front line, regarded fascism as the main enemy, and formed the base on which Communism later built.

The first attempt at a Popular Front in Latin America was the National Liberation Alliance formed in 1935 in Brazil, led by Communist chief Luiz Carlos Prestes; however, dictator Vargas arrested him and his associates in 1937 and outlawed the Alliance. The second Latin American Popular Front appeared in Chile, in 1936, consisting of the Communists, Socialists, and Radicals. The Popular Front candidate for president, Aguirre, won the 1939 election, and the Front was dominant during the war years.

CONCLUSIONS

According to Robert Strausz-Hupé of the Pennsylvania Foreign Policy Research Institute and Stefan Possony:

> There seems hardly any doubt, in view of the long collaboration between Russia and Germany, that the Soviet-Nazi pact corresponded more closely to Soviet expectations and projections than would have a Soviet-Western pact. . . . It seems likely that the real reason behind the well-publicized Soviet negotiations with the West was to force the errant Hitler back into an alliance with the Soviet Union.[21]

Looking back on the Soviet and Communist policy of the Popular Front, it can be seen that the objective was twofold: 1) to increase vastly the Communist penetration of the masses via the anti-fascist crusade; 2) to suggest to the West the idea of an alliance with the U.S.S.R., out of which the U.S.S.R. would extract maximum concessions. But, as has been outlined above, the Soviets concluded somewhere in 1938, that although they were making headway on the first objective, they were not making comparable headway on the second. Furthermore, what was good for the U.S.S.R. was beginning to take precedence over what was good for the French, British, and other Communist

21. Robert Strausz-Hupe and Stefan Possony, *International Relations* (New York, McGraw-Hill, 1954), p. 581.

parties. However much the Popular Front was taking in Socialists and liberals, little benefit was accruing to the Soviet
Union. Therefore, the effort was made to guide Hitler back into
the Rapallo habit (the German-Soviet treaty of 1922) and remind
Germany of the danger of a two-front war.

Primacy of the Soviet Party over other parties has always been
the basis of USSR policy. By late 1938 the Soviet Party (i.e. the
Government) had not benefited from the united front as had the
parties of the West. Indeed the USSR had become increasingly
isolated. Thus there was need for a change of tactics.

Chapter 5

THE HITLER-STALIN PACT 1939–1941

The fact that the Soviet leaders were banking heavily on the traditional eastern orientation of Germany and fear of a two-front war is suggested by a statement which Soviet Foreign Commissar Litvinov made to an American journalist in 1937:

> Hitler and the generals who control Germany read history. They know that Bismarck warned against war on two fronts. They know that he urged the reinsurance policy with Russia. They believe that the Kaiser lost the First World War because he forgot Bismarck's admonition. When the Germans are prepared at last to embark upon their new adventures, these bandits will come to Moscow to ask us for a pact.[1]

It is possibly true that Stalin might have signed a pact with the British and French if the Germans had not signified their

1. John T. Whittaker, *We Cannot Escape History* (New York, MacMillan, 1937), p. 268.

readiness to come to terms with the Soviet Union. Whatever
faith the Soviet Union ever may have had in the will of the
French to fight would appear, however, to have been short-lived
indeed. In 1935 the Franco-Russian pact was signed. Yet in 1937
Litvinov, the promotor of collective security and reputedly the
great friend of the West, confided to an American publicist that
France was through and would never fight.[2]

We have seen, in the previous chapter, how the Soviet Union,
late in 1938, began to believe that the Popular Front stratagem,
however successful it was in penetrating Spanish, French,
Chinese, American and other societies, and however much
influence and prestige it gave to local Communist parties posing
as anti-fascist, was not adequately serving the needs of the Soviet
Union itself in world affairs. Britain and France were unwilling
to force Rumania and Poland to make concessions to the
U.S.S.R. in order to buy Soviet assistance in building a 'cordon
sanitaire' around Nazism. Furthermore, the Soviets could not be
certain that Germany might not leave France and Britain alone,
and move east. Therefore, on April 17, 1939, the Soviet ambassador to Germany, Merekalov, paid an unexpected call on
German State Secretary Weizsäcker, which launched the Soviet-
initiated conversations with Nazi Germany culminating in the
Nazi-Soviet Pact of August 23, 1939. The State Secretary's notes
on the Merekalov visit follows:

> The [Soviet] Ambassador thereupon stated approximately as
> follows: Russian policy had always moved in a straight line.
> Ideological differences of opinion had hardly influenced the
> Russian-Italian relationship, and they did not have to prove a
> stumbling block with regard to Germany either. Soviet Russia
> had not exploited the present friction between Germany and
> the western democracies against us, nor did she desire to do
> so. There exists for Russia no reason why she should not live
> with us on a normal footing. And from normal, the relations
> might become better and better.[3]

Soviet Foreign Commissar Litvinov, associated in many minds

2. Ibid., p. 269.
3. U. S. Dept. of State, *Nazi-Soviet Relations 1939–1941*, 1948, p. 2.

with the pro-Western Soviet tactics during the Popular Front era, was replaced on May 3, 1939, by Molotov, suggesting a reorientation of Soviet foreign policy. A telegram from the German *chargé* in Moscow (Tippelskirch) explains:

> Sudden change has caused greatest surprise here, since Litvinov was in the midst of negotiations with the English delegation . . . his dismissal seems to be result of spontaneous decision by Stalin. The decision apparently is connected with the fact that differences of opinion arose in the Kremlin on Litvinov's negotiations. Reason for difference of opinion presumably lies in deep mistrust that Stalin harbors toward the entire surrounding capitalist world. At last Party Congress Stalin urged caution lest Soviet Union be drawn into conflicts. Molotov (no Jew) is held to be "Most intimate friend and closest collaborator" of Stalin. His appointment is apparently to guarantee that the foreign policy will be continued strictly in accordance with Stalin's ideas.[4]

Meantime the British and French delegations to Moscow were continuing their negotiations with the Soviets in an effort to form a common front against Germany, unaware of the Soviet initiative in conversations with Germany. According to German Ambassador Schulenberg (in Moscow), to State Secretary Weizsäcker (in Berlin):

> It is extraordinarily difficult here to learn anything at all about the course of the English-French-Soviet negotiations. My British colleague . . . preserves an iron silence. Even neutral diplomats have not been able to learn anything.[5]

An indication of some possible Soviet foreign policy movements was gleaned from comments made to German Under-Secretary of State Woermann by Bulgarian Minister Draganoff on June 1, 1939; Draganoff (clearly operating as a "plant") was reporting opinions expressed to him by the Soviet *chargé d'affaires* in Berlin:

4. Ibid., p. 6.
5. Ibid., p. 8.

The Soviet Union faced the present world situation with hesitation. She was vacillating between three possibilities, namely
the conclusion of the pact with England and France, a further
dilatory treatment of pact negotiations, and a rapprochement
with Germany. This last possibility, with which ideological
considerations would not have to become involved, was
closest to the desires of the Soviet Union.[6]

In the latter part of July, and early August, Nazi-Soviet negotiations drew closer to agreement although many problems
between the two countries remained to be settled. In his telegram
of August 4, 1939, German Ambassador Schulenberg informed
his superiors in Berlin of his conversation that day with Soviet
Foreign Commissar Molotov, including a reference to negotiations the Soviets were then also carrying on with the French and
British:

> From M.'s whole attitude it was evident that the Soviet
> government was in fact more prepared for improvement in
> German-Soviet relations, but that the old mistrust of
> Germany persists. My overall impression is that the Soviet
> government is at present determined to sign with England and
> France if they fulfill all Soviet wishes.[7]

But, according to professors Strausz-Hupe and Possony, "the
main stumbling block" to a Soviet-French-British rapprochement was "Russian insistence on incorporation of the
Baltic countries into the Soviet Union and, as during the Berlin
crisis, on free passage of Russian troops through Poland." It is
the view of these scholars that:

> The pact with Germany was, then, Russia's main desire; and
> she negotiated with the West in order to extract the agreement
> from the Nazis. The various discussion points raised by the
> Soviets were "red herrings" to delay the negotiations till late
> in summer when the Germans had to make up their mind, or
> delay the war.[8]

6. Ibid., p. 20.
7. Ibid., p. 41.
8. Strausz-Hupe & Possony, *International Relations*, pp. 586–587.

During the Summer of 1939 the German and Soviet negotiators drew closer and closer together, although the Germans were not certain that the Soviets were not about to conclude some agreement with France and Britain, just as the Soviets were not sure of Germany's attitude. On August 18, 1939, in response to Germany's inquiry, Molotov gave Schulenberg, the German Ambassador to the U.S.S.R., the following message:

> If, however, the German government now undertakes a change from the old policy in the direction of a sincere improvement in political relations with the U.S.S.R., the Soviet government can look upon such a change only with pleasure and is on its own part prepared to alter its policy in the direction of an appreciable improvement in relations with Germany. . . . The government of the U.S.S.R. is of the opinion that the first step toward such an improvement in relations . . . could be the conclusion of a trade and credit agreement . . . the second step, to be taken shortly thereafter, could be the conclusion of a non-aggression pact or the reaffirmation of the neutrality pact of 1926, with the simultaneous conclusion of a special protocol which would define the interests of the signatory parties . . . and which form an integral part of the pact.[9]

In the meantime Germany increased its pressure on Poland, while the diplomats took steps to conclude their negotiations for a German-Soviet agreement. German Foreign Minister Ribbentrop met with Stalin and Molotov in Moscow to bring the negotiations to a conclusion. All three agreed that the principal enemies were Britain and France, as the following memorandum from the Carmen Foreign office makes clear:

> Herren Stalin and Molotov commented adversely on the British Military Mission in Moscow, which had never told the Soviet government what it really wanted. The Reich Foreign Minister stated in this connection that England had always been trying and was still trying to disrupt the development of good relations between Germany and the Soviet Union. England was weak and wanted to let others fight for its presump-

9. *Nazi-Soviet Relations*, p. 59.

tuous claim to world domination. Herr Stalin eagerly con-
curred . . . If England dominates the world . . . this was due to
the stupidity of the other countries that always let themselves
be bluffed.[10]

Stalin proposed a toast to Hitler, as follows:

I know how much the German nation loves its Fuhrer; I
should therefore like to drink to his health.[11]

Following further toasts, a Treaty of Non-aggression, and also
the far more important Secret Protocol, were concluded later on
the same day, August 23, 1939. Here is the text of the Secret Protocol:

On the occasion of the signature of the Non-Aggression Pact
between the German Reich and the Union of Soviet Socialist
Republics the undersigned plenipotentiaries of each of the two
parties discussed in strictly confidential conversations the
question of the boundary of their respective spheres of
influence in Eastern Europe. These conversations led to the
following conclusions:

1. In the event of a territorial and political rearrangement in
the areas belonging to the Baltic states (Finland, Estonia,
Latvia, Lithuania), the northern boundary of Lithuania shall
represent the boundary of the spheres of influence of Germany
and the U.S.S.R. In this connection the interest of Lithuania
in the Vilna area is recognized by each party.

2. In the event of a territorial and political rearrangement of
the areas belonging to the Polish state the spheres of influence
of Germany and the U.S.S.R. shall be bounded approximately by the line of the rivers Narew, Vistula, and San.

The question of whether the interests of both parties make

10. Ibid., p. 79.
11. Ibid., p. 75.

desirable the maintenance of an independent Polish state and how such a state shall be bounded can only be definitely determined in the course of further political developments. In any event both governments will resolve this question by means of a friendly agreement.

3. With regard to Southeastern Europe attention is called by the Soviet side to its interest in Bessarabia. The German side declares its complete political disinterestedness in these areas.

4. This protocol shall be treated by both parties as strictly secret. Moscow, August 23, 1939.

For the Government of the German Reich:
V. RIBBENTROP

Plenipotentiary of the Government of the U.S.S.R.:
V. MOLOTOV

When the Nazi-Soviet Pact of August 23, 1939, was announced, Communist parties abroad suddenly found themselves faced with the task of abandoning the Popular Front against Nazism, and taking up the thesis that Britain and France were jeopardizing a peace maintained by Germany and Russia. The French party, until August 23 proudly claiming to be in the forefront of patriotic defense against the Axis imperialists, was now suddenly obliged to concentrate its hatred on the Polish landlords to justify Soviet occupation of eastern Poland, and to agitate for peace with Hitler. On September 26, the party was dissolved by the French government. On October 4, the party's leader, Maurice Thorez, who was serving as a N.C.O. in the French army, deserted from his unit.

In the United States, Communists suddenly demanded an isolationist policy—no aid to Britain and France: "The Yanks are not coming" was the chief slogan. Economic and military sabotage took place in the form of the industrial strikes and an attempt to paralyze production in the aircraft industry. But the greatest Communist and pro-Communist effort was concentrated in a front organization known as the American Peace Mobilization, designed to block American intervention in behalf of Britain and France, thus giving free rein to the Nazi-Soviet partners as they overran Europe. The National Secretary was a Vanderbilt scion, Frederick Vanderbilt Field. Referring to the American Peace Mobilization, journalist Eugene Lyons writes:

> It instantly received the endorsement of the California, Wisconsin, Connecticut and Washington C.I.O. State councils. These are the states in which defense strikes were particularly numerous and embittered in the following year. Endorsement also came quickly from the National Maritime Union, the International Woodworkers Union, the Farm Equipment Workers Organizing Committee, the Maritime Federation of the Pacific, the Federation of Architects, Chemists, Engineers and Technicians, the Fur and Leather Workers Union, the American Newspaper Guild, and the Greater New York Industrial Council—all C.I.O. affiliates. Joe Curran's Maritime Union prepared to send seven hundred delegates to the American Peace Mobilization convention the American Youth Congress undertook to provide a delegation of four hundred or more and several hundred were announced by the National Negro Congress. Locals of the United Automobile Workers Union—locals which would soon figure in defense production blockades—sent a thousand delegates.[12]

A large number of prominent Americans became members of the National Council of the American Peace Mobilization, while Poland and the Baltic states were being overrun by the Nazis and Communists. Among these were: James Carey, Max Yergan, Carl Sandburg, Richard Wright, Langston Hughes, Carey McWilliams, Earl Robinson, Michael Quill, Abraham Cronbach, Franz Boas, and George Seldes.

The American Peace Mobilization picketed the White House, opposing American aid to the victims and intended victims of totalitarian aggression. Until the German attack on Russia, its members conducted a persistent pro-isolationist and anti-defense campaign while Europe was being overrun.

Four days before the Hitler-Stalin pact was signed, Germany and the Soviet Union had already begun to strengthen each other's economies through trade agreements. According to a German Foreign Office memorandum:

---

12. Eugene Lyons, *The Red Decade* (Indianapolis, Bobbs-Merrill, 1941), p. 385.

In order that we (Germany) might secure an immediate benefit from the credit agreement, it was made a condition from the beginning that the Soviet Union bind itself to the delivery, starting immediately, of certain raw materials as current business. . . . The Russian commitments . . . amount to 180 million Reichsmarks. . . . It is a question, in particular, of lumber, cotton, feed grain, oil cake, phosphate, platinum, raw furs, petroleum, and other goods . . .[13]

THE WAR BEGINS

German troops invaded Poland at the beginning of September and entered Warsaw nine days later. This occasioned a telephone message of congratulations from Molotov to German Ambassador Schulenberg which the latter relayed to Berlin:

I have received your communication regarding the entry of German troops into Warsaw. Please convey my congratulations and greetings to the German Reich government. Molotov[14]

In the meantime the Soviet Union prepared to carry out its part of the invasion of Poland, justifying such action by the "necessity" of "protecting" the "Russian" minorities. In a telegram to the Foreign Office in Berlin, Schulenberg said:

Molotov summoned me today (September 14) . . . Soviet action could . . . take place sooner than he had assumed. For the political motivation of Soviet action (The collapse of Poland and protection of Russian "minorities") it was of the greatest importance not to take action until the governmental center of Poland, the city of Warsaw, had fallen. Molotov therefore asked that he be informed as nearly as possible as to when the capture of Warsaw could be counted on.[15]

Naturally the Germans did not like the Soviet "motivation"

13. Nazi-Soviet Relations, p. 84.
14. Ibid., p. 89.
15. Ibid., p. 92.

and suggested that the Soviets simply invade Poland as planned, without any public announcement; however the Soviets demurred, as related in this telegram of September 16, sent by Schulenberg to Berlin:

> Molotov added that . . . the Soviet government intended to motivate its procedure as follows: the Polish State had collapsed and no longer existed; therefore all agreements concluded with Poland were void; third powers might try to profit by the chaos which had arisen; the Soviet Union considered itself obligated to intervene to protect its Ukrainian and White Russian brothers and make it possible for these unfortunate people to work in peace . . . Molotov conceded that the projected argument of the Soviet government contained a note that was jarring to German sensibilities but asked that in view of the difficult situation of the Soviet government we not let a trifle like this stand in our way.[16]

On September 28, 1939, the Nazi and Soviet governments issued several protocols and agreements among which were:

> Both parties will tolerate in their territories no Polish agitation and inform each other concerning suitable measures for this purpose . . . After the government of the German Reich and the government of the U.S.S.R. have, by means of the treaty signed today, definitely settled the problems arising from the collapse of the Polish state and have thereby created a sure foundation for a lasting peace in eastern Europe, they mutually express their conviction that it would serve the true interests of all peoples to put an end to the state of war. . . . Should, however, the efforts of the two governments remain fruitless, this would demonstrate the fact that England and France are responsible for the continuation of the war, whereupon, in case of the continuation of the war, the governments of Germany and the U.S.S.R. shall engage in mutual consultations with regard to necessary measures.[17]

Even prior to this joint declaration, the Soviets had begun to

16. Ibid., p. 95.
17. Ibid., p. 107.

exert pressure against the Baltic states, and the day before German Foreign Minister Ribbentrop departed for Moscow to finalize the accord with the U.S.S.R., he received the following telegram from the German mission in Estonia, quoting the Estonian Foreign Minister:

> The Estonian government, under the gravest threat of imminent attack, perforce is prepared to accept a military alliance with the Soviet Union.[18]

The most serious Soviet action in the Baltic area was the invasion of Finland. The Finns, not knowing about the Secret Protocol of August 23, hoped that Germany might help oppose Soviet pressures. However, as the following instructions from Berlin to the German missions abroad makes clear, they had no chance of help from Germany:

> In your conversations regarding the Finnish-Russian conflict please avoid any anti-Russian note. According to whom you are addressing the following arguments are to be employed: The inescapable course of events in the revision of treaties following the last Great War. The natural requirement of Russia for increased security of Leningrad and the entrance to the Gulf of Finland . . .[19]

These instructions were supplemented on December 6, 1939:

> In conversations regarding the Finnish-Russian conflict, you are requested to make use of the following considerations: Only a few weeks ago Finland was about to come to an understanding with Russia, which might have been achieved by a prudent Finnish policy. An appeal to the League of Nations by the Finnish government is the least suitable way of solving the crisis. There is no doubt that British influence on the Finnish government . . . induced the Finnish government to reject Russian proposals and thereby brought on the present

18. Ibid., p. 104.
19. Ibid., p. 127.

conflict. England's guilt in the Russo-Finnish conflict should
be especially emphasized. Germany is not involved in these
events. In conversations, sympathy is to be expressed for the
Russian point of view. Please refrain from expressing any
sympathy for the Finnish position.[20]

The Germans received economic compensation for this diplomatic support of Soviet aggression. On February 11, 1940 the
following memorandum on the German-Soviet Commercial
Agreement was signed.

Soviet deliveries. According to the Agreement, the Soviet
Union shall within the first 12 months deliver raw materials in
the amount of approximately 500 million Reichsmarks. The
most important raw materials are the following:
1,000,000 tons of grain for cattle, and of legumes, in the
amount of 120 million Reichsmarks.
900,000 tons of mineral oil in the amount of approximately
115 million Reichsmarks.
100,000 tons of cotton in the amount of approximately 90
million Reichsmarks.
500,000 tons of phosphates
100,000 tons of chrome ore
500,000 tons of iron ore
300,000 tons of scrap iron and pig iron
2,400 kg. of platinum
Manganese ore, metals, lumber, and numerous other raw materials.

On April 9, 1940, Germany advanced into Denmark and
Norway. The Germans explained this to their Russian allies as a
preventive measure against British pressures. German Ambassador Schulenburg reported the following Soviet reaction to
the German move:

Molotov declared that the Soviet government understood the
measures which were forced upon Germany. The English had
certainly gone much too far; they had disregarded completely

20. Ibid., p. 129.

the rights of neutral nations. In conclusion, Molotov said literally: "We wish Germany complete success in her defensive measures."

A similar Soviet reaction resulted after the Germans informed Moscow of the invasion of the Low Countries, also explained as being a defensive measure:

> Molotov appreciated the news and added that he understood that Germany had to protect herself against Anglo-French attack. He had no doubt of our success.[21]

During this entire period, the British, as well as other Western countries, were unaware of the Secret Protocol, and still assumed that Russia might be amenable to Western overtures leading to a possible coalition against Germany. Therefore, at the end of May, 1940, the British government sent left-wing Laborite Sir Stafford Cripps to Moscow to discuss matters with Stalin. This is the way the Germans sized up the Cripps mission:

> There is no reason for apprehension, concerning the Cripps mission, since there is no reason to doubt the loyal attitude of the Soviet Union toward us and since the unchanged direction of Soviet policy toward England precludes damage to Germany or vital German interests.

As the Germans moved into the Low Countries and invaded France, the Soviets completely took over Lithuania, Latvia, and Estonia, as reported by German Ambassador Schulenberg:

> The unresisted reinforcement of Russian troops in Lithuania, Latvia and Estonia and the reorganization of the governments of the Baltic states, sought by the Russian government to bring about more reliable cooperation with the Soviet Union, are the concern of Russia and the Baltic states . . .

21. Ibid., pp. 138, 142.

Molotov summoned me this evening to his office and
expressed warmest congratulations of the Soviet government
on the splendid success of the German armed forces.
Thereupon, Molotov informed me of the Soviet action against
the Baltic states. He referred to the reasons published in the
press and added that it had become necessary to put an end to
all the intrigues by which England and France had tried to sow
discord and mistrust between Germany and the Soviet Union
in the Baltic states.

A few days after the Soviets achieved consolidation of their
newly acquired Baltic possessions, they made demands on the
Rumanian government for Bessarabia and northern Bucovina.
Molotov informed German Ambassador Schulenburg on June
23, 1940:

The solution of the Bessarabian question brooked no further
delay. The Soviet government was still striving for a peaceful
solution, but it was determined to use force, should the Rumanian government decline a peaceful agreement. The Soviet
claim likewise extended to Bucovina, which had a Ukrainian
population.

Four days later Schulenburg reported:

Molotov just informed me by telephone that he had summoned the Rumanian Minister at 10 o'clock this evening, had
informed him of the Soviet government's demand regarding
the cession of Bessarabia and the northern part of Bucovina,
and had demanded a reply from the Rumanian government
not later than tomorrow, i.e., on June 27.

The Rumanian government, not knowing about the Secret
Protocol of August 23, 1939, requested support from the German
government against these Soviet demands. German Foreign
Minister Ribbentrop instructed the German Minister in
Bucharest to inform the Rumanian government that:

The Soviet government has informed us that it has demanded the cession of Bessarabia and the northern part of Bucovina from the Rumanian government. In order to avoid war between Rumania and the Soviet Union, we can only advise the Rumanian government to yield to the Soviet government's demand.[22]

Meantime the Soviet Union continued to repulse Western attempts to establish an anti-German alliance. On July 13, 1940, Molotov sent to Ambassador Schulenberg the following description of Stalin's answers to the inquiries of British emissary Cripps:

The Soviet government was, of course, very much interested in present events in Europe, but he (Stalin) did not see any danger of the hegemony of any one country in Europe and still less any danger that Europe might be engulfed by Germany. Stalin observed the policy of Germany, and knew several leading German statesmen well.

He had not discovered any desire on their part to engulf European countries. Stalin was not of the opinion that German military successes menaced the Soviet Union and her friendly relations with Germany. These relations were not based on transient circumstances, but on the basic national interests of both countries.

However, during the late summer of 1940 there were several incidents which caused friction between Germany and the U.S.S.R. Germany, still unhappy with Russia's demands on Rumanian Bucovina, joined with Italy to bring about a territorial cession from Rumania to Hungary—the province of Transylvania. This did not please the Soviets. There was also some bad feeling on both sides regarding their respective attitudes toward, and actions in, Finland. Nonetheless, on October 13, Germany made overtures to the U.S.S.R. with regard to joining Germany, Japan, and Italy in a grand coalition of totalitarians against the Western Powers, designed to exclude the United States and

22. Ibid., p. 163.

Britain from the Eurasian continent forever. On this date Ribbentrop sent a letter to Stalin which stated:

> I should like to state that, in the opinion of the Führer, also, it appears to be the historical mission of the Four Powers—the Soviet Union, Italy, Japan, and Germany—to adopt a long-range policy and to direct the future development of their peoples into the right channels by delimitation of their interests on a worldwide scale.

This letter invited Molotov to come to Berlin to discuss ways and means of bringing the dictators together. Stalin replied as follows:

> I agree with you that a further improvement in the relations between our countries is entirely possible on the permanent basis of a long-range delimitation of mutual interests. Herr Molotov admits that he is under obligation to pay you a return visit in Berlin. He hereby accepts your invitation.

Conversations between Molotov, Hitler, and Ribbentrop took place in Berlin on November 13, and 14, 1940. They discussed their aspirations and common problems, and considered how they, together with the Japanese and Italians, might be able to work out a New World Order. Some conception of the scope of these conversations can be gleaned from this memorandum (of German State Secretary Weizsäcker) of Hitler's talk with Molotov:

> After the conquest of England, the British Empire would be apportioned as a gigantic worldwide estate in bankruptcy of 40 million square kilometers. In this bankrupt estate there would be for Russia access to the ice-free and really open ocean. Thus far, a minority of 45 million Englishmen had ruled 600 million inhabitants of the British Empire. He was about to crush this minority. Even the United States was actually doing nothing but picking out of this bankrupt estate a few items. . . . The conflict with England would be fought to the last ditch, and he (Hitler) had no doubt that the defeat of

the British Isles would lead to the dissolution of the Empire. ... Under those circumstances there arose worldwide perspectives. During the next few weeks they would have to be settled in joint diplomatic negotiations with Russia, and Russia's participation in the solution of these problems would have to be arranged. All the countries which could possibly be interested in the bankrupt estate would have to stop all controversies among themselves and concern themselves exclusively with the partition of the British Empire. This applied to Germany, France, Italy, Russia, and Japan.

Germany proposed to the U.S.S.R. that:

The focal points in the territorial aspirations of the Soviet Union would presumably be centered south of the territory of the Soviet Union in the direction of the Indian Ocean. ... Germany, Italy, and the Soviet Union would jointly exert their influence to the end that the Straits Convention of Montreux, presently in force, would be replaced by another convention which would accord to the Soviet Union the unrestricted right of passage through the Straits for her warships at any time, whereas all other powers except the other Black Sea countries, but including Germany and Italy, would renounce in principle the right of passage through the Straits of their warships.[23]

After Molotov returned to Moscow, the Soviet government further discussed concrete implementation of the general issues considered in Berlin, and as a result of a conversation between Molotov and Ribbentrop on November 26, 1940, a draft of a secret protocol was written, including the following provisions:

The Soviet Union declares that her territorial aspirations center south of the national territory of the Soviet Union in the direction of the Indian Ocean.

Later that day Ambassador Schulenberg reported to Berlin this further Soviet reaction to the German proposals:

23. Preceding extracts from *Nazi-Soviet Relations*, pp. 216, 242, 250.

The Soviet government is prepared to accept the draft of the
Four Power Pact which the Reich Foreign Minister outlined
in the conversation of November 13, regarding political
collaboration and reciprocal economic support subject to the
following conditions: . . . Provided that within the next few
weeks the security of the Soviet Union in the Straits is assured
by the conclusion of a mutual assistance pact between the Soviet Union and Bulgaria, which is geographically situated inside the security zone of the Black Sea boundaries of the Soviet Union, and by the establishment of a base for land and
naval forces of the U.S.S.R. within range of the Bosporus and
Dardanelles by means of a long-term lease. Provided that the
area south of Batum and Baku in the general direction of the
Persian Gulf is recognized as the center of aspirations of the
Soviet Union.

As usual, a draft secret protocol was proposed by the Soviets,
which provided for:

. . . a fifth secret protocol between Germany, the Soviet
Union, and Italy, recognizing that Bulgaria is geographically
located inside the security zone of the Black Sea boundaries of
the Soviet Union and that it is therefore a political necessity
that a mutual assistance pact be concluded between the Soviet
Union and Bulgaria, which in no way shall affect the internal
regime of Bulgaria, her sovereignty or independence.

The Nazi-Soviet documents clearly show that the U.S.S.R.
wanted the Four Power Pact, with emphasis on protecting Soviet
spheres of influence in Eastern Europe. But Hitler finally tired of
the Soviet insistence on a special role in the Black Sea area.

After considering Soviet demands, particularly those relating
to Bulgaria, Hitler concluded that rather than bring the U.S.S.R.
into the Axis, the better course would be to eliminate the Communist element in the world equation. On December 18, 1940,
Hitler therefore issued the top secret "Operation Barbarossa," a
massive plan envisaging invasion of the Soviet Union in the
spring of 1941. Meantime, of course, Germany went through the
motions of continuing its alliance with the Soviets, and, in spite
of certain suspicions in Moscow, induced the Kremlin to believe

that Germany was considering specific implementation of the November, 1940 conversations with Molotov in Berlin.

Soviet suspicions of German actions stemmed primarily from German actions in Bulgaria, as the following Soviet statement of January 17, 1941, makes clear:

> According to all reports, German troops in great numbers are in Rumania and are now prepared to march into Bulgaria, having as their goal the occupation of Bulgaria, Greece, and the Straits. There can be no doubt that England will try to forestall the operations of German troops, to occupy the Straits, to start military operations against Bulgaria into a theater of operations. The Soviet government has stated repeatedly to the German government that it considers the territory of Bulgaria and of the Straits as the security zone of the U.S.S.R. and that it cannot be indifferent to events which threaten the security interests of the U.S.S.R. In view of all this the Soviet government regards it as its duty to give warning that it will consider the appearance of any foreign armed forces on the territory of Bulgaria and of the Straits as a violation of the security interests of the U.S.S.R.

But the Soviet threat was not carried out. All that happened was that the U.S.S.R. indicated its unhappiness with the German action, and its lack of support for that action:

> It is to be regretted that despite the caution contained in the *démarche* of November 25, 1940, on the part of the Soviet government, the German Reich government has deemed it possible to take a course of action that involves injury to the security interests of the U.S.S.R. and had decided to effect the military occupation of Bulgaria. In view of the fact that the Soviet government maintains the same basic position as its démarche of November 25, the German government must understand that it cannot count on support from the U.S.S.R. for its acts in Bulgaria.[24]

In March, 1941, Japanese Foreign Minister Matsuoka tra-

24. Ibid., p. 278.

veled to Moscow, on to Berlin, back to Moscow, and then home, in an effort to ascertain Soviet and German moods, and arrive at some agreement with the U.S.S.R. in the Far East with respect to mutual security interests. German Ambassador Schulenberg reported to Berlin that:

> Matsuoka explained to me and the Italian Ambassador that he had for thirty years been of the opinion that relations between Japan and the Soviet Union should be good. His further pursuit of this policy, therefore, was nothing new.

When Matsuoka arrived in Berlin, Hitler did not tell him that Germany was planning to attack Russia, but did indicate (through Ribbentrop) that Russo-German relations had cooled:

> Confidentially he (the Reich Foreign Minister) could inform Matsuoka that present relations with Russia were correct, to be sure, but not very friendly. After Molotov's visit, during which accession to the Three Power Pact was offered, Russia had made conditions that were unacceptable. They involved the sacrifice of German interests in Finland, the granting of bases on the Dardanelles and a strong influence on conditions in the Balkans, particularly Bulgaria. The Führer had not concurred because he had been of the opinion that Germany could not permanently subscribe to such a Russian policy. Germany needed the Balkan peninsula above all for her own economy and had not been inclined to let it come under Russian domination.[25]

Matsuoka told Hitler, on March 27th, that he foresaw a grand alliance of the Axis and the Soviet Union against the Anglo-Saxon powers. According to the notes of the German Foreign Office:

> Matsuoka then continued that he had discussed with Stalin his ideas about the New Order and had stated that the Anglo-Saxon represented the greatest hindrance to the establishment

25. Ibid., pp. 280, 284.

of this order and that Japan therefore was compelled to fight against them. He had told Stalin that the Soviets on their part also were coming out for something new and that he believed that after the collapse of the British Empire the difficulties between Japan and Russia could be eliminated. He had represented the Anglo-Saxons as the common foe of Japan, Germany, and Soviet Russia. Stalin had arranged to give him an answer when he passed through Moscow again on his return journey to Japan.

Matsuoka then returned to Moscow, where he reached agreement with Stalin on a Japanese-Soviet neutrality pact, which gave the Japanese freedom of action to the south with fore-knowledge of security in the west. German Ambassador Schulenburg telegraphed Berlin on April 13, 1941, that:

> Matsuoka has just visited me in order to make his farewell call. He stated to me that a Japanese-Soviet Neutrality Pact had been arranged at the last moment, and, in all likelihood, would be signed this afternoon at 2 p.m. local time.[26]

Later that same day, Schulenburg telegraphed a further report, indicating, among other things, that the Soviet Union at this time still considered itself a faithful adherent of the Hitler-Stalin pact:

> To a question from the Italian Ambassador to Matsuoka as to whether at the conversation between Matsuoka and Stalin the relationship of the Soviet Union with the Axis had been taken up, Matsuoka answered that Stalin had told him that he was a convinced adherent of the Axis and an opponent of England and America. The departure of Matusoka was delayed for an hour and then took place with extraordinary ceremony. Apparently, completely unexpectedly for both the Japanese and the Russians, both Stalin and Molotov appeared and greeted Matsuoka and the Japanese who were present in a remarkable friendly manner and wished them a pleasant journey. Then Stalin publicly asked for me, and when he found me he came

26. Ibid., pp. 297, 322.

up to me and threw his arm around my shoulders: "We must remain friends and you must now do everything to that end." Somewhat later Stalin turned to the German acting military attaché, Colonel Krebs, first made sure that he was a German, and then said to him: "We will remain friends with you—in any event." Stalin doubtless brought about this greeting of Colonel Krebs and myself intentionally, and thereby he consciously attracted the general attention of the numerous persons who were present.

Further evidence of the Soviet solidarity with the Axis was manifest in the following telegram sent from the German Embassy in Moscow to Berlin on April 16:

The Japanese Ambassador, on whom I called today, told me that the conclusion to the Soviet-Japanese Neutrality Pact had created a very favorable atmosphere on the part of the Soviet government, of which he was convinced by Molotov, who today had asked him to call immediately in order to continue the negotiations regarding a commercial treaty. The conclusion of the treaty had caused disappointment and anxiety in America, where Matsuoka's journey to Berlin and Rome had been followed with interest. Members of the Japanese Embassy here maintain that the Pact is advantageous not only to Japan but also to the Axis, that the Soviet Union's relations with the Axis will be favorably affected by it, and that the Soviet Union is prepared to cooperate with the Axis. Stalin's manner toward the Ambassador at the railroad station when Matsuoka left is also interpreted in the same way by the diplomatic corps here. The view is frequently expressed that Stalin had purposely brought about an opportunity to show his attitude toward Germany in the presence of the foreign diplomats and press representatives; this, in view of the persistently circulating rumors of an imminent conflict between Germany and the Soviet Union is considered to be especially noteworthy. At the same time the changed attitude of the Soviet government is attributed to the effect here of the success of the German armed forces in Yugoslavia and Greece.

That same day, a Commercial Agreement Protocol was signed between Germany and the U.S.S.R.:

The plenipotentiaries of the Government of the German Reich and the Government of the Union of Soviet Socialist Republics acting in pursuance of article 10 of the Commercial Agreement between Germany and the Union of Soviet Socialist Republics of February 11, 1940, have, on the basis of their inquiry into the observance of the above-mentioned agreement as of February 11, 1941, agreed as follows: According to Soviet calculations, the Soviet deliveries on February 11, 1941, amounted to 310.3 million Reichsmarks. The Germans will, by May 11, 1941, make deliveries from Germany in at least this amount.[27]

Meantime it was inevitable that war rumors should spread, and on April 24, the German Naval *Attaché* in Moscow reported that the British Ambassador had predicted June 22 as the day of the outbreak of war. This prediction was exact, and the wonder is that the Soviet Union seemingly ignored the warning:

Rumors current here speak of alleged danger of war between Germany and the Soviet Union and are being fed by travelers passing through from Germany. According to the Counselor of the Italian Embassy, the British Ambassador predicts June 22 as the day of the outbreak of war. May 20 is set by others. I am endeavoring to counteract the rumors, which are manifestly absurd.[28]

A most authoritative analysis of Soviet foreign policy during this period is provided in the conversation which took place on April 28, 1941, in Berlin, between Hitler and Ambassador Schulenburg, an account of which follows:

The Führer thereupon asked me what devil had possessed the Russians to conclude the Friendship Pact with Yugoslavia. I expressed the opinion that it was solely a matter of the declaration of Russian interests in the Balkans. Russia had done something each time that we undertook anything in the Balkans. . . . The Führer then said that it was not clear who had pulled the strings in the overthrow of the Yugoslav

27. Preceding extracts from *Nazi-Soviet Relations*, pp. 324, 326, 327.
28. Ibid., p. 330.

government. England or Russia? In his opinion it had been the British, while the Balkan peoples all had the impression that Russia had been behind it. I replied that, as seen from Moscow, there was nothing to support the theory that Russia had had a finger in the pie. . . . Now Russia was very apprehensive at the rumors predicting a German attack on Russia. The Führer insisted that the Russians had been the first to move, since they had concentrated needlessly large numbers of divisions in the Baltic states. . . . He [Hitler] did not, it was true, believe that Russia could be brought to attack Germany, but strong instincts of hatred had survived, nevertheless, and, above all, Russian determination to approach closer to Finland and the Dardanelles was unchanged, as Molotov had allowed clearly to be seen on his visit. When he considered all this, he was obliged to be careful. I pointed out that Cripps had not succeeded until six days after the conclusion of the Russo-Yugoslav treaty in even speaking to Molotov's deputy, Vishinsky. I further reminded him that Stalin had told Matsuoka he was committed to the Axis and could not collaborate with England and France, as well as of the scene at the railroad station, which Stalin had purposely brought about in order to demonstrate publicly his intention to collaborate with the Axis. In 1939 England and France had taken all conceivable means to win Russia over to their side, and if Stalin had not been able to decide in favor of England and France at a time when England and France were both still strong, I believed that he would certainly not make such a decision today, when France was destroyed and England badly battered. On the contrary, I was convinced that Stalin was prepared to make even further concessions to us. . . . The Führer then took leave of me.[29]

The above conversation suggests that in Schulenburg's view the Soviets would remain on Germany's side, and that Schulenburg, if he was aware of "Operation Barbarossa," sought unsuccessfully to dissuade Hitler from attacking Russia.

Schulenburg was not the only member of the Nazi hierarchy who had doubts about the desirability of war with Russia. German State Secretary Weizsäcker made one final estimate of the situation, in the form of a memorandum to his superior, Foreign Minister Ribbentrop, dated April 28, 1941:

29. Ibid., p. 332.

I can summarize in one sentence my views on a German-Russian conflict: If every Russian city reduced to ashes were as valuable to us as a sunken British warship, I should advocate the German-Russian war for this summer; but I believe that we would be victors over Russia only in a military sense, and would, on the other hand, lose in an economic sense. It might be considered an alluring prospect to give the Communist system its death blow and it might also be said that it was inherent in the logic of things to muster the Eurasian continent against Anglo-Saxondom and its following. But the sole decisive factor is whether this project will hasten the fall of England. . . . A German attack on Russia would only give the British new moral strength. It would be interpreted there as German uncertainty as to the success of our fight against England. We would thereby not only be admitting that the war was going to last a long time yet, but we might actually prolong it in this way instead of shortening it.

On May 7, 1941, Stalin took over the chairmanship of the Council of People's Commissars in place of Molotov. Ambassador Schulenburg's estimate of the meaning of this action follows:

It can be stated with great certainty that if Stalin decided to take over the highest government office, it was done for reasons of foreign policy. . . . We must bear in mind particularly that Stalin personally has always advocated a friendly relationship between Germany and the Soviet Union. . . . It is remarkable that groups representing the most divergent opinion agree in the presumption that Stalin is pursuing a policy of rapprochement with Germany and the Axis.

Whatever suspicions the Soviets may have had about Germany did not prevent them from continuing to deliver raw materials to Germany, under various trade agreements, in the spring of 1941, as this memo from the German Foreign Office on May 15, 1941, demonstrates:

The status of Soviet raw material deliveries still represents a favorable picture. Of the most important items of raw materials, the following deliveries were made in April:

Grain	208,000 tons
Petroleum	90,000 tons
Cotton	8,300 tons
Nonferrous metals	6,340 tons
cotton, tin, and	
nickel.	

The transit route through Siberia is still operating. The shipments of raw materials from East Asia, particularly of raw rubber, that reach Germany by this route, continue to be substantial (raw rubber during the month of April, 2,000 tons by special trains, 2,000 by regular Siberian trains). . . . I am under the impression that we could make economic demands on Moscow which would even go beyond the scope of the treaty of January 10, 1941. . . . The quantities of raw materials now contracted for are being delivered punctually by the Russians, despite the heavy burden this imposes on them, which, especially with regard to grain, is a notable performance.[30]

On May 24, Schulenburg sent another telegram to Berlin restating his conviction that Soviet foreign policy would continue to be pro-German:

. . . the two strongest men in the Soviet Union—Stalin and Molotov—hold positions which are decisive for the foreign policy of the Soviet Union. That this foreign policy is, above all, directed at the avoidance of a conflict with Germany, is proved by the attitude taken by the Soviet government during the last few weeks, the tone of the Soviet press, which treats all the events which concern Germany in an unobjectionable manner, and the observance of the trade agreements concluded with Germany.

As late as eight days before the German invasion of the Soviet Union, Molotov informed Schulenburg that the Soviet news agency *TASS* had been asked to refute rumors of an impending war between Germany and Russia:

30. Ibid., p. 340.

Despite the obvious absurdity of these rumors, responsible circles in Moscow have thought it necessary, in view of the persistent spread of these rumors, to authorize *TASS* to state that these rumors are a clumsy propaganda maneuver of the forces arrayed against the Soviet Union and Germany, which are interested in a spread and intensification of the war.

TASS declares that:

1. Germany has addressed no demands to the Soviet Union. . . .

2. According to the evidence in the possession of the Soviet Union, both Germany and the Soviet Union are fulfilling to the letter the terms of the Soviet-German Non-Aggression Pact, so that in the opinion of Soviet circles the rumors of the intention of Germany to break the Pact and to launch an attack against the Soviet Union are completely without foundation. . . .

3. The Soviet Union, in accordance with its peace policy, has fulfilled and intends to fulfill the terms of the Soviet-German Non-Aggression Pact; as a result, all the rumors according to which the Soviet Union is preparing for a war with Germany are false and provocative. . . .

But Hitler's Operation Barbarossa was not to be dissuaded.

At 4 a.m., June 22, 1941, Ribbentrop summoned Soviet Ambassador Dekanasov, and declared:

The hostile policy of the Soviet government toward Germany, which had reached its climax in the conclusion of a pact with Yugoslavia at the very time of the German-Yugoslav conflict, had been evident for a year. At a moment when Germany was engaged in a life-and-death struggle, the attitude of Soviet Russia, particularly the concentration of the Russian military forces at the Soviet border, had presented so serious a threat to the Reich that the Führer had to decide to take military counter-measures . . .

Already German forces were moving across the border on the entire front.

The Nazi-Soviet alliance, which lasted from August 23, 1939, to June 22, 1941, was possibly the only one in which the Soviets came out second best. For a time, however, they did very well indeed. They were able to move into Finland, the Baltic states, Bessarabia, and northern Bucovina, without getting involved in war with the West. Because the secret protocol was secret, many in the West actually believed that the Soviets were neutral and even "biding their time" to gain strength against a German attack they always knew was coming. The Nazi-Soviet documents demolish this myth. To the extent that the Soviets are capable of sincerity (in pursuance of their goal of Communism), they were sincere about the Hitler-Stalin pact. The only trouble was that Hitler spoiled everything with his unexpected invasion on June 22, 1941.

Chapter 6

ALLIANCE WITH THE WEST 1941–1945

From the moment of the German invasion, Soviet strategy was to demand American and British aid, to demand the opening of a second front in Europe against the Germans, to maintain the neutrality pact with Japan, and to agitate for territorial changes in eastern and central Europe beneficial to the Soviet Union. From the very start the Soviets were concerned with political objectives extending into the postwar era, while the United States and Britain were almost completely immersed in immediate military goals.

In order to carry out these political objectives, the cooperation, or at least the lack of opposition from the Western Powers was necessary. The Soviets exploited to the maximum the cooperative attitude in leading American and British circles, and the international Communist movement, as the instrumentality of Soviet foreign policy, bent its efforts toward fostering pro-Soviet attitudes in the United States and Great Britain.

When Germany invaded Russia on June 22, 1941, foreign Communists abandoned their neutralist, pro-German, and anti-British attitudes, and advocated all-out cooperation between the western democracies and the Soviet Union against Germany and Italy. Meantime foreign Communists supported the Soviet-Japanese neutrality pact. In the United States, Frederick Vanderbilt Field's American Peace Mobilization, which had picketed the White House with signs stating "The Yanks Aren't Coming," evaporated, and Field volunteered to enter Army Intelligence. Communists flocked to the colors and demanded the opening of a second front to take the pressure off Russia. In France and elsewhere on the continent, Communists, who had collaborated with the Vichy regime and other German-oriented regimes, joined the underground and played an active and often dominant role in the resistance movement.

The Communist cause was immensely strengthened by virtue of the fact that prominent non-Communists in the United States and Britain advocated practically unrestricted aid to "our gallant Soviet ally," and praise of that "ally." On November 8, 1942, for example, Vice-President Henry Wallace addressed a gathering in Madison Square Garden on the occasion of the celebration of the Bolshevik Revolution. He said:

> Russia has probably gone further than any other nation in the world in practicing ethnic democracy . . . It is because Stalin pushed educational democracy with all the power that he could command that Russia today is able to resist Germany.

In February, 1942, Joseph P. Davies, former Ambassador to the Soviet Union, declared in an address in Chicago:

> By the testimony of performance and in my opinion, the word of honor of the Soviet Government is as safe as the Bible . . . (Communism) is protecting the Christian world of free men.

Davies went on to urge all Christians to embrace the Soviet Union: . . .

> . . . by the faith you have found at your mother's knee, in the name of the faith you have found in temples of worship.

In 1943 Senator Elbert D. Thomas of Utah, writing for the Communist magazine *New Masses,* stated:

> In the future when we make an estimate of Soviet leadership, we will see that it is based on the finest of democratic principles, the cultivation and the development of the people by providing proper education, proper health, proper hospitalization.

A year later Thomas wrote a book called *The Four Fears* in which he informed his readers:

> All close students were in agreement that Stalin had abandoned all hopes of world revolution or world conquest ... anti-Russian forces ... will make every attempt to discredit Russia, to throw doubts on her motives and intention, and to make Americans especially believe that Russia is the most to be feared of all powers. . . . They will make us believe that the Russians have deep-laid plans to rule the world, to change all governments by force, to absorb all Europe.[1]

Right after the German invasion of Russia, both the United States and Britain proclaimed their willingness to grant the Soviets maximum aid and support against Germany. This was prior to Pearl Harbor, when there was as yet no state of war between the United States and Germany. United States help to both Britain and Russia naturally increased after Pearl Harbor, when the United States came openly into the conflict. No sooner did the German invasion take place than President Roosevelt dispatched his personal adviser Harry Hopkins to London to discuss matters of supply and strategy with Churchill and his advisors:

> In London Hopkins had found a glimmer of hope that the Soviet forces would be able to hold out until winter. Churchill

---

1. Five preceding quotations from Louis Budenz, *The Cry Is Peace* (Chicago, Regnery, 1952), pp. 3, 4, 8, 60.

had been struck by the fact that Stalin, while urging Britain to make greater military effort, did not show any sense of desperate dependence on help; that, in fact, he had seemed more intent on talking about frontiers and spheres of influence after the war than anything else.[2]

It is remarkable that the Soviets, with their backs to the wall, were seemingly more concerned about exporting Socialism than survival. Meantime, President Roosevelt expedited military aid to the Russians:

He issued unusual orders to his administrators; as when on July 21, he directed that the Russian requests be reviewed at once, and that he be given, within forty-eight hours, a list of what could and ought to be shipped at once. He saw to it these orders were heeded.[3]

Soviet demands on the United States and Britain were great, and Winston Churchill writes of Britain's reaction:

We endured the unpleasant process of exposing our own vital security and projects to failure for the sake of our new ally— surly, snarly, grasping, and so lately indifferent to our survival.[4]

Churchill suspected that the Soviets might have been thinking of making another deal with the Germans. And yet in spite of great provocation, the Western Powers continued to plead with the Russians to accept Western aid:

. . . To Roosevelt Churchill had confided the next day that although nothing in Maisky's (Soviet Ambassador to London) language . . . warranted the assumption, he could not exclude the impression that the Russians might be thinking of

2. Herbert Feis, *Roosevelt, Churchill, Stalin* (Princeton, Princeton University Press, 1960), p. 11.
3. Feis, *Roosevelt, Churchill, Stalin*, p. 21.
4. Winston Churchill, *The Grand Alliance* (Boston, Houghton-Mifflin, 1950), p. 452.

separate terms. This possibility had not caused the American and British governments to modify their military plans. But it had impelled them to hasten the dispatch of their joint mission to Moscow.

The British and American visitors had arrived in Moscow on September 28. Both Beaverbrook and Harriman in their first words to the Russians tried to convey the eagerness of their countries to bring help. Yet at first the mission's reception had been, to use Churchill's word, 'bleak' . . . Stalin had been rude to the point of insult . . . At Stalin's request the program of prospective supply was put in the form of a written protocol signed at the Kremlin on October 1. This set out the quantities of each item to be supplied for shipment to the Soviet Union from October 1, 1941, to July 1, 1942. These included 400 planes a month, among them 100 bombers; 500 tanks a month; a substantial number of scout cars and trucks; antiaircraft and antitank guns; telephone equipment of all kinds; aluminum . . . tin, lead, nickel, copper, magnesium, steel, oil, chemicals, rubber, leather, shoes, wool, army cloth, wheat, and medical supplies. All these goods and more were promised without requiring full information about total Soviet needs or Soviet stocks—information of the sort that was asked of every other country seeking Lend-Lease aid.[5]

Although it was the Soviets who were in the desperate position militarily, and the United States, and to a lesser degree Britain, who were relatively safe, it was the Soviets who exerted pressure on the West for political (i.e. territorial) concessions.

In December, 1941, British Foreign Secretary Anthony Eden arrived in Moscow and discovered that Stalin was not satisfied with Western assurances of support against Germany:

. . . The pledge of alliance and of mutual good conduct based on familiar principles had not satisfied the Soviet rulers. What they sought was a definition of what the Soviet Union was to have at the end of the war . . . Stalin asked first of all recognition of Soviet boundaries as they were roughly before the German attack in June, 1941. The Baltic States, the detached part of Finland, and the province of Bessarabia were to be kept within the Soviet Union. The boundary between

5. Feis, *Roosevelt, Churchill, Stalin*, pp. 15–17.

Poland and the Soviet Union was to be based on the so-called
Curzon line, which meant, in effect, retention of all of eastern
Poland that the Soviet Union had occupied in 1939. Rumania
was to grant special facilities for Soviet air bases. Addi-
tionally, Molotov had hinted that the Soviet government
would also ask that its frontiers be carried into East Prussia,
and that it wanted additional air and naval bases in Finland.[6]

Meantime Japan had struck at Pearl Harbor, and Prime
Minister Churchill was on his way to a meeting with President
Roosevelt. Upon receiving Eden's report of Stalin's demands,
Churchill told his cabinet in a message:

> Stalin's demand about Finland, Baltic States, and Rumania
> are directly contrary to the first, second and third articles of
> the Atlantic Charter to which Stalin has subscribed.[7]

On July 30, 1941, the Soviet Union and the Polish government-in-exile signed an agreement stipulating that the Soviet-
German treaties of 1939 concerning the partition of Poland were
no longer valid: "The government of the U.S.S.R. recognizes
that the Soviet-German treaties of 1939 relative to territorial
changes in Poland have lost their validity."

Both the United States and Britain supported this agreement,
Under-Secretary of State Sumner Welles stating that it "was in
line with the United States policy of non-recognition of territory
taken by conquest."[8]

The extent of Soviet good faith towards Poland was measured
by the mass murder of 10,000 Polish officers by the Soviets in the
fall of 1941 in the Katyn forest, west of Smolensk. The guilty
party blamed the Germans for the atrocity. So anxious were the
British and American governments not to criticize the U.S.S.R.
that they refrained from supporting a Polish demand for an
investigation by the International Red Cross. The same was true
of the British and American reaction to the Soviet execution of
the Polish Jewish socialist leaders Henryk Ehrlich and Wiktor
Alter.

6. Ibid., p. 26.
7. Churchill, *The Grand Alliance*, p. 630.
8. Jan Ciechanowski, *Defeat In Victory* (New York, Doubleday, 1947), p. 39.

According to the Stanislaw Mikolajczyk, who later became the Polish Premier:

> We in London could not raise our voices. Nothing was to be said that would embarrass Stalin. We were told by the British to hold our peace, not only in the face of the arrest of many relief workers, but also despite the fact that hundreds of thousands of Poles were forced to become Russian citizens. Those who resisted were jailed, shot, or sent to slow death in the labor camps. . . .
>
> The picture of Russia became distorted. Ambassador Jan Ciechanowski reported from Washington that pro-Soviet elements had moved into important places in some of the United States war agencies and that any American who attempted to bring up such distasteful matters as, for instance, the cold-blooded murders of the Polish Jewish socialist leaders, Henryk Ehrlich and Wiktor Alter, was pilloried as a 'Fascist Saboteur and German spy. . . .' We turned from Churchill to Roosevelt, then back to Churchill. They both were uniformly sympathetic but continued to impose silence upon us, as they were reluctant to inject anything into their relations with Stalin that might displease him. . . .[9]

Initially the Western Powers resisted Soviet demands for European territories. On January 8, 1942, Prime Minister Churchill wrote Anthony Eden:

> The transfer of peoples of the Baltic States to Soviet Russia against their will would be contrary to all the principles for which we are fighting this war and would dishonor our cause. This also applies to Bessarabia and to northern Bucovina, and in a lesser degree to Finland, which I gather it is not intended to subjugate and absorb . . . In any case there can be no question of settling frontiers until the Peace Conference. I know President Roosevelt holds this view as strongly as I do, and he has several times expressed his pleasure to me at the firm line we took at Moscow.[10]

9. Stanislaw Mikolajczyk, *The Rape of Poland* (London, Whittlesey House, 1948), pp. 24–26.
10. Churchill, *The Grand Alliance*, p. 695.

President Roosevelt appealed to Stalin on March 2, 1942, to refrain from making territorial demands in connection with the prospective treaty, but Stalin's answer was noncommital. But the Western stand on principle began to waver in view of Soviet persistence. Churchill told Roosevelt on March 7:

> The increasing gravity of the war has led me to feel that the principles of the Atlantic Charter ought not to be construed so as to deny Russia the frontiers she occupied when Germany attacked her.

Although President Roosevelt still opposed agreement in advance concerning territorial claims by the Soviet Union, he:

> . . . scurried about in search of a compromise—or he called it that. This was to the effect that the Finns, the Lithuanians, the Latvians, and the Estonians who did not wish to be incorporated in the Soviet Union should have the right to leave these territories with their properties.[11]

Also on March 7 Roosevelt invited Molotov to come to Washington to discuss ways and means of increasing American aid to Russia. But Stalin refused to permit the visit unless there was some prior American and British agreement to Soviet territorial demands.

For a short time there was a belief in American circles that it might be possible to open a second front in Europe in 1942. But this belief was ill-founded, and when Churchill so informed Stalin, the latter stated:

> With regard to . . . the question of creating a second front in Europe, I am afraid it is not being treated with the seriousness it deserves. Taking fully into account the present position on the Soviet-German front, I must state in the most emphatic

11. Feis, *Roosevelt, Churchill, Stalin,* p. 60.

manner that the Soviet government cannot acquiesce in the postponement of a second front in Europe until 1943.[12]

Indeed Stalin went so far as to tell Churchill, whose British forces had been fighting the Germans the year and one half that Stalin was Hitler's ally:

> . . . a great many disagreeable things, especially about our being too much afraid of fighting the Germans, and if we tried it like the Russians we should find it not so bad . . .[13]

Stalin continually complained to Roosevelt and Churchill that they were not sending him enough aid. In spite of terrible losses incurred by convoys taking the northern route to the Soviet Union around the Cape of Norway and through the Arctic Seas to Murmansk, the Soviet complaints kept coming in, and the British and Americans redoubled their efforts to keep the ships coming. On May 17, Churchill instructed his military chiefs as follows:

> Not only Premier Stalin but President Roosevelt will object very much to our desisting from running the convoys now. The Russians are in heavy action, and will expect us to run the risk and pay the price entailed by our contribution. The United States ships are queueing up. My own feeling, mingled with much anxiety, is that the convoy ought to sail on the 18th. The operation is justified if a half gets through. Failure on our part to make the attempt would weaken our influence with both our major Allies. There are always the uncertainties of weather and luck, which may aid us. I share your misgivings, but I feel it is a matter of duty.[14]

While the battle for Stalingrad was going on, Stalin continually complained about the alleged failure of the British and Americans to get enough supplies through to him. After

12. Winston Churchill, *The Hinge of Fate* (Boston, Houghton-Mifflin, 1950), p. 271.
13. Ibid., p. 486.
14. Ibid., p. 261.

receiving a "rough and surly" message from Stalin in this connection, Churchill noted in his Memoirs:

> I did not, however, think it worth while to argue out all this with the Soviet government, who had been willing until they were themselves attacked to see us totally destroyed and share the booty with Hitler, and who even in our common struggle could hardly spare a word of sympathy for the heavy British and American losses incurred in trying to send them aid.[15]

Not only did the Western Powers send arms to the U.S.S.R. via the Arctic, but also via Iran:

> ... an operating organization headed by General Donald H. Connally, an army engineer, had been recruited and flown to Iran. Diesel engines built for American railways had been requisitioned. Ships to transport construction materials and railway supplies had been found despite the competing demands of TORCH (North African landing). The immediate results were only scantily praised by the Soviet authorities, but they no doubt counted closely the enlarging volume of supplies that began during the autumn to reach the Soviet Union over this route.[16]

On December 2, 1944, General John R. Deane, the United States lend-lease expeditor in Moscow, complained to General George C. Marshall (U.S. Chief of Staff), about the absence of Soviet reciprocity in the matter of aid:

> After the banquets we send the Soviets another thousand airplanes and they approve a visa that has been hanging fire for months. We then scratch our heads to see what other gifts we can send and they scratch theirs to see what they can ask for ... In our dealings with the Soviet authorities the United States Military Mission has made every approach that has been made ... In short, we are in the position of being at the same time, the givers and the supplicants.

15. Ibid., p. 270.
16. Feis, *Roosevelt, Churchill, Stalin*, p. 88.

This is neither dignified nor healthy for United Stages prestige.[17]

After the Americans had succeeded in North Africa and were preparing for the invasion of Sicily, Stalin again bluntly referred to the matter of the second front, on March 15, 1943:

> ... I deem it my duty to warn you in the strongest possible manner how dangerous would be from the viewpoint of our common cause further delay in the opening of the second front in France.[18]

At the same time that he hinted at a separate agreement with Hitler if his demands were not met, Stalin repelled continued American requests for cooperation in the war against Japan. Time and time again, on the advice of the Joint Chiefs of Staff, Roosevelt tried to get Stalin to agree at least to start preliminary talks looking toward combined operations in the Far East theaters of war, but Stalin brushed all such queries aside in the plea that all Russian forces were needed on the western front. (Feis, p. 117).

Soviet foreign policy objectives at this time were summed up by Harry Hopkins on March 16, 1943, following a talk with Soviet Ambassador, Maxim Litvinov:

> I called to see the Ambassador this evening and asked him what he believed the Russian demands at the Peace Table would be. He said that they, of course, would want the Baltic States ... Litvinov said he thought Russia had no desire to occupy all of Finland ... but that Russia would insist on moving the line about to a point where the Russian armies were at the end of the Finnish War ... He said that Russia would agree to Poland having East Prussia but that Russia would insist on what he called "her territorial rights" on the Polish frontier. Said he did not anticipate any great difficulty with Poland about this although Poland, he said, would make "outrageous" demands. He felt that Great Britain and the United States should decide what was to be done about Po-

---

17. John R. Deane, *Strange Alliance* (New York, Viking, 1946), p. 84.
18. Churchill, *The Hinge of Fate*, p. 751.

land and "tell them" rather than ask them. He said he
assumed that everybody would agree that Russia should have
Bessarabia . . . He said he was sure Russia would like to see
Germany dismembered.[19]

The Soviets were also interested in Yugoslavia. The Communist movement there, led by Tito Broz, did not fight the
Germans and Italians as did the Chetnik underground of General
Mihailovich (representing the Yugoslav government-in-exile)
until after Germany invaded Russia. Thereafter, Tito represented himself as the only effective anti-fascist force in Yugoslavia. Tito's supporters in Britain and America encouraged
this line of thinking, and by the end of 1943, the United States
and Britain were giving Tito, rather than Mihailovich, their support.

In the summer of 1943, President Roosevelt sent a new
representative to Moscow, someone known to the Soviets as a
long time supporter of the U.S.S.R. in the United States:

> . . . (The President) wanted an alert and zealous proponent of
> cooperation in the post . . . the President asked Joseph E.
> Davies to leave at once on a special trip to Moscow. He had
> served there as Ambassador before, in the thirties, and ever
> since had portrayed Russia as a land of friendly people and
> the Soviet rulers as sincere men of good will.[20]

Roosevelt instructed Davies to inform Stalin of Roosevelt's
desire for a face-to-face meeting with Stalin to discuss military
and political problems. While Davies was in Moscow, the Soviets
announced that the Communist International would be
dissolved, a step designed to accelerate wishful thinking about
Communist global intentions:

> What seemed to the Western Allies conclusive proof of
> Stalin's change of heart was the dissolution of the Comintern
> in May 1943. 'Dissolution,' to be sure, did not even lead to the

19. Robert Sherwood, *Roosevelt and Hopkins* (New York, Harper, 1948), p. 713.
20. Feis, *Roosevelt, Churchill, Stalin*, p. 131.

dispersal of the Comintern staff in the U.S.S.R., let alone disturb Soviet control of its foreign apparatus or weaken the loyalties of foreign Communists to the U.S.S.R. It may in fact, have strengthened the Kremlin's hand by reducing lateral communication between parties while leaving vertical lines from Moscow untouched. By that time, however, the alleged conversion of Stalin into a 'nationalist' leader was a widespread article of faith in the West. Those who knew little of the U.S.S.R.—except perhaps, as some had learned in school, that "Trotsky wanted world revolution, while Stalin only wanted socialism in one country"—found it easy to believe or did not dare to doubt that Stalin was a Tsar in commissar's clothing.[21]

The Soviets reproached the West for the postponement of the 1943 cross-channel landings, and Stalin refused to reply to messages sent to him during the summer of 1943. The Russians were going on with their plans for Eastern Europe, regardless of the Western reaction. Yet the Western leaders felt that they could not reject the Soviet demand for the establishment of such a joint Commission out of hand. Indeed it appears likely that the Soviets may have used their demand for a voice in Italian matters as a political lever to extract even greater Western concessions with respect to eastern and central Europe. President Roosevelt, according to Herbert Feis:

> . . . recognized that Russia had the power to grasp whatever parts of central and eastern Europe it wanted. But he planned to try to get it to abstain from doing so by making the resultant world reaction clear. He meant to appeal to the (presumed) Soviet wish for collective security and an equal place at the council tables. He was also going to try to satisfy Stalin's wish for more direct security by agreeing to join in the sponsorship of such protective measures as the dismemberment of Germany. He hoped his views could be made more persuasive by offers of American help in repairing war damage in the Soviet Union. In sum, in return for moderation and trust, Russia was to win merit, recognition of its place

---

21. Donald Treadgold, *Twentieth Century Russia* (New York, Rand McNally, 1959), p. 375.

among the great powers, promises of protection against future enemies, and aid in regaining a normal peaceful life.[22]

Pressing for the creation of a Military-Political Commission, with immediate pertinency to Italy, the Soviets suggested not only the immediate creation of the Commission, but that it promptly issue orders to the provisional government of Premier Badoglio, and direct the political reconstruction of Italy. But the Americans and British, although agreeing to the establishment of such a group, succeeded in keeping it advisory to the Commander-in-Chief of Italian operations. Nevertheless, Communism thrived and prospered under American-British auspices, partly due to pro-Communist influences within the Allied Control Commission for Italy. According to Professor Thomas R. Fisher, who served with the American Occupation forces, the Regional Commissioner for Milan, of the Allied Control Commission, "gave orders . . . to appoint no labor officer who was not recommended by the Communist party."

On December 12, 1943, the Soviets concluded an agreement with the Czech leader Benes providing for the reorganization of the Czech exile committee into a provisional government giving due recognition to Communists and Communism. The leading prewar anti-Communist party was to be outlawed, and later, Czechoslovakia gave the U.S.S.R. control of the easternmost Czech province, Ruthenia. Benes accepted Soviet assurances that there would be no Communist intervention in internal Czech affairs. Not only did this set the stage for further Communist penetration of Czechoslovakia, but the Soviets, having convinced Benes of their good intentions, used Benes and the December 12 agreement in an attempt to convince the Americans and the British, and to pressure the Polish and Yugoslav exile governments in London, into adopting policies congenial to Soviet ambitions in central and eastern Europe. At the same time the Soviets actively discouraged British thinking in terms of landing Western military forces in the Balkans, because the presence of such forces would hamper Communist operations there at the time of liberation.

With respect to the United States war against Japan, the So-

---

22. Feis, *Roosevelt, Churchill, Stalin*, p. 174.

viets consistently rejected any cooperative role. However, Stalin did tell Secretary of State Cordell Hull on October 30, 1943, that the U.S.S.R. would enter the war against Japan after the defeat of Germany. The extent to which the Soviets convinced Hull, and most U.S. leaders of their good intentions is measured by the exuberant language of the following address delivered by the Secretary of State to the Congress upon returning from the October, 1943, Moscow Conference of Foreign Ministers:

> As the provisions of the Four-Nation Declaration are carried into effect, there will no longer be need for spheres of influence, for alliances, for balances of power, or any other of the special arrangements through which, in the unhappy past, the nations strove to safeguard their security or to promote their interests.[23]

The first face-to-face meeting among Roosevelt, Churchill, and Stalin took place at Teheran, in November, 1943. The Soviet dictator refused to travel any further to meet the Western chiefs of State. Among other things, the three discussed postwar spheres of influence. Even though the U.S.S.R. and Japan were not at war, President Roosevelt suggested that Russia might have an interest in the port of Dairen:

> It was Roosevelt who mentioned the possibility that Russia might have access to the port of Dairen in Manchuria . . . Stalin immediately expressed the opinion that the Chinese would object to this proposal, but Roosevelt said he thought they would agree to having Dairen made a free port under international guarantee.[24]

After Roosevelt suggested that the Chinese could be induced to accept Soviet participation in the internationalization of the port of Dairen, Stalin indicated Soviet interests in the Far East as follows:

23. William H. Chamberlin, *America's Second Crusade* (Chicago, Regnery, 1950), p. 175.
24. Sherwood, *Roosevelt and Hopkins*, p. 792.

1) . . . Stalin looked with favor on making Dairen a free port
for all the world, with the idea that Russian trade could move
over the Manchurian railways and through this port in bond.

2) Stalin had agreed that the Manchurian railways should become the property of the Chinese government.

3) Stalin wanted all of the other half (southern) of the Island
of Sakhalin and all the Kurile Islands for Russia.[25]

Turning to European problems, the Soviets also made their demands very clear at Teheran. As they related to Finland, there
would have to be acceptance of permanent Soviet control of the
areas taken by the Russians during their invasion of Finland in
1939–1940. In addition:

Stalin said that he did not want money, but within, say, five or
eight years the Finns would be well able to make good the
damage they had done to Russia by supplying her with paper,
wood, and many other things. He thought the Finns should be
given a lesson, and he was determined to get compensation
. . . he could not diverge from several conditions:

1) Restoration of the 1940 treaty.

2) Hango or Petsamo. (Here he added that Hango was leased
to the Soviet Union, but he would propose to take Petsamo.)

3) Compensation in kind as to 50 percent for damage. Quantities could be discussed later.[26]

Stalin also outlined at Teheran the Soviet claims in other parts
of Europe: 1) retention of areas occupied by the Soviets during
the Hitler-Stalin pact, and 2) cession to Russia of northern East
Prussia, including Koenigsberg. (Churchill, *Closing the Ring*, pp.
400, 403).

The essence and scope of Soviet policies, as they became more
clear during the Teheran Conference, was summed up by one of
the American participants:

25. Feis, *Roosevelt, Churchill, Stalin*, p. 225.
26. Ibid., p. 236.

... Germany is to be broken up and kept broken up. The states of eastern, southeastern, and central Europe will not be permitted to group themselves into any federations or association. France is to be stripped of her colonies and strategic bases beyond her borders and will not be permitted to maintain any appreciable military establishment. Poland and Italy will remain approximately their present size, but it is doubtful that either will be permitted to maintain any appreciable armed force. The result would be that the Soviet Union would be the only important military and political force on the continent of Europe. The rest of Europe would be reduced to military and political impotence.[27]

Stalin was very pleased with the results of the Teheran Conference:

... The Soviet government had been given a firm pledge that the invasion of the West would start within a few months. Soviet territorial aims in Europe had been advanced, and he (Stalin) had managed to get all proposals that might have resulted in opposed strength discarded or deferred. The promise to enter the Pacific War left time and opportunity to decide what advantage might be secured in that connection. Substantial as these benefits were, it is quite possible that Roosevelt's responsiveness may have caused Stalin to think that they would be even greater than they turned out to be, and more easily had.[28]

Stalin was anxious to obtain some Western approval of Soviet ambitions relative to Poland, at the Teheran Conference. Roosevelt was inclined to let Churchill and Stalin deal with this matter for the time being:

... According to the American (Bohlen) memo made of this conversation the President went on to explain that a national election in the United States was due in 1944; that while he would rather not run again he might have to if the war was still in progress. There were between six and seven million

27. Ibid., p. 275.
28. Ibid., p. 278.

Americans of Polish extraction in the United States and he
did not want to lose their votes . . .[29]

Stalin made it clear that he intended to keep those Polish territories which had been invaded and occupied by the Russians
during the Hitler-Stalin Pact:

Stalin said . . . that the Poles could not be allowed to seize the
Ukraine and White Russian territory. That was not fair. Ac-
cording to the 1939 frontier, the soil of the Ukraine and White
Russia was returned to the Ukraine and White Russia. Soviet
Russia adhered to the frontiers of 1939, for they appeared to
be ethnologically the right ones.
    Eden asked if this meant the Ribbentrop-Molotov Line.
    "Call it whatever you like," said Stalin.
    Molotov remarked that it was generally called the Curzon
Line.
    "No," said Eden, "there are important differences."[30]

Actually the Curzon Line was only a temporary armistice line
between Polish and Russian armies in the winter of 1920–1921,
and the only definitive boundary line which had been accepted by
the two states was the Riga Line of 1921, reaffirmed by both
parties in various agreements thereafter until the Hitler-Stalin
Pact. But the Soviets now succeeded in inducing the Western
Powers to label what was actually the Molotov-Ribbentrop Line,
the Curzon Line. The Curzon Line, for example, had never included Galicia, but under the new definition it was now construed
as extending to the Czech frontier.

After Teheran the Soviet Union launched verbal attacks
against the Polish government-in-exile and hinted at the creation
of a Soviet-sponsored Polish emigré committee should the
London government not meet Soviet territorial and other claims.
Roosevelt tried to keep out of the dispute, because of the election
in the United States, and Churchill tended to the view that the
Poles must make concessions to the Russians because the latter
were more important.

29. Ibid., p. 285.
30. Winston Churchill, *Closing the Ring* (Boston, Houghton-Mifflin, 1950), p. 395.

In August, 1943, the Soviet Union recognized the French Committee of National Liberation, led by de Gaulle, "as representative of the state interests of the French Republic," by which it attempted to strengthen Soviet influence in France, as well as the hand of the Communist party in that country. Moscow could also hope by this gesture that French Communists would gain influence, both within the French Committee and in occupied France. On March 14, 1944, the Soviets, without consulting their Allies, announced an arrangement to exchange diplomatic missions with the Badoglio government in Italy. These and other Soviet unilateral actions caused U.S. Ambassador Averill Harriman to comment:

> . . . When the Soviets do not like our proposals they certainly do not hesitate to be abrupt with us. We may look forward to a Soviet policy of playing the part of world bully if we don't follow this procedure of firmness now in connection with each incident.[31]

While the Teheran Conference was assembling, Communist leader Tito Broz in Yugoslavia brought the partisan groups under his leadership firmly within the Communist orbit, and the U.S.S.R. established open contact with what amounted to a government-in-opposition to the recognized Yugoslav government-in-exile. Winston Churchill wrote:

> . . . we have seen the entry of a grandiose Russian Mission to Tito's Headquarters, and there is little doubt that the Russians will drive straight ahead for a Communist Tito-governed Yugoslavia, and will denounce everything done to the contrary as "undemocratic."[32]

The Soviets were also busily engaged in stirring up trouble within the Greek government-in-exile by instigating a rebellion among army and navy units in Cairo, and by setting up a Com-

31. Feis, *Roosevelt, Churchill, Stalin*, p. 237.
32. Churchill, *Closing the Ring*, p. 477.

munist-led Committee of National Liberation in Greece in March, 1944.

In March, 1944, the Red Army crossed the Pruth River and entered Rumania at several points, although the Soviets still disclaimed territorial ambitions other than Bessarabia and Bucovina, which the Soviets had gained during the Hitler-Stalin Pact. Coming on top of Communist actions in Italy, Yugoslavia, and Greece, these new adventures alarmed Churchill, who wrote to Eden:

> A paper should be drafted for the Cabinet . . . setting forth . . . the brute issues between us and the Soviet government which are developing in Italy, in Rumania, in Bulgaria, in Yugoslavia, and above all in Greece . . . Broadly speaking, the issue is, are we going to acquiesce in the Communisation of the Balkans and perhaps of Italy?[33]

In the summer of 1944 the Polish question became acute. Polish Prime Minister Mikolajczyk went to Washington in June, where he was advised by President Roosevelt to come to some accommodation with the Soviet Union on the matter of borders. Furthermore, Roosevelt suggested that the United States would not support the Polish stand on the restoration of the 1939 border which had existed prior to the German-Russian invasion of Poland:

> . . . you Poles must find an understanding with Russia. On your own, you'd have no chance to beat Russia, and let me tell you now, the British and Americans have no intention of fighting Russia.[34]

Mikolajczyk then went to Moscow, largely as a result of American and British urging, even though Stalin made clear in advance that Mikolajczyk would be coolly received.

On the eve of the Polish Prime Minister's arrival in Moscow (July 29, 1944), a Moscow radio station (called Kosciuszko) ap-

---

33. Ibid., p. 708.
34. Mikolajczyk, *The Rape of Poland*, p. 60.

pealed to the Polish underground in Warsaw to rise up and join
with the approaching Red Army to destroy the Germans:

> No doubt Warsaw already hears the guns of the battle that is
> soon to bring her liberation . . . Poles, the time of liberation is
> at hand! Poles, to arms! There is not a moment to lose![35]

In response to this plea, the Polish underground forces com-
manded by General Bor began their uprising on August 1, 1944.
But Soviet military aid to these forces against the common
German enemy was not forthcoming. Indeed, Stalin ignored the
rapidly developing events in Warsaw, and rejected cooperation
with the British who, at Churchill's request, began air sorties
from Italy to drop supplies to the Poles in Warsaw.

Meantime the Soviet leaders brushed aside Mikolajczyk's urgent requests for a common military effort against the Germans,
as they did those of Churchill and Roosevelt. Stalin's message to
Mikolajczyk stated:

> . . . the Warsaw action . . . is a thoughtless adventure causing
> unnecessary losses . . . it should be mentioned that a calum-
> nious campaign has been started by the Polish London
> government which seeks to present the illusion that the Soviet
> Command deceived the Warsaw population. In view of this
> state of affairs the Soviet Command cuts itself away from the
> Warsaw adventure and cannot take any responsibility for it.[36]

In response to continuing U.S. and British pressures, Soviet
spokesman Vishinsky informed U.S. Ambassador Harriman and
British Ambassador Clark-Kerr on August 16:

> The Soviet government cannot of course object to English or
> American aircraft dropping arms in the region of Warsaw,
> since this is an American and British affair. But they decidedly
> object to American or British aircraft, after dropping arms in
> the region of Warsaw, landing on Soviet territory, since the

35. Ibid., p. 69.
36. Ibid., p. 82.

Soviet government does not wish to associate themselves either directly or indirectly with the adventure in Warsaw.[37]

On October 2, 1944, what was left of the fighting Poles surrendered after sixty-three days of the most awful fighting. The strongest element in the Polish government-in-exile's underground armies had been lost. As Churchill wrote of the final outcome:

> When the Russians entered the city three months later they found little but shattered streets and the unburied dead. Such was their liberation of Poland, where they now rule.[38]

While the fighting was going on in Warsaw, Stalin informed Prime Minister Mikolajczyk that he would have to accept the "Curzon Line," that the Polish government in London would have to be dissolved, and that the Soviet Union was dealing with its puppets—the Polish Committee of National Liberation. Mikolajczyk returned to London empty-handed and disconsolate, while Stalin installed the Polish Committee of National Liberation (Communist-dominated) as the administrative power of Poland, with headquarters in Lublin.

The Soviets could hardly have achieved what they did without a favorable attitude in the United States. Harry Hopkins, top aide to President Roosevelt, produced at the 1944 Quebec Conference (which dealt primarily with Germany's postwar position), a document entitled "Russia's Position":

> Russia's postwar position in Europe will be a dominant one. With Germany crushed, there is no power in Europe to oppose her tremendous military forces . . . Since Russia is the decisive factor she must be given every assistance and every effort must be made to obtain her friendship. Likewise, since without question she will dominate Europe on the defeat of the Axis, it is even more essential to develop and maintain the most friendly relations with Russia. Finally, the most im-

37. Winston Churchill, *Triumph and Tragedy* (Boston, Houghton-Mifflin, 1950), p. 133.
38. Ibid., p. 145.

portant factor the United States has to consider in relation to Russia is the prosecution of the war in the Pacific. With Russia as an ally in the war against Japan, the war can be terminated in less time and at less expense in life and resources than if the reverse were the case. Should the War in the Pacific have to be carried on with an unfriendly or a negative attitude on the part of Russia, the difficulties will be immeasurably increased and operations might become abortive.[39]

In the Far East, meanwhile, the Soviets not only reneged on a commitment to grant bases to the United States Air Force in the Maritime Provinces from which to bomb Japan, but they also concluded an agreement with Japan on March 30, 1944, dealing with fishing rights and a Japanese commitment to liquidate Japanese concessions in northern Sakhalin. With respect to China, the Soviets called for the establishment of a coalition government, from within which the Communists could weaken and finally destroy the Kuomintang:

> ... the general Soviet program for both Europe and Asia called for the establishment of coalition governments. In those very years (1943–1945) such coalition governments were initiated in Yugoslavia, Poland, and Czechoslovakia ... they enabled the Communists to occupy key positions and to begin the disintegration of their partners from within ... In China this meant a coalition between Chiang Kai-shek and Mao Tse-Tung ... and the subsequent weakening of the Kuomintang until the Communists could dominate the government. Soviet insistence on such a reorganization of the Chinese regime was not confined to the press. In diplomatic negotiations, at the Conference in Teheran and Yalta, the Soviet government followed the same line. It soon found receptive ears in the West, and the Soviet press could, with considerable satisfaction, quote American publications which seemed to have swallowed the Moscow line.[40]

Stalin claimed that Chiang Kai-shek had many faults, and that

39. Sherwood, *Roosevelt and Hopkins*, p. 748.
40. David Dallin, *Soviet Russia in the Far East* (New Haven, Yale University Press, 1948), p. 220.

the Chinese Communists were not real Communists. He said, for example:

> The Chinese Communists are not real Communists; they are 'margarine communists.' (Still) they are real patriots and they want to fight the Japanese.[41]

Turning back to Europe, Soviet military pressure against Finland increased while the U.S.S.R. made urgent territorial and political demands on the country the Red Army had initially invaded in 1939. But the Finns fought on, believing that they would become satellites to the Soviets in the event of surrender. Naturally the Germans urged the Finns to stay in the war as a way of tying up more Soviet troops. But on September 5, 1944, the Finns had to give up the unequal fight and were forced to accept a Soviet-dictated peace.

By late August, Soviet troops were beginning to cross into Rumania and Bulgaria, and the U.S.S.R. made clear its intention of controlling the situations in those countries. New governments came into power in Bucharest, Rumania and Sofia, Bulgaria, which made agreements, under pressure, with the U.S.S.R. which led to increasing Communist influence in these countries. The Soviet armed forces often helped the cause of the local Communists by liquidating not only pro-Nazi elements, but also anti-Communist leaders.

In Yugoslavia, Communist leader Tito Broz took advantage of pro-Tito sentiments in the British government which pressured the exile government of King Peter to come to terms with Tito. As the Russian forces came closer to Yugoslavia, Tito drew away from the British, and followed a policy of ignoring the existence of King Peter's representative, Ivan Subasic (a Croatian politician), whom Churchill hoped might help find common ground between the Communists and the exile regime.

Communism threatened in Greece, too. The pro-Communist front organization, known as the EAM, threatened civil war against the Greek government-in-exile which was preparing to return to Greece with British assistance.

In August, 1944, Great Power delegations met at Dumbarton

41. Feis, *Roosevelt, Churchill, Stalin*, p. 407.

Oaks, in Washington, D.C., to discuss the establishment and organization of a new international organization to replace the defunct League of Nations. At one point Soviet delegate Gromyko demanded sixteen votes for the U.S.S.R. in the new organization—one for each Soviet republic. The Soviets also insisted on full use of the veto power, and got their way in spite of suggestions from others present, especially the United States, that the use of the veto be curtailed.

Shortly after the Dumbarton Oaks meeting, Secretary of State Cordell Hull became disturbed about Soviet unilateral actions and totalitarian methods in central Europe:

> . . . He was at the same time becoming disturbed over Soviet claims of right to dictate what was done about Hungary, Rumania, and Bulgaria. He sent Harriman, on September 18, a perplexed query, which said he was beginning to wonder whether the Soviets had decided to reverse the policies "apparently" decided on at Moscow and Teheran of cooperation with the Western Allies and to pursue a contrary course. He invited the Embassy to comment on this question, particularly as regards the causes of the change in Soviet policy. The inquiry bewildered the Embassy. Had the scores of messages it had sent on the many signs of Soviet disregard of American and British wishes not been understood?[42]

In mid-October, 1944, Churchill also went to Moscow, where he discussed with Stalin and Ambassador Harriman the future of central Europe. Stalin agreed to Churchill's proposal: "So far as Britain and Russia are concerned, how would it do for you to have ninety percent predominance in Rumania, for us to have ninety percent of the say in Greece, and go fifty-fifty about Yugoslavia?"[43] But the Soviets soon proved their willingness not only to take their share, but most if not all of the West's share as well. The first instance was Hungary:

> . . . Stalin had agreed on paper that the British should have a part equal to that of the Russians in the direction of Hun-

42. Ibid., p. 434.
43. Churchill, *Triumph and Tragedy*, p. 227.

garian affairs. But what the Soviet government now asked made it clear that this balance would be hard to maintain. It sought control arrangements that were almost the same as the ones adopted for Rumania—in which country Russia had been accorded the most say—and would have allowed the Soviet commander-in-chief to impose his unrestrained will on Hungary.[44]

The Churchill-Stalin talks then turned to a discussion of Poland, and Polish Prime Minister Mikolajczyk was invited to Moscow to join the discussions. Stalin continued to insist on the Soviet version of the "Curzon Line," and the creation of a new Polish regime based largely on the Communist-dominated Committee of National Liberation. Churchill supported Stalin against Mikolajczyk's Polish government-in-exile. Molotov then informed Mikolajczyk for the first time that President Roosevelt had already agreed, at Teheran, to support Soviet claims to eastern Poland; when he said to Churchill and Harriman: "If your memories fail you, let me recall the facts to you. We all agreed at Teheran that the Curzon Line must divide Poland. You will recall that President Roosevelt agreed to this solution and strongly endorsed the line. And then we agreed that it would be best not to issue any public declaration about our agreement."[45] Later that same evening (October 13), Churchill and Stalin met with the Communist leaders of the Polish Committee of National Liberation. Churchill made this observation about them:

> . . . It was soon plain that the Lublin Poles were mere pawns of Russia. They had learned and rehearsed their part so carefully that even their masters evidently felt they were overdoing it.[46]

The great pressure that was brought to bear on Mikolajczyk to make concessions finally forced him to agree to the Curzon Line, including Lwow, and the formation of a new Polish regime,

44. Feis, *Roosevelt, Churchill, Stalin*, p. 452.
45. Mikolajczyk, *The Rape of Poland*, p. 96.
46. Churchill, *Triumph and Tragedy*, p. 235.

which would represent the London Poles and the Communists equally. But Stalin insisted that the Communists be dominant, and in the absence of support from Churchill, Mikolajczyk was faced with a *fait accompli.*

On October 14, with the American General John R. Deane and Ambassador Harriman present, Churchill and Stalin discussed Soviet entry into the Pacific war. Stalin described how Soviet forces would enter China and Korea, and the British and Americans were enthused over the prospect:

> . . . The great visualized spread southward of the Red Army caused no alarm . . . The satisfaction of the American government at all this progress and preparation for Soviet entry into the Pacific war was not spoiled by the fact that Stalin had made it clear that the Soviet government expected a reward for doing so.[47]

Stalin declared that the Soviet Union would enter the war three months after the defeat of Germany, but went on to say, however,

> . . . there were also certain political aspects which would have to be taken into consideration. The Russians would have to know what they were fighting for. They had certain claims against Japan.[48]

As the Allied armies closed in on the Germans in the winter of 1944–45, American and British commanders gave the Russians full details of their battle plans and asked the Russians for theirs. But the Russians repeatedly rebuffed Western inquiries. General Deane, the U.S. military representative in Moscow during the war, took note of Soviet non-cooperation:

> When the Red Army was back on its heels, it was right for us to give them all possible assistance with no questions asked . . . However, they are no longer back on their heels; and, if

47. Ibid., p. 236.
48. Feis, *Roosevelt, Churchill, Stalin*, pp. 465–466.

there is one thing they have plenty of, it's self-confidence. The
situation has changed, but our policy has not. We still meet
their requests to the limit of our ability, and they meet ours to
the minimum that will keep us sweet.

The truth is that they want to have as little to do with
foreigners, Americans included, as possible. We never make a
request or proposal to the Soviets that is not viewed with suspicion. They simply cannot understand giving without taking, and as a result even our giving is viewed with suspicion.
Gratitude cannot be naked in the Soviet Union. Each
transaction is complete in itself without regard to past favors.
The party of the second part is either a shrewd trader to be ad-
mired or a sucker to be despised.[49]

Soviet foreign policy objectives were greatly furthered as a
result of the momentous decisions arrived at during the historic
Yalta Conference, beginning on February 4, 1945. Although the
U.S. leaders were informed of the preparation of the atomic
weapon, and in spite of the fact that the Japanese navy and air
forces were incapable of further major action:

... neither the establishment of our command of the air and
seas near Japan nor this forecast of a new weapon that would
make that command indisputable caused the Joint Chiefs of
Staff to make any substantial changes in their plans or
schedules for the further conduct of the war against Japan or
waver in their opinion that Russian entry (into the war) would
be of great value.[50]

Although the Chinese, Americans, and the British Commonwealth forces had been fighting the Japanese for some years, they
demanded little or nothing from Japan. But the Soviets, planning
to come into the war against Japan at the very end, demanded
substantial territorial concessions.

At the Yalta Conference the United States recognized the
Communist control of Outer Mongolia, Soviet "pre-eminent
interests" in an "internationalized" port of Dairen, the leasing of

49. Deane, *Strange Alliance*, p. 84.
50. Feis, *Roosevelt, Churchill, Stalin*, p. 502.

Port Arthur to the Soviet Union as a naval base, Soviet "pre-eminent interests" in the jointly operated (with China) Chinese Eastern Railroad and South Manchurian Railroad, as well as Soviet control over the former Japanese areas of southern Sakhalin and the entire Kurile Islands chain. Because most of these territories belonged to America's Chinese ally, Stalin asked Roosevelt to obtain Chiang Kai-shek's consent to the agreements. The Soviets sought to lull possible American and Chinese concern by stating that:

> For its part the Soviet Union expresses its readiness to conclude with the National government of China a pact of friendship and alliance between the U.S.S.R. and China in order to render assistance to China with its armed forces for the purpose of liberating China from the Japanese yoke.[51]

The Soviets reneged on this agreement, while they helped and encouraged the Chinese Communists in their struggle to overthrow the Chinese government. Soviet territorial and political gains in the Far East resulting from the Yalta Conference set the stage for further expansion of Communism in China and Korea.

At Yalta the Soviets also got their way on Poland. The Soviets refused to make any concessions, demanding strict adherence to the "Curzon Line" including Lwow,* and a limited enlargement of the Lublin Communist group which would then be recognized as the Polish government. Prime Minister Mikolajczyk, made the following observations about the predicament of the Polish government-in-exile and his own attempts to retain Western support through compromise:

> On the one side, I was confronted with the heavy Russian demands, the accomplished facts, and the appalling reality of what was happening inside Poland. Thousands of Home Army men were being arrested and shipped into Russia. Villages were being burned by the Red Army. Citizens were

---

51. U. S. Department of State, *The Conferences at Malta and Yalta*, 1955, p. 984.

*Although Roosevelt had asked Stalin to allow Poland to keep the all-Polish city of Lwow.

being murdered and the land stripped of its industry. On the
other side, I had to take into consideration the exact extent of
the support we could thereafter expect from the British and
Americans. We were becoming increasingly isolated. The Big
Three regarded us either openly or privately as 'saboteurs' of
their unity, because of our refusal to yield on all points. My
own cabinet felt that what I had agreed to represented too
much of a compromise . . .[52]

Stalin proceeded to recognize the Lublin regime as the
government of Poland, in spite of President Roosevelt's contrary
pleas. With respect to the borders of Poland, it was agreed at
Yalta that the Curzon Line, with minor modifications, was the
eastern boundary, and that the western boundary should be determined at the Peace Conference. The Yalta formula about the
government of Poland read as follows:

The provisional government which is now functioning in Poland should therefore be reorganized on a broader democratic
basis with the inclusion of democratic leaders from Poland itself and from Poles abroad. This new government should then
be called the Polish Provisional Government of National
Unity.

Churchill unsuccessfully complained that:

If the Conference is to brush aside the existing London
government and lend all its weight to the Lublin government,
there will be a world outcry. As far as can be foreseen, the
Poles outside of Poland will make a virtually united protest.
There is under our command a Polish army of 150,000 men,
who have been gathered from all who have been able to come
together from outside Poland. This army fought, and is still
fighting, very bravely. I do not believe it will be at all rec-
onciled to the Lublin government, and if Great Britain
transfers recognition from the government it has recognized
since the beginning of the war, they will look on it as a betrayal.[53]

52. Mikolajczyk, *The Rape of Poland*, p. 104.
53. Churchill, *Triumph and Tragedy*, p. 378.

But Stalin's own interpretation of the Yalta agreement was eventually to prevail in Poland. The newly accepted Polish Provisional Government became simply the Communist-dominated Lublin Committee under a new name. There was a promise to hold free and unfettered elections in Poland, but the Soviets refused to allow international supervision of these elections.

On the question of Germany, Stalin demanded twenty billion dollars in reparations from Germany, of which the U.S.S.R. was to get half. Roosevelt and Churchill agreed to this as a basis for discussion later (at Potsdam). The Three Powers also agreed at Yalta that they

> . . . shall possess supreme authority with respect to Germany. In the exercise of such authority they will take such steps, including the complete disarmament, demilitarisation and dismemberment of Germany as they deem requisite for future peace and security.

Definitive settlement of the German question had to await defeat of the German armed forces and a future conference (Potsdam). Shortly prior to the Yalta Conference, the British intervened in Greece to support the Greek government against a Communist revolt. *This was the only instance in which the West used force to resist Communist encroachments.*

In Yugoslavia, after efforts to obtain Stalin's consent to the inclusion in Tito's regime of representatives of the Yugoslav government-in-exile had failed, Churchill and Roosevelt acquiesced at Yalta in the formation of a government subject to Tito's will.

In Rumania, the Soviets were also rapidly imposing their will, with the result that the Communist-dominated National Democratic Front at the time of Yalta was actively seeking to establish a monopoly of power. The Western Powers had protested the highhanded tactics of the Soviet High Command in Rumania without avail. Roosevelt and Churchill were soon to discover that the Yalta pledge about the peoples of Europe solving by "democratic means their pressing political and economic problems" was a sham and a fraud.

The hopes of the Americans and British who had expected that the Soviets would reciprocate their material assistance in time of desperation, and their good will, were about to be shattered. Agreements about the establishment of democracy in Soviet-occupied areas were shown to be without substance by Soviet actions:

> But Soviet actions evidenced an unwillingness to trust the outcome of the democratic political contest, and a ruthless will to make sure that all of central and eastern Europe was governed by its dependent supporters. This set purpose was not affected by association in combat or appeals to principle. Nor could it be diverted by the vision pursued at San Francisco at the founding conference of the United Nations of a world in which all countries would join together to protect each and to maintain peace. The Soviet Union wanted space, satellite peoples and armies, additional economic resources, and a favorable chance for Communism to spread its influence.[54]

In Hungary Soviet Marshal Voroshilov disregarded prior agreements to consult with and inform the American and British members of the Allied Control Commission, and in spite of all protests, directed the course of political events in Hungary along Soviet lines. In Czechoslovakia, the Soviet-trusting Benes was beginning to discover that the Soviets were taking advantage of him. He was pushed into granting the Communists and their associates a greater number of posts in the government than he had wished or expected. His comment was that "It might have been worse."

It was in the establishment of the Polish Provisional Government of National Unity that the Soviets showed their real intent to have their own way regardless of the consequences. They wanted the Lublin Committee to become the Provisional Government, with minor window dressing added, whereas it was the American and British desire that a substantial democratic element, especially from London, be included. According to Churchill:

> As the weeks passed after Yalta it became clear that the Soviet government was doing nothing to carry out our

54. Feis, *Roosevelt, Churchill, Stalin*, p. 563.

agreements about broadening the Polish government to include all Polish parties and both sides. . . . Time was on the
side of the Russians and their Polish adherents, who were
fastening their grip upon the country by all kinds of severe
measures, which they did not wish outside observers to see.[55]

The Soviets insisted that nobody be included in the Provisional
Government who was critical of Yalta. This ruled out almost all
patriotic Poles. The West agreed to the ban against almost all ex-
cept Mikolajczyk, but even he was opposed by Molotov, who
together with Harriman and the British representative, Clark-
Kerr, were supposed to "broaden" the Lublin group to include
democratic Poles. In addition, the Soviets rejected American and
British suggestions for a visit to Poland by Harriman and Clark-
Kerr. Churchill became so worried that he told Roosevelt on
March 13, 1945:

At Yalta we agreed to take the Russian view of the frontier
line. Poland has lost her frontier. Is she now to lose her
freedom? . . . we are in the presence of a great failure and an
utter breakdown of what was settled at Yalta . . . The moment
that Molotov sees that he has beaten us away from the whole
process of consultations among Poles to form a new government, he will know that we will put up with anything . . .[56]

But Roosevelt refused to join Churchill in taking a strong
stand on the Polish issue. He advised patience and forebearance
in negotiating with the Russians. After Roosevelt died, Churchill
asked President Truman to join him in a strong stand on Poland,
but Truman, too, refused, stating that such a stand might antagonize the Soviets and jeopardize the San Francisco United Nations Conference.

In late April, 1945, in violation of the Yalta agreement and
over strong American and British protests, the Soviet government concluded a treaty of mutual assistance with the
Lublin Committee, while simultaneously turning over to its
administration not only Poland west of the "Curzon Line" but

55. Churchill, *Triumph and Tragedy*, p. 418.
56. Ibid., p. 426.

also the German territory lying between the Oder-Neisse river line and the old Polish-German frontier. On May 5, Stalin informed Churchill that sixteen Polish leaders loyal to the London exile government, who were under a safety guarantee by the Russians, and who were to be considered by the Allied Commission on Poland as prospective members of the Provisional Government, had been seized by the Red Army and incarcerated. According to Prime Minister Churchill:

> Nothing more was heard of the victims of the trap until the case against them opened on June 18. It was conducted in the usual Communist manner. The prisoners were accused of subversion, terrorism, and espionage, . . . Thirteen were found guilty, and sentenced to terms of imprisonment ranging from four months to ten years . . . This was in fact the judicial liquidation of the leadership of the Polish underground which had fought so heroically against Hitler. The rank and file had already died in the ruins of Warsaw.[57]

Soviet hostility to the West was also shown in the spring of 1945 when German officers made contact with U.S. representatives on the possibility of a German surrender. The United States dutifully reported this fact to the Soviets, who immediately accused the United States and Britain of trying to negotiate a separate peace with Germany and demanded representation at future meetings with the Germans. Stalin's suspicions and accusations spurred President Roosevelt to reply, on April 5, just before his death:

> . . . it would be one of the great tragedies of history if at the very moment of the victory now within our grasp, such distrust, such lack of faith, should prejudice the entire undertaking . . . Frankly I cannot avoid a feeling of bitter resentment toward your informers, whoever they are for such vile misrepresentations of my actions or those of my trusted subordinates.[58]

Ambassador Harriman, On April 4, commented on Soviet

57. Ibid., p. 498.
58. Ibid., p. 448.

policy, as paraphrased by Herbert Feis, in the following way:

> ... we now have ample proof that the Soviet government views all matters from the standpoint of their own selfish interests. They have publicized to their own political advantage the difficult food situation in areas liberated by our troops such as Italy, Belgium, and France ...

> The Communist party or its associates everywhere are using economic difficulties in areas under our responsibility to undermine the influence of the Western allies to promote Soviet concepts and policies ... The Soviet Union and the minority governments that the Soviets are forcing on the people of eastern Europe have an entirely different objective. We must clearly recognize that the Soviet program is the establishment of totalitarianism, ending personal liberty and democracy as we know and respect it.[59]

Yet Mr. Harriman, during this period and later, including his role in Laos in 1961, failed to grasp the inevitability of Communist expansion (unless blocked by the West) based on the necessity to fulfill the Marxist-Leninist imperative of transition from capitalism to socialism.

But the new President, Harry S. Truman, resisted the counsel, so ably presented by Churchill, that the United States and Britain should take a firm stand together against Communist expansionism in Europe. Meantime Truman and General Eisenhower, and particularly the latter, decided to downplay the political aspects of the liberation and let the Russians take full credit for the liberation of Czechoslovakia and Berlin. They permitted Russian troops to enter Prague and Berlin, even though in both cases American or British troops could have gotten there first. The American view of Soviet intentions proved less realistic than that of Churchill's, as the war in Europe came to an end:

> ... But even while tired soldiers gave thanks, and hats were tossing in the air, the governments of the West were worrying over what Communist Russia had in mind for Europe. Chur-

59. Feis, *Roosevelt, Churchill, Stalin*, p. 597.

chill was advocating that the American, British, and French forces which had won their hard way forward from the Channel and the Mediterranean should stay where they were long enough to prove that the war had been fought so that the people of Europe should be able to live freely and without fear in the future. Emerging from the Nazi realm of cruelty and arrogance, were they to pass into the Soviet realm of compulsion?[60]

When Soviet forces entered Vienna, they shortly announced that they were recognizing as the provisional government a group of men presided over by the veteran Socialist Karl Renner. At the same time the Soviets refused to permit Allied missions to fly into Vienna. Allied protests were unavailing. Meanwhile Tito's forces, backed up by the Russians, rushed towards Trieste and threatened to overrun the entire Venezia Giulia area of Italy.

As the Russians moved into Germany, Churchill expressed his concern about Soviet policy in these words:

> I fear terrible things have happened during the Russian advance through Germany to the Elbe. The proposed withdrawal of the United States Army to the occupational lines which were arranged with the Russians and Americans in Quebec ... would mean the tide of Russian domination sweeping forward 120 miles on a front of 300 or 400 miles. This would be an event, which, if it occurred, would be one of the most melancholy in history ... the Allies ought not to retreat from their present positions to the occupational line until we are satisfied about Poland, and also about the temporary character of the Russian occupation of Germany, and the conditions to be established in the Russianized or Russian-controlled countries in the Danube Valley, particularly Austria and Czechoslovakia, and the Balkans.[61]

As the war in Europe came to a close, the United States government began to realize that as a result of its military successes in the Far East and the development of the atomic bomb, Russian intervention in that theater was no longer as urgent or even desirable as it had seemed at Yalta. George Kennan, in charge of the Moscow Embassy in Harriman's absence, warned

60. Ibid., p. 616.
61 Churchill, *Triumph and Tragedy*, p. 502.

of Soviet intentions in the Far East:

> It would be tragic, if our natural anxiety for the support of the
> Soviet Union at this juncture, coupled with Stalin's use of
> words which mean all things to all people . . . were to lead us
> into an undue reliance on Soviet aid or even Soviet acqui-
> escence in the achievement of our long term objectives in
> China.[62]

But this warning was not heeded, and Soviet forces entered
Manchuria, occupied south Sakhalin and the Kuriles, and set the
stage of a Communist expansion in Asia which led to the conquest of China, the invasion of Korea, and the guerrilla warfare
in southeast Asia. Japan was defeated only to make way for
another threat to peace in the Far East.

One of the striking aspects of Soviet policy from 1941 to 1945
was that *even when the Soviets had their backs to the wall, as was
the case the last half of 1941 and the first half of 1942, they were
insisting on spheres of influence in the postwar world*. They were
most insistent about Poland, both with respect to the "Curzon
Line" and the Lublin Committee. The Soviets also applied
pressure on the Western Allies for control of east-central Europe,
East Prussia, and Manchuria. They exploited the good will and
even naïveté of the Western leaders, and extracted substantial
concessions at the wartime conferences.

What the Soviets could not get in conference, they took
through military invasion ("liberation") in the last half of 1944
and 1945. They also used the strategy of asking for things they
knew they could not get (such as a voice in the occupation of
Italy and Japan, trusteeship for Tripolitania, etc.) in order to give
them more leverage for the things they really wanted (in east-
central Europe).

President Truman gradually realized that conciliation of the
U.S.S.R. was impossible:

> I had hoped that the Russians would return favor for favor,
> but almost from the time I became President I found them
> acting without regard for their neighboring nations and in
> direct violation of the obligations they assumed at Yalta.[63]

62. Feis, *Roosevelt, Churchill, Stalin*, p. 639.
63. Harry S Truman, *Memoirs* (New York, Doubleday, 1955), Vol. I., p. 217.

Chapter 7

SOVIET EXPANSIONISM 1945–1950

THE NEW SOVIET POLICY

After the threat to Stalingrad ended, and even more clearly after the Teheran Conference of 1943, Soviet foreign policy became less and less defensive, and increasingly offensive in character. As soon as the Soviet leaders realized that Germany was going to be defeated, their military, diplomatic, political, and economic programs became integrated into a long-range anti-Western orientation. At the same time that the United States and Britain were approaching the zenith of their sympathy for, and cooperation with, the Soviet Union, the Soviets were beginning to recognize that the real enemy was no longer Germany, but the West.

James Burnham, in his brilliant *The Struggle for the World* (John Day, 1947) holds that the "cold war"—a new war, World War III—began in April, 1944, when Soviet agents directed the anti-Greek government mutiny in Cairo. Taking advantage of United States and British good will and even the willingness of these two countries to renege on pledges to the exiled governments of Poland and Yugoslavia in order to remain on good terms with the U.S.S.R., the Soviets not only extracted maximum political concessions from them at Teheran, Yalta, and Potsdam, but also used direct pressures in eastern Europe and later in China to advance the cause of the international Communist movement.

Not only did the Greek experience in 1944 suggest that the international Communist movement was no longer directed primarily at Germany, but so did the situation in Poland. After urging the Polish underground army to rise up against the Germans, the Soviets proceeded to stand by as spectators to watch the Germans defeat the Poles in August and September, 1944. The last remaining authority of the Polish exile government having been destroyed, the Soviets then felt free to move into Warsaw with their "own Poles"—the Lublin Committee—which subsequently became accepted as the government of Poland. In China, the Communists followed the 1937 admonition of Mao Tse-tung:

> The war between China and Japan is an excellent opportunity for the development of our party. Our determined policy is 70 percent expansion, 20 percent dealing with the Kuomintang, and 10 percent fighting Japan. . . . The first stage is to compromise with the Kuomintang, with the view of maintaining our existence. The second stage is to fight for a balance of power vis a vis the Kuomintang to achieve equilibrium. The third stage is to infiltrate deeply into central China, to establish bases there, in order to launch counter-offensives against the Kuomintang . . .[1]

The change in Soviet strategy was also manifested in 1945 when the international Communist movement ordered the replacement of U.S. Communist leader Earl Browder by William Z. Foster, precisely because Browder had predicted, in his book *Road to Teheran*, "generations of peace" between Russia and the United States. The Attorney General of the United States declared in 1950:

---

1. "Strategy and Tactics of World Communism—Communism in China," House Committee on Foreign Affairs, 1949, p. 24.

With the end of hostilities in Europe in 1945, the Communist party was instructed by the leaders of the world Communist movement, including Jacques Duclos, a leader of the French Communist International, Dmitri Manuilsky, a leader of the Communist party of the Soviet Union and formerly general secretary of the Communist International, to re-establish itself in the United States for the purpose of again carrying forward the program and activities to which it had adhered from 1919 to 1944.[2]

Communism began to spread into east-central Europe as the German armies retreated and as the Soviets followed them in the so-called "liberation." In this Communist expansion Allied diplomacy played a role, as we have seen from the previous chapter, and so did the power of the Soviet Army. Establishment of these satellite governments did not come about through popular uprisings or by a peaceful penetration of ideas. The Soviet influence spread as a consequence of ruthless application of well elaborated devices of direct and indirect pressure under the shadow of the Red Army. Indeed Stalin is quoted as saying at the Potsdam Conference that the Soviets would not allow freedom of expression in east-central Europe because such freedom would result in anti-Communism: "Any freely-elected government in these countries will be an anti-Soviet government and we cannot allow that."[3]

SOVIET AND COMMUNIST ACTIONS: EAST-CENTRAL EUROPE

Let us now briefly review the step-by-step events and policies through which Communism came to east-central Europe as a Soviet foreign policy.

Following the defeat of the Polish underground army in the fall of 1944 by the Germans (while the Soviets stood by and watched), the Soviets moved into the country and installed their puppets into power, the Lublin Committee. Proclaimed as the provisional government of Poland on December 31, 1944, it was

2. As quoted in *The New York Times*, Nov. 23, 1950.
3. Phillip Mosely, "Across the Green Table From Stalin," *Current History* (September, 1948), p. 131.

recognized as such a few days later by the Soviet Union. Eastern Poland was ceded to the Soviet Union at Yalta, at which time Britain and the United States agreed to recognize the provisional government after it was reorganized to include non-Communist Poles, and after it held free elections. But the only prominent non-Communist Pole allowed back was the Polish peasant leader Mikolajczyk, and he had to flee the country in October, 1947, to avoid arrest and judicial murder. Elections were held, but they were not free. According to American Ambassador Arthur Bliss Lane:

> The reports received from the United States Embassy in Poland in the period immediately prior to the elections, as well as its subsequent reports based upon the observations of American officials who visited a number of Polish voting centers, confirmed the fears which this government had expressed that the elections would not be free . . . The United States government considers that the Polish provisional government has failed to carry out its solemn pledges . . .[4]

Nevertheless the United States, after withdrawing recognition from the Polish government-in-exile, proceeded to recognize the Communist government of Poland as it was organized in June, 1945. *Communist strategy in Poland, as elsewhere in the middle European area, was to take over power gradually.* First the Soviet Army moved in, sweeping aside opposition, and giving favored treatment to Communist emigres who returned from Moscow and their collaborators. A sham coalition was created, with the Communists controlling the key ministries of Justice and Interior (police). Single slate elections were then held, after which time the Communists consolidated power and fused the satellite country politically, economically, and militarily with the Soviet Union.

Instead of attempting to introduce the Soviet system in one sweeping move, the Communist parties entered or created in each country a coalition government, the members of which were chosen or approved by the Communists. These pseudo-coalition

4. Arthur Bliss Lane, *I Saw Poland Betrayed* (New York, Doubleday, 1949), p. 291.

governments were called in Yugoslavia, 'National Liberation Front'; in Albania, 'Democratic Front'; in Bulgaria, 'Fatherland Front'; in Hungary, 'National Independence Front,' and in Rumania, 'National Democratic Front.'

From the very beginning the Communists seized the positions of power and gradually eliminated the independent leaders of the non-Communist parties. Then a few intimidated politicians or disguised Communists were proclaimed as representatives of some of the non-Communist splinter parties and the coalition went on happily; the difference between a fake coalition and the one party system is only nominal. Throughout this evolution it has been a constant habit to give formal authority to non-Communists, and to concentrate effective control of power positions in the hands of Communists or fellow-travellers. To implement this policy the Communists asked invariably for the ministry of interior, for in European countries this ministry controls the police.

The Soviet Army entered Hungary in the fall of 1944, and Communist organizers were supplied money, automobiles, sound trucks, gasoline, newsprint, literature, and films in the Hungarian language by the Soviet army. A Soviet-inspired provisional government was established in Debrecen in December, 1944; in January an armistice was signed in Moscow forcing Hungary to pay Russia 200 million dollars in reparations. Following the "liberation" of Budapest in February, 1945, the Soviets dominated the Allied Control Commission, and ignored the noble sentiments of the Yalta agreement which called for "the establishment, through elections, of governments responsive to the will of the people." When, in spite of the Soviets, the anti-Communist Smallholder Party won 57 percent of the popular vote, the Soviets proceeded to prevent the Smallholders from making effective their mandate. The Communist-controlled Socialist Vice-Premier Szakasits declared:

If the Smallholder party really wants democracy it must renounce the hope of governing with a Smallholder majority . . . electoral arithmetic cannot form the basis of our political life.[5]

5. Hal Lehrman, *Russia's Europe* (New York, Appleton-Century, 1947), p. 208.

The Soviets discredited and kidnapped Smallholder leaders, and finally forced the resignation of Premier Ferenc Nagy by kidnapping his son. Nagy was succeeded by the Communist Rakosi, and the philosophy of the New Order was expressed by Interior Minister Rajk as follows:

> The peaceful and quiet governing of a country is possible only when functional parties do not threaten the unity of National Assembly.[6]

Former Premier Nagy later admitted:

> I went far—perhaps too far—in trying to placate the Communists. I was willing to go to great lengths to hold our coalition together . . .[7]

The Soviet Union then gained complete control over the Hungarian economy through the establishment of theoretically joint companies which were actually under exclusive Russian management. These joint companies gave the Russians control of Hungarian aviation, river transport, crude oil and petroleum refining industries, the bauxite industry, and other connected industries and enterprises.

The Hungarian Communist debt to the Soviet Union was expressed by Joseph Revai, one of the chief Communist theorists in Hungary:

> Our force, the force of our Party and the working class, was multiplied by the fact that the Soviet Union and the Soviet army were always there to support us with their assistance.[8]

In Rumania, the Soviets blocked the anti-Communist efforts of King Michael, and Vishinsky bullied him into giving the Communists control of the ministries of Interior and Justice. The pro-

6. Michael Florinsky, "Hungary," Current History (September, 1947), p. 155.
7. *Saturday Evening Post* (September 6, 1947), p. 28.
8. *Foreign Affairs*, Vol. 28 (1949), p. 143.

Communist Groza was installed as premier, and in May, 1946, the Soviets ratified their control through sham elections. Communist leader Bodnares said: "We will win no matter what."

The U.S. and Britain recognized this new Soviet-dominated government, and the Soviets gained control of the Rumanian economy as they had that of the Hungarians through joint companies. Russia requisitioned almost all of Rumania's grain supply, and for the first time in its history, Rumania had to import grain to feed its people.

On September 7, 1944, the Soviet Union declared war on Bulgaria and invaded the country. The Bulgarian government was overthrown by a joint putsch of Communists and the Fascist Zveno organization. The Communist-dominated Fatherland Front controlled the new government, and the Soviet occupation forces purged the country of anti-Communists. Zveno leader Stainov once told American correspondent Hal Lehrman:

> You Americans must be patient with the Russians; you must allow for their peculiar mentality, and win their confidence.[9]

Not much later, Stainov, his usefulness to the Communists having ended, was denounced in the Communist press as a "dirty fascist dog."

In striking at Nikola Petkov, chief spokesman for the opposition, Bulgarian Communist leader Georgi Dimitrov was aiming not so much at Petkov the man as at the United States and western democracy. Dimitrov declared:

> If we execute Petkov this will demonstrate to the entire opposition how powerless the great democracies are to defend them, and how senselessly futile their opposition to communism has therefore become. And now that the democracies have made their empty protests on his behalf, our little demonstration will be doubled, reinforced.[10]

9. Lehrman, *Russia's Europe*, p. 266.
10. G. M. Dimitrov, "Bravest Democrat of All," *Saturday Evening Post* (December 6, 1947), p. 28.

With respect to Yugoslavia, Tito and his Soviet sponsors effectively sabotaged the Yalta agreement, which supposedly provided for a coalition government representing both Communist and monarchist elements. Ever since he had entered Belgrade on the heels of the Soviet Army, Tito was determined to maintain a monopoly of political power. One of his Politburo members, Moshe Pijade declared: "The altar lamp of terror must never be extinguished; the people must have fear. It is the duty of the police and the army to see that the people have fear."[11]

Tito's foreign minister Kardelj proclaimed:

> We have made several concessions to the capitalist world, in order to gain time. But when the hour strikes we must be ready to pass on to the offensive. The proletarian revolution is on the march. It is linked to the Soviet Union through agreements of mutual political and economic assistance. It is creating, as Stalin has said, a union of all the many parts of the Revolution ... into one system. That Revolutionary system will go into a frontal attack against the Imperialist system ... Between us and America there is an unbridgeable chasm. We are two worlds. They cannot be united. When we are victorious over the American world, the world will be one.[12]

In the fall of 1945 Tito purged his principal opponents, and election laws were passed which paved the way for a rubber stamp Communist-controlled legislature. Serb patriot Mihailovich (who had led the resistance against Germany in the name of the Yugoslav exile government in London) was arrested and executed, and Archbishop Stepinac was put in jail. Meantime Tito received recognition and aid not only from Russia but also the United States. In 1948 Tito and Stalin had a falling out, occasioned probably by Tito's complaints about Russia's influence on the Yugoslav economy and secret police. Tito remains a dedicated Communist, however, and since 1948 his policy has wavered between so-called "Titoism" (sometimes called national or independent Communism) and a rapprochement with Moscow.

The story of the Communist conquest of Albania is no more

11. Martin Ebon, *World Communism Today* (New York, McGraw-Hill, 1948), p. 131.
12. Ibid., p. 118.

than an appendix to the story of Tito's conquest of Yugoslavia. As early as 1942 Moscow subordinated the Albanian Communists to Tito, and messages from Moscow to the Albanian Politburo passed through Tito's hands; the international representatives controlling the action of the Albanian Communists were Tito-appointed Communists.

The Soviet and Tito-supported Albanian Communist leader Hodja found his task during the war facilitated by American and British diplomacy which not only cast aside the anti-Communist Mihailovich in favor of the Communist Tito in Yugoslavia, but did precisely the same thing in Albania. Indeed, pro-Western and anti-Communist leaders throughout the Balkans were uniformly dumped or passed by:

> In practice, therefore, nothing at that period could provide a Balkan leader with a more effective passport to eternity than unswerving loyalty to the West.[13]

In Albania, accordingly the anti-Communist and pro-British Albanian guerrilla leader Abbas Kupi was abandoned by the British and Americans, who even denied him asylum. Britain gave Moscow a mighty boost by deciding to support and recognize the Communist-dominated National Committee of Liberation (LNC) headed by Hodja.

In Czechoslovakia, Moscow's program was facilitated by the collaboration of the Czech leader Benes. As the Russian troops entered the eastern part of Czechoslovakia, they started, in pursuance of the negotiations between Benes and Stalin in 1943, to treat the Carpatho-Ukraine as their own territory, and they officially annexed it soon after the end of the war. In March, 1945, Benes flew from London to Moscow. There Stalin demanded that the Czech Communist leader Gottwald be made Vice-Premier in the Czech regime that was to be carried into the homeland by the Russian Army, and that Communists control the ministries of Interior, Propaganda, Education, and Industry. Benes gave in to Stalin's wishes, and Czechoslovakia, which had resisted Nazism more weakly than its neighbors, resisted Communism scarcely at all. Elections in 1946 made the Communists

13. Franz Borkenau, *European Communism*, p. 502.

the largest single political party. Although without a majority in Parliament, they dominated the government and the country. Benes thought that if he cooperated with the Soviets and the Czech Communists, he could save Czechoslovakia from the fate of Poland and Yugoslavia. He had told Stalin in 1943: "Mr. Stalin, I have complete confidence that we have signed an agreement for non-intervention in domestic affairs, and I know you will keep it."[14]

But Stalin was not to be appeased. He instructed the Communists, who were aided by the Socialist party, to set the stage for a complete take-over of Czechoslovakia. This preparation took place between 1945 and 1948. In February, 1948, the Communists, with Socialist support, seized power in a coup d'etat engineered by Soviet Ambassador Zorin. The new Premier, Gottwald, declared:

> When February was a success, some comrades voiced the opinion that we had unnecessarily lost all the time between 1945 and 1948 . . . There would be no greater mistake than to leave even a shadow of such thinking in our ranks. Our party and our people inevitably had to go through this schooling of three years in order to make what happened in February possible.[15]

A leading authority on Soviet methods of penetration in eastern Europe has summarized the story of Communist take-overs in that area in the following language:

> After World War II eventually all Eastern European countries one after the other, fell into the same pit. Countries that resisted the German aggression now finally have the same fate as the former Axis satellites. Poland, Yugoslavia and Czechoslovakia have been original members of the United Nations. Their fate is not likely to increase the faith of small nations in moral principles in international politics. . . . Negotiations conducted during the war in Moscow, Teheran and

14. *The New York Times*, Feb. 26, 1948.
15. Ivo Duchachek, *The Strategy of Communist Infiltration* (New York, Holt-Rinehart, 1949), p. 24.

Yalta are evidences of the confidence of American statesmen in Soviet pledges. The Soviets were considered as unjustly neglected and unfairly treated step-children of human society, who needed patience, education and whose mischief was not to be taken seriously. Leading western statesmen had great hopes that the Soviet Union could somehow be brought into a democratic world community. . . . In this period, some in the West watched with half-closed eyes, others almost incredulously, the first Soviet violations of international obligations . . . The failure of western diplomatic moves in connection with the installation of minority regimes in Yugoslavia, Poland, Rumania, Hungary and Czechoslovakia is a long, pathetic and painful history. Irrespective of the noble intentions with which they were conceived, the Four Freedoms, the Atlantic Charter, the United Nations, and other solemn declarations of principle have become meaningless phrases to those eastern European nations who during the Nazi oppression awaited their liberation by the western world.[16]

Soviet diplomacy during 1946 consolidated Communist gains in east-central Europe, notably at the Paris Peace conference late that year. This conference did little else than to ratify Soviet-imposed armistice agreements on the satellites. United States Secretary of State Byrnes declared that the "achievements" of the Paris Peace conference were "not the best which human wit could devise." These treaties not only modified the boundaries of these formerly independent countries to the advantage of the Soviet Union, but also forced them to pay hundreds of millions of dollars in reparations to the U.S.S.R., rendering them economic satraps of the Soviet Union.

The Paris conference first of all strengthened Communist Yugoslavia by ceding to Yugoslavia the Istrian peninsula (including part of Trieste) and generally moving the boundary line between Italy and Yugoslavia about twenty miles to the west. In addition Italy was forced to pay 100 million dollars in reparations each to the U.S.S.R. and Yugoslavia.

Second, the conference approved for the Finnish, Rumanian and Hungarian treaties the figure of 300 million dollars in

---

16. Stephen Kertesz in W. Gurian (ed.), *The Soviet Union* (South Bend, Ind., University of Notre Dame Press), p. 136.

reparations, each, to the Soviet Union, as per the Soviet armistice terms of 1945. To make it harder for the defeated and occupied nations, each had to pay the Soviets in deliveries to be valued on the basis of 1938 prices. This had the effect of enslaving the economies of the countries concerned, particularly the Finnish, Hungarian, and Rumanian economies.

Third, the conference acquiesced in the Soviet absorption of northern Bucovina (Rumanian), Petsamo (Finnish) and a modification of the Russo-Finnish border to the benefit of the U.S.S.R. At about the same time, the international Communist movement showed its contempt for the free world when Yugoslavia shot down an American Army transport plane and forced down several more, and when Albania shot at British shipping and sank a British destroyer.

In addition to retaining control over Lithuania, Latvia, and Estonia, gaining control of Poland, Czechoslovakia, Hungary, Rumania, Yugoslavia, and Albania, and extracting economic benefits from Italy and Finland, the Soviets made a serious effort to conquer Greece, and to institute civil war in France, while striving to extend Soviet and Communist influence elsewhere in southern and western Europe.

SOVIET AND COMMUNIST ACTIONS: SOUTHERN AND WESTERN EUROPE

In 1943 the Communist fifth column in Greece, known as the EAM, with its military force (the ELAS), established a "provisional government" in the Pindus mountains, thus flaunting the authority of the Greek government-in-exile. A year later a small group of Russian Army officers parachuted into ELAS headquarters; these Soviet agents were from Moscow by way of Belgrade. At the same time EAM agents in Cairo initiated a mutiny in the Greek armed forces, and the Greek premier was persuaded to bring five members of the EAM into the exile government's cabinet. These five men joined the Greek government on September 1, 1944, upon receiving instructions to do so from the Soviet legation in Cairo.

When the Greek government returned to Greece near the end of 1944, it was confronted by an uprising of the EAM-ELAS, and was able to maintain its authority only with British armed assistance. Meantime the Communist guerrilla forces fled to Yugoslavia for re-grouping, supplying, and training. With assistance also from Communist Bulgaria and Albania, the Soviet-directed assault against Greece broke out again in December, 1946. The UN was prevented from acting owing to the Soviet veto,* although a UN observation commission found the three Communist states guilty of aiding and abetting the uprising in Greece. Subsequently, in 1948, U.S. aid to Greece and Tito's temporary defection from the Soviet bloc ended, at least for the time being, the threat of Communist dominance in Greece.

As far as Western Europe was concerned, the Soviets were not able to render as much assistance and direct support to local Communist parties as they did in eastern Europe. But with the end of World War II, the Soviets explicitly considered western Europe, and its traditional allies, the United Kingdom and the United States, as its enemies, especially when the defeat of Germany was assured. In his speech of February 9, 1946, Stalin dropped any remaining pretense that the defeat of the Axis had eliminated the danger of war and reaffirmed the menace of capitalistic encirclement as the central factor in postwar Soviet policy.

The main postwar Soviet objective was to render Germany impotent and extend Communist influence as far west as possible. The Soviets occupied eastern Germany and tried to influence the United States and Britain to keep western Germany as weak as possible. The American Morgenthau Plan, inspired by Treasury Under Secretary Harry Dexter White in 1944, would almost certainly have destroyed forever Germany's industrial power and reduced that country to a pastoral plain. White was subsequently identified by ex-Communists Whittaker Chambers and Elizabeth Bentley as a Soviet espionage agent. Although the Morgenthau Plan was not implemented at the Potsdam Conference (mid-1945), some of the anti-German spirit of the Plan was carried out, and the Soviets made important gains at that Conference. The U.S.S.R. won control of East Prussia, a zone of occupation in East Germany (which became in effect a part of the Soviet satellite network), reparations from West Germany, and control of all former German external assets along the Danube river. In

*The U. N. Balkan Commission's report implicitly suggested sanctions, as provided in Chapter 7 of the U. N. Charter, Articles 41 and 42.

addition, thousands of Russians, Ukrainians, Balts, and Poles who had fled the invading Soviet armies during 1944 and 1945 into West Germany, were claimed by the Soviets to be Soviet citizens, and the United States and Britain forced these unfortunate people, at point of bayonet, to return to Communist slavery or death. The London *Economist* made this prescient comment on Potsdam:

> The Potsdam Declaration will not last ten years, and when it breaks down there will be nothing but the razor-edge balance of international anarchy between civilization and the atomic bomb. . . . It has in it not a single constructive idea, not a single hopeful perspective for the postwar world. At the end of a mighty war to defeat Hitlerism the Allies are making a Hitlerian peace. This is the real measure of their failure.[17]

In East Germany the Soviets forced a shotgun wedding between the Socialists and Communists, calling the new party the Socialist Unity Party (S.E.D.). Controlled by the Communists, it has ruled East Germany for the Soviets since 1945. The Soviets also won a zone of occupation in Austria, but later withdrew, after exacting a pledge from Austria (to be enforced by the Great Powers) of permanent neutrality.

Communism made the most headway, outside the Soviet bloc, in France and Italy. French Communist leader Thorez, who had deserted his regiment in 1940 and fled to Moscow, returned after the liberation to be welcomed as a hero by leftists; the Communist party, the largest in France since 1945, was a member of the government coalition between 1945 and 1947. The Communists followed a tactic, both subtle and dangerous, which consisted of masquerading as a government party while retaining a virtual monopoly of revolutionary hope and action.

In September, 1947, Thorez attended the international Communist conference in Warsaw where Soviet leader Zhdanov announced the creation of the Cominform, successor to the Comintern. Thorez and his Italian colleague Togliatti were given a new "hard" line to implement. Upon returning to their respective countries they withdrew from the French and Italian

17. As quoted in Chamberlin, *America's Second Crusade*, p. 322.

governments and launched a series of bloody strikes, which many observers felt was a prelude to civil war. Meantime Thorez referred to the Marshall Plan as "an attempt by warmongering American capitalists to enslave Europe." After 1949, Soviet and Communist policy in France aimed at sabotaging the Atlantic Pact and neutralizing France by suggesting peace on Soviet terms.

We have seen in an earlier chapter how the Soviets tried to influence Italian developments through their representation in the Allied Control Commission without much success. However the Soviet-financed Italian Communists are a formidable force, especially in conjunction with their sometime allies, the Socialists of Pietro Nenni. As in France, they dominated the general confederation of labor, and participated in Italian governments from April, 1944 to May, 1947. Togliatti for a time controlled the Justice ministry, but Communists never captured the ministries of Foreign Affairs, Interior, or Defense. In 1948 Premier De Gasperi and his ruling Christian Democratic party won a great victory, and the Communists and their Socialist allies have taken a definite second seat since. Italian Communists were hampered until mid-1948 by Soviet insistence that Trieste be given to Tito, something which was most unpopular in Italy.

SOVIET POLICY AND COMMUNIST OPERATIONS: FAR EAST

During the Second World War, and until the last week of the fighting, the Soviet Union and Japan acted out their partnership based on the treaty of April 14, 1941, and the principle of non-aggression. Soviet espionage agent Victor Sorge, and leaders of the Institute of Pacific Relations of Japan, passed on important information to Moscow and appear to have influenced Japan's decision not to attack Russia, but rather to confine its aggression in a southerly direction. Sorge and his espionage associates had as one of their objectives: "To influence Japanese policy away from an attack on the Soviet Union and toward an attack on the United States, Great Britain, and the Dutch East Indies." (Senate Internal Security Subcommittee, Hearings on Institute of Pacific Relations, July 2, 1952, p. 180).

Meantime the Soviets played a role toward China which initially consisted of favoring Chiang Kai-shek as the symbol and figurehead of the united front, until the Chinese Communists felt themselves strong enough to make a challenge for leadership. By the end of 1943 the international Communist movement decided to attack Chiang Kai-shek as "reactionary" and "corrupt," and to champion the cause of Mao Tse-tung's "agrarian reformers."

On August 8, 1943, Moscow's *War and the Labor Class* magazine published a long article criticizing the Chinese government. The article, written by Vladimir Rogov, *Tass* correspondent in China, alleged that there were "appeasers, defeatists and surrenderists" in the Chinese government scheming to prevent military reforms and industrial construction, and that this had reduced China's combat strength. Rogov also predicted that civil war would soon break out in China. According to President Chiang Kai-shek:

> This [article] led people in and outside the American government to believe that there were "die-hards" in Kuomintang bent on fomenting civil war. The *Tass* agency had actively paved the way in its propaganda for the complete change-over by the Chinese Communists. . . . Thereafter international Communists worked overtime to turn American public opinion and American diplomacy against the Republic of China and Chinese government. Such adjectives as "corrupt," "incompetent," "reactionary" and "dictatorial" were flung on our government and on me personally. Their aim was to sabotage relations between China and the United States so as to isolate China. The Sino-Japanese War was then at its most difficult state. They wanted it to fall short of victory so as to enable the Chinese Communists to seize power. This was Moscow's plot, but few could see it at the time.[18]

In 1944 while the Russo-German war was raging in Europe, Soviet Russia annexed Tannu Tuva, part of China's territory in Outer Mongolia. As early as 1921 Russian troops had invaded Tannu Tuva, which has been called Soviet Russia's first satellite. In 1941 a Communist puppet regime in Tannu Tuva sided with Russia against Germany.

After V-J day, Soviet and American forces began to fill the political vacuum caused by the defeat of Japan. Commenting on

18. Chiang Kai-shek, *Soviet Russia in China*, (London, Harrap, 1956), p. 111.

the situation in September, 1945, historian David Dallin wrote:

> Only a few weeks before it had been Japan that confronted Soviet policy and Soviet forces everywhere in the Far East. . . . And now, within a matter of weeks, Soviet policy and Soviet forces were everywhere confronting—the United States. . . . Soviet aspirations had not been satisfied, however. Only the points enumerated in the Yalta and subsequent agreements had been fulfilled. Stalin's great designs for the Far East were still far from realization, and it was the United States that barred the roads to their achievement.[19]

Although the Soviet Union had entered the Pacific war for only the last few days of the fighting, it demanded a voice equal to that of the United States in determining Japan's future. But General MacArthur refused to accede to Communist demands, leading *Pravda* to state: "The American policy jeopardizes peace in Asia and the relations among the Allies." (Sept. 17, 1945).

The Soviet Union was excluded from any decisive part in ruling Japan (except for south Sakhalin and the Kuriles, gained at Yalta), and direct Soviet policy in Japan was limited to opposition and propaganda; Japanese Marxists assumed greater importance in the fulfillment of Moscow's purposes.

The Soviets did, however, assume control of North Korea. At the Potsdam conference it had been agreed that Soviet forces could accept Japanese surrenders north of the 38th parallel. But the Soviets used this as an excuse to establish permanent Communist domination of North Korea: "It was then (1945) considered a line for short range military convenience. Now the Soviets made it a solid political and economic border."[20]

Soviet and Communist aspirations in China depended to a large degree on the attitude of the United States. During 1944, according to David Dallin:

> The attitude of the United States government, more influential in China than any other, began to veer in the di-

---

19. David Dallin, *Soviet Russia in the Far East* (New Haven, Yale Univeristy Press), p. 236.
20. Ibid., p. 261.

rection prompted by Moscow. President Roosevelt subscribed
to the idea of a united front in China; he did it not so much out
of sympathy for the Communist elements as in an effort to appease the Soviet Union during the war. He sought to fulfill as
many of Stalin's demands as he could afford to. When he sent
Vice President Wallace on a tour of Siberia and Russia, in
1944, he had two objectives in mind; to improve Russo-
Chinese relations and, to this end, to bring about a rapprochement between the Central Government and the Communists in China.[21]

As a result of the Yalta agreement, Soviet power flowed into
Manchuria, and the Soviets later turned over captured Japanese
equipment to the Chinese Communists. In the Sino-Soviet
Treaty of August, 1945, the U.S.S.R. promised to recognize only
the Chinese Nationalist government, as well as its sovereignty in
Manchuria, but these promises were broken shortly thereafter.
This treaty also affirmed the Soviet territorial gains realized at
Yalta. Speaking of this treaty, Chiang Kai-shek declared:

> Even such great sacrifices as China has been forced to make
> under the Sino-Soviet Treaty of Friendship and Alliance have
> failed to satisfy Soviet Russia. Obviously nothing short of
> complete domination of China would satisfy Stalin's ap-
> petite.[22]

Since the United States had already indicated its complete
unwillingness to use force to lead Nationalist troops into areas
where Nationalist sovereignty had been recognized at Yalta,
Chiang tried the "soft" approach:

> When the Soviet "dismantling" of Manchurian industry and
> the Soviet-protected Communist drive into Manchuria were
> at their height, Chiang Kai-shek made a friendly gesture
> toward Russia, stating, on October 15, 1945, that he "felt sure
> that Soviet forces in Manchuria would be withdrawn in accor-
> dance with the Sino-Soviet pact."[23]

21. Ibid., p. 228.
22. Chiang Kai-shek, *Soviet Russia in China*, p. 149.
23. Dallin, *Soviet Russia in the Far East*, p. 254.

Meantime the war-weary Chinese Nationalists, who had borne the brunt of the fighting against Japan, found that the United States was not prepared to give them the same aid against the new aggressor—Communism—that had been rendered against the Japanese invader.

Soviet foreign policy objectives were furthered by Communist and pro-Communist influences in an unusually influential private organization known as the Institute of Pacific Relations. Among the conclusions of the bipartisan Senate Internal Security Sub-committee of the United States Senate which conducted a thorough investigation of this organization in 1952, were:

> The IPR has been considered by the American Communist party and by Soviet officials as an instrument of Communist policy, propaganda and military intelligence.
>
> The effective leadership of the IPR used IPR prestige to promote the interests of the Soviet Union in the United States.
>
> A group of persons operating within and about the Institute of Pacific Relations exerted a substantial influence on United States far eastern policy.
>
> The IPR was a vehicle used by the Communists to orientate American far eastern policies toward Communist objectives.
>
> A group of persons associated with the IPR attempted, between 1941 and 1945, to change United States policy so as to accommodate Communist ends and to set the stage for a major United States policy change, favorable to Soviet interests, in 1945.[24]

A leading analyst of Soviet Far Eastern policy makes this assessment of the situation:

> The political consequences of the avalanche of propaganda in favor of the Chinese Communists in Yenan and Moscow, in-nocently taken up in Washington and carried out in China, made themselves felt during the last period of the war and for at least a year, after its conclusion. Long after the military alliance of the United States and Russia had ended and all the motives for the appeasement of the Soviet Union had ceased

24. "The Institute of Pacific Relations," hearings before the Senate Internal Security Subcommittee, 1952, pp. 223–225.

to operate, the policy of the United States in China continued to labor under the impact of the propaganda campaign of 1944–45.

Seldom has the Soviet government been more successful than in this case in attaining its goals by a really brilliant maneuver.[25]

The same writer then describes developments in China as they relate to the Soviet power position in these words:

Considerable American pressure was exerted on Chungking [seat of the Nationalist government] to make various offers and concessions to the Communists. In the first stages of these negotiations the American Ambassador, Patrick J. Hurley, played an important part; he visited Moscow, Chungking, and Yenan, attempting to bring together all the partners of the proposed agreement. He was later succeeded by Gen. George C. Marshall, whose efforts lasted for another year. After almost three years of futile effort the upshot was the only one possible—a complete fiasco. The parleys, in broad outline, reflected the course of American-Soviet relations and depended on the general trends of Soviet policy. From the vantage point of the Soviet power position in Asia, collaboration between Moscow and Washington in the Far East became, with the end of the war, superfluous and even undesirable. The removal of American forces and influence from China, Japan, and Korea became the immediate Soviet concern in 1946. Accordingly the government of Chiang Kai-shek again became an enemy and the Chinese Communists the sole force to be relied upon in China.[26]

Secretary of State James Byrnes declared on November 27, 1945:

The wise course would be to try to force the Chinese government and the Chinese Communists to get together on a compromise basis, perhaps telling Chiang Kai-shek that we will stop the aid to his government unless he goes along with this.[27]

25. Dallin, *Soviet Russia in the Far East*, p. 230.
26. Ibid., p. 230.
27. Walter Millis, *The Forrestal Diaries* (New York, Viking, 1951), p. 104.

Subsequent policy statements by the President of the United States, the Secretary of State and other American officials made it clear that the United States favored a coalition government which included the Communists in China.

Accordingly, General Marshall was sent to China to try to persuade Chiang to bring Communists into his government; failing that Chiang was to be threatened with the elimination of American aid. Unable to gain his objective, General Marshall recommended, and President Truman adopted, an embargo on further military equipment to Nationalist China. This embargo was in effect from early August, 1946, to the end of May, 1947.

The Chinese Nationalists, demoralized and defeated, retreated to the island of Taiwan in December, 1949. Chinese Communist leader Mao Tse-tung asserted that if it had not been for Soviet aid, his cause could not have prevailed. The Central Committee of the Chinese Communist party declared in 1953:

> The victory of the people's revolution in China and the development of the Chinese People's Republic are inseparable from the support and help of the Communist party of the Soviet Union, the Soviet government, and the Soviet people.[28]

In southeast Asia, the international Communist movement now sought to capture the leadership of nationalist and anti-western movements. In Vietnam and in Indonesia such Moscow-trained operatives as Ho Chi-minh, Tan Malakka and Muso built Communist organizations on the residue of the Japanese puppet regimes. In Vietnam the fighting broke out with a vengeance on Christmas day, 1946, when Vietminh (Communist) guerrillas massacred thousands of European residents in Hanoi. Four years later the U.S.S.R. and Communist China recognized the "Vietnam Democratic Republic" (Vietminh), and the Peiping newspaper *Jen Min Jin-pao* announced:

> The Chinese people extend a warm welcome to the Vietnam Democratic Republic as their friendly neighbor, and are confident that the establishment of diplomatic relations between China and Vietnam will mark a great event in the struggle for national liberation in the Orient.[29]

28. Dallin, *Soviet Russia in the Far East*, p. 342.
29. *Izvestia*, Jan. 21, 1950.

Communist influence in Burma and Indonesia gained during the period 1945–1950. The Burmese government itself was Socialist and in world affairs struck an attitude of benevolence toward the U.S.S.R. and the Chinese Communists. In Indonesia, the Communists supported nationalist leader Sukarno, who was to become President of that newly-created state, until 1948 when they staged an ill-fated revolt against him. Not long afterwards, however, the Communists were again permitted to organize openly, and very soon they were dominant in labor and education, and were even influential in the government.

In Thailand, Malaya, and the Philippines, Communist guerrilla forces fought to expel western influences and overthrow the governments concerned. This guerrilla effort is still very active in Malaya.

Beginning in 1949, developments in China paralleled those of the U.S.S.R. in an earlier era, and Mao Tse-tung wrote in his pamphlet *On People's Democratic Dictatorship,* published in July, 1949, that: "The Communist party of the U.S.S.R. is our very best teacher, and we must learn from it." During 1949, both the U.S.S.R. and Communist China stepped up the "hate America" campaign as a prelude to the Communist invasion of Korea in 1950.

By 1949 the U.S.S.R. claimed that its forces had withdrawn from Korea, leading to a United States evacuation in June, 1949. But on June 25, 1950, the large North Korean army, "trained and equipped by the Soviets, attacked, plainly on Stalin's orders."[30] Writing in 1948, David Dallin summarized Soviet policy in the Far East:

> The Moscow government has given its answer to the all-important problem of the Far East. In the pursuit of its policy of expansion, in its boundless dynamism, it is developing the area into a new fortress, subjected once again to all the vicissitudes of military operations. Its dynamism has increased far beyond the accomplishments of its imperial predecessor at the peak of its successes in the Far East, in the decade from 1895 to 1904 . . .
>
> The new Far Eastern Cominform is destined to be one of the principal channels of this policy. In November, 1947, the

30. Treadgold, *Twentieth Century Russia*, p. 436.

first postwar conference of the Eastern Communist parties took place in Harbin, the Russo-Chinese capital of Northern Manchuria. In his Christmas report of 1947 to the Central Committee of the Chinese Communist party, Mao Tse-tung, the "Chinese Stalin," referred to the new Communist International which had been set up for nine European parties in Belgrade, and declared that a similar organization should be established "to coordinate the liberation movements of the billion people of the Far East." The reluctance to proceed with such an organization was understandable since the alleged independence of Chinese Communism from international Communism had been successfully played up as a political propaganda asset by the Chinese Communists. But now this propaganda had lost its persuasive power and could readily be discarded. The way was open for the creation of a Far Eastern Cominform.

For the vast Soviet sphere in Asia—in China, Korea, and Mongolia—the specific weight of the Russian Far East lies not in its numbers or size, but in its backdrop, the Soviet Union in Europe. It is in Moscow that the currents are generated which build up the Russian Far East into a mighty fortress on the shores of the Pacific and which aim relentlessly at expanding to the south, penetrating into the island empire to the east, and erecting a Soviet "co-prosperity sphere" for the Chinese, Mongol, Korean, and Japanese peoples under Soviet Russian leadership.[31]

SUMMARY

The period 1945 to 1950 was, for the international Communist movement, one of expanding the area of control of the Soviet bloc as far as possible, and capitalizing on American demobilization and the western desire for peace. In Western Europe the Soviets achieved their greatest influence in France and Italy, while using their bridgeheads of power in East Germany and Czechoslovakia to intimidate all of Western Europe. In Asia and especially the Far East, the Soviets took advantage of the concessions made to them at the Yalta conference, and helped the Chinese Communists to extend their zone of influence at precisely the same time that the United States insisted that Communists be included in the Chinese National government. When

31. *Soviet Russia in the Far East*, p. 379.

Chiang refused, the American embargo on arms aid to Nationalist China was imposed, leading ultimately to the defeat of the Nationalist armies.

Stefan Possony's comment on the 1945–1950 balance of power change is an apt conclusion to this chapter:

> The Communists helped each other; the non-Communists did not—they helped the Communists. The Soviets won by commission; the United States lost by omission. The Communist flood was not contained, but broke through the dams that never had been built.[32]

32. Possony, *International Relations*, p. 351.

Chapter 8

FROM KOREA TO HUNGARY 1950–1956

THE SOVIET "PEACE" OFFENSIVE

Soviet policy in Europe achieved a high-water mark in 1948 with the coup d'etat in Czechoslovakia, bringing that country into the Soviet orbit. That same year the Soviet blockade of Berlin was over-flown by the United States airlift into that city, and the defection of Tito from the Soviet bloc led to a gradual cessation of the Soviet-directed attack against Greece. United States aid to Greece was also a factor.

It appeared that the Zhdanov-directed Cominform efforts to stress further penetration into Europe had been checkmated. Zhdanov's death and the rise of Malenkov to influence coincided with the rapid expansion of Communism in China, and the simultaneous United States withdrawal from China. From 1948 to 1955, major Soviet and Communist gains were made in the Far East. Then, beginning with the Soviet shipment of arms to Egypt in September, 1955, Soviet and Communist influence in the Middle East rose sharply, and during 1958 became the dominant factor in the political life of Egypt, Iraq and Syria.

As Soviet gains in Europe tapered off, and the main Communist emphasis began to shift to the Far East, the international Communist movement launched its so-called "peace offensive." Its objective was first to check, and then to disintegrate the effects of the gradual awakening in the West to Soviet and communist expansion, and the tangible results of that awakening in the form of the North Atlantic Treaty Organization, the Marshall Plan, Truman Doctrine, Berlin Airlift, etc. The Third Cominform Congress convened in Hungary in November, 1949, at which time Soviet spokesman Suslov discussed the expanding "peace movement":

> The strength and power of the peace movement lies further in the fact that it has assumed an organized character. The champions of peace increasingly consolidate and organize themselves on a local, national, and international scale . . . National peace congresses were held in a number of countries. The wave of strikes, popular demonstrations and meetings of protests against the ratification of the North Atlantic agreement swept the whole of Western Europe. In many countries, national committees in defense of peace were formed. . . . The movement of the fighters for peace also gains ground in the United States of America and Great Britain.[1]

Suslov referred to Communists and their allies in the "peace" movement as "partisans of peace." This was not an accidental term. During World War II the Communists controlled large groups of partisans in Yugoslavia, Greece, France, Italy and elsewhere who carried on an active campaign of sabotage behind the enemy lines under instructions similar to the following:

> Make every effort to have the tanks, airplanes, and armoured cars produced by you to go out of commission soon. See to it that the mines and shells do not explode. Disorganize railroads. Dislocate the transportation systems . . . Disorganize traffic, blow up bridges . . . Sabotage the production of guns, tanks, ammunition; call strikes. Blow up . . . am-

---

1. House Un-American Activities Committee, *Report on the Communist "Peace" Offensive*, 1951, p. 5.

munition dumps and storehouses. Disorganize their military shipments.[2]

Among the various national "peace" meetings convened at the behest of the Soviet Union, and under its control, was the Scientific and Cultural Conference for World Peace, arranged by the National Council of the Arts, Sciences, and Professions, and held in New York City on March 25–27, 1949. Most of the sponsors were veteran supporters of Soviet and Communist causes. The U.S. Department of State referred to the gathering as a "sounding board for Communist propaganda." The purpose of the conference was:

1. To provide a propagandist forum against the Marshall Plan, the North Atlantic defense pact, and American foreign policy in general.

2. To promote support for the foreign policy of the Soviet Union.

3. To mobilize American intellectuals in the field of arts, science, and letters behind this program even to the point of civil disobedience against the American government.

4. To prepare the way for a subsequent world peace congress in Paris on April 20 to 24, 1949, with similar aims on a world scale and under similar Communist auspices.

5. To discredit American culture and to extol the virtues of Soviet culture.[3]

Thus, the Soviet-controlled Permanent Committee of the World Peace Congress met in Stockholm, Sweden, between March 15 and 19, 1950, with 120 delegates in attendance. General Secretary Jean Lafitte, French Communist, reported that 52 National Committees in Defense of Peace were affiliated with parent Committee of the World Peace Congress. Another

2. *Manifesto*, Second All-Slavonic Congress, Moscow, April 4–5, 1942.
3. *Report on the Communist "Peace" Offensive*, p. 11.

leading speaker, Louis Saillant, general-secretary of the Communist-controlled World Federation of Trade Unions, sounded
the following call: "We should state that one of the essential
duties of the defenders of peace is the refusal to work on and
produce war material in all capitalist countries."[4]

The most far-reaching decision made by the World Peace
Congress at its Stockholm meeting was to launch a worldwide
signature drive, the "World Peace Appeal." This was the boldest
and most extensive piece of psychological warfare ever conducted
by any organization on a world scale. The World Peace Appeal
was launched three months before the outbreak of Communist
armed aggression against the Republic of Korea. By soliciting
names and addresses from "peace" petition signers, the Communists were in a position to establish huge mailing lists to be
used for the circulation of propaganda, and to recruit new
members into the international Communist apparatus. Re-
prisals* were taken against non-signers within the Soviet bloc,
and in some instances, outside the bloc as well.

A second World Peace Congress was scheduled for November,
1950, in Sheffield, England, but the locale was changed after
British Prime Minister Clement Attlee denounced the meeting as
a . . . "bogus forum of peace with the real aim of sabotaging national defense."

Attlee refused to admit most of the delegates, so the conference was convened in Warsaw, Poland. American "aggression" in Korea was condemned, and delegates gave a
standing ovation to the North Korean Communist delegate.

In 1952 Stalin pointed out that the "fight for peace" was
simply part of the fight to overthrow capitalism:

> . . . the fight for peace will develop here or there into a fight
> for socialism. But then it will no longer be the present-day
> peace movement; it will be a movement for the overthrow of
> capitalism.[5]

Ever since Stalin's death, the international Communist
movement has taken advantage of fear of possible nuclear war,

4. Ibid., p. 31.
*Including threats regarding jobs, housing, travel permits, relatives abroad, etc.
5. *Soviet Weekly*, Oct. 30, 1952.

together with the rising tide of pacifism, to generate peace at any price movements in the West. In this connection, Communists have always distinguished between just and unjust wars (the latter constituting resistance to Communist aggression). Coincidentally, "war" (except "just" and "national liberation" wars), meaning also Free World resistance to Communist expansionism, is anathema to the international Communist movement. The draft program of the 22nd Communist Party Congress (U.S.S.R.) urged:

> Steadfastly to pursue a policy of consolidating all the forces fighting against war. All the organizations and parties that strive to avert war, the neutralist and pacifist movements and the bourgeois circles that advocate peace . . . will meet with understanding and support on the part of the Soviet Union . . .

> To be highly vigilant with regard to the aggressive circles, which are intent on violating peace; to expose, in good time, the initiators of military adventures; to take all necessary steps to safeguard the security and inviolability of our Socialist country and the Socialist camp as a whole.

> The C.P.S.U. and the Soviet people as a whole will continue to oppose all wars of conquest, including . . . local wars aimed at strangling people's emancipation movements, and consider it their duty to support the sacred struggle of the oppressed peoples and their just anti-imperialist wars of liberation.[6]

THE INVASION OF KOREA

Following the Communist victory in China, the Soviets decided to risk massive retaliation by invading the Republic of Korea. The Soviets did not consider the risk too great, however, especially after U.S. Secretary of State Acheson declared in January, 1950, that the United States did not consider Korea or Formosa to be within its Pacific security line. There is some evidence that the international Communist movement laid plans for the invasion of Korea during a meeting of the World Federation

6. Salisbury, *Khruschev's Mein Kampf*, p. 92.

of Trade Unions at the end of 1949:

> Anyone who has read the published proceedings of the so-
> called "labor conference" staged by the World Federation of
> Trade Unions at Peiping during November and December of
> 1949 knows full well that Korean aggression was planned
> months before the North Koreans plunged southwards
> towards Seoul.[7]

When the North Korean Communist regime invaded the Republic of Korea on June 25, 1950, its army had been trained by
Soviet Marshal Malinovsky, and all its equipment was of
Russian make. Because the United States had withdrawn its
forces from South Korea and refused to train and equip an ade-
quate military establishment in South Korea, the invading Communist forces won the early battles of the war. But at the end of
September, 1950, General MacArthur carried out the Inchon
landings, cutting off most Communist forces from the rear. Seoul
was liberated, and the United Nations, by its resolution of
October 7, 1950, authorized MacArthur to liberate North Korea.
As Percy Spender, Australian Minister for External Affairs said
over the UN Radio on October 5, 1950:

> The UN would be courting disaster . . . if it were for one
> moment to contemplate stopping short at the 38th parallel . . .
> Why on earth go through all the effort and bloodshed of the
> last three months if we are going to do no more than restore
> the status quo.

MacArthur liberated North Korea but, upon reaching the
Yalu, was confronted with a Chinese Communist invasion of the
peninsula. Failing to obtain permission to retaliate against the
enemy's privileged sanctuary in Manchuria, MacArthur was
forced to retreat. The evidence suggests that the International
Communist movement had reasonable assurance that there
would be no retaliation north of the Yalu if Red China entered
the war.

7. Richard Deverall, "The Situation in Korea," *America* (Jan. 20, 1951).

The United Nations invited Red China to New York in December, 1950, to discuss a settlement in Korea, but nothing came of these talks. Meantime Communist propaganda throughout the world urged that the UN forces stop their counter-offensive at the 38th parallel. Even after April, 1951, when President Truman removed General Douglas MacArthur, who had publicly opposed the Administration's ban on bombing north of the Yalu, MacArthur's successor, General James Van Fleet, was leading victorious UN armies north towards the North Korean capital of Pyongyang. At this point the Soviet Union decided to intervene and attempted to win through diplomacy what was being lost on the battlefield. Jacob Malik of the USSR, speaking on the radio from New York, 'suggested' that the time might be ripe for talk of a cease fire.

The United States accepted this proposal, even though the UN forces were marching north, and victory was in sight:

> Washington immediately directed General Mathew B. Ridgeway to broadcast an announcement to the Communist field commanders that the United Nations was willing to discuss an armistice. This was not only done in great haste; it was done without denouncing the 38th parallel as a line of demarcation. The Communists, therefore, concluded that the United Nations Command needed an armistice, and that the 38th parallel would be a truce line acceptable to the United States.[8]

During this time, Communist propaganda suggested that if the UN forces tried to achieve military victory, this would "spread the war" and bring the Soviets into the war. Actually Van Fleet's armies had all but won the war already, and every senior military commander in Korea was convinced at the time that the Soviets would hardly have entered a losing battle in which they would have had to supply their forces via the long and vulnerable Trans-Siberian rail line.

Having retreated from the original objective of liberating North Korea to that of seeking a negotiated peace, the UN Command under Admiral Joy (and later, General Harrison) was

---

8. D. Turner Joy, *How Communists Negotiate* (New York, Macmillan, 1955), p. 165.

directed by Washington to adopt a conciliatory attitude toward the Communist side. Admiral Joy described the Communist objective at the Panmunjom conference in these words:

> You have increasingly presented evidence before the world that you did not enter these negotiations with sincerity and high purpose, but rather that you entered into them to gain time to repair your shattered forces and to try to accomplish at the conference table what your armies could not accomplish on the field.[9]

A final concession made to the Communists concerned North Korean prisoners taken by the Republic of Korea (South Korea), eighty percent of whom had decided not to return to Communism. The UN had made a commitment to the South Korean government that these prisoners would simply be released and would be free to choose their own future. Instead, the UN Command agreed to the Communist demand to force these anti-Communist prisoners, together with Anti-Communist Chinese prisoners, to be forcibly detained by Indian guards for four months, during three of which they were to be forced to listen to the appeals of professional brain-washers from eastern Europe.

When South Korean President Syngman Rhee heard about this intended betrayal of commitment, he instructed his guards to release the anti-Communist Koreans from their prison camps. This action upset the impending truce and incensed both the Chinese Communists and official Washington. American soldiers were ordered to round up the escaped anti-Communist Koreans and turn them over for interrogations. But few of the Koreans were found, and the truce was finally signed July 27, 1953. The Communists were allowed to hold almost all North Korea, while the U.N. Command returned 132,000 prisoners to them in return for less than 12,000 captured by the Communist side. Among those not returned by the Communists were 11,000 UN prisoners of war murdered by their Communist captors, 63,000 Korean prisoners impressed into the Communist armies, 944 Americans and untold thousands of Koreans.[10]

9. Ibid., p. 157.
10. Ibid., p. 167.

Part of the Panmunjom Agreement specified that neither side should increase its military strength either through reinforcements or through the introduction of new weapons. A "neutral" nations commission (Poland, Czechoslovakia, India, Sweden, and Switzerland) was supposed to inspect in both the north and south for violations. But the Communists never permitted genuine inspection in the north, while the Poles and Czechs engaged in espionage in the south. This uneven performance continued for four years, with the UN forces remaining static while the Communist side introduced additional military strength.

During the same month that the Panmunjom Agreement was signed by the Communists and the UN (but not by the Republic of Korea), the Soviet occupation army in East Germany and its puppet Communist East German regime were confronted with a popular uprising which began in the east zone of Berlin. German workers, farmers, and housewives, fed up with totalitarianism, fought Soviet tanks with bare hands and rocks. Most East German policemen joined the revolt, and the Soviets had to rush in tank units and troops from Poland. But without help from the West, the unarmed German population was unable to resist long:

> There remains the question whether the 1953 uprising is now no more than a stirring memory, or whether that extraordinary event still exerts an influence on Soviet Zone developments. The answer is that the latter unquestionably holds true. The people of Eastern Germany would long ago have given up the struggle if it were not for the assurance the seventeenth of June has given them that the Communist leaders are not invincible—There is not the slightest doubt, however, that the will to oppose will die if the Western Powers should appear ready to accept the Soviet proposal of a European security system based on the present division of Germany.[11]

COMMUNIST PENETRATION IN SOUTHEAST ASIA

Fighting in French-dominated Vietnam had reached a crescendo in early 1954 with the battle of Dienbienphu, at which

11. Stefan Brant, *The East German Rising* (New York, Praeger, 1957), p. 201.

the Vietminh (Communist rebels) inflicted a severe defeat on the French colonial troops. On the one hand, some French and American military men argued in favor of United States intervention to help defeat the rebels, while on the other, defeatists and those tired of the fighting urged a negotiated settlement akin to Panmunjom. The upshot was the 1954 Geneva Conference, at which French Premier Mendes-France decided to accept partition of Vietnam, with the Communists taking over control of twelve million people north of the 17th parallel. Another "neutral nations commission" consisting of Poland, India, and Canada was created in an attempt to insure compliance with the Geneva Agreement, and anti-Communist refugees from the north were supposed to be free to escape to the south. But Communist leader Ho Chi-minh became alarmed at the great numbers of people who wished to go south:

> Such an exodus of people became embarrassing to Ho Chi-minh and he began hindering individuals who wanted to leave. . . . People were beaten, tortured, and abused in many ways. . . . Though the Communist Vietminh signed the agreements, they have consistently violated every one of them and have again demonstrated that the word of a Communist is worthless.[12]

The Western retreat at Geneva was followed by neutralization of Cambodia, Communist infiltration into Laos, a temporary reevaluation by Thailand of its pro-Western stand, and stepped-up Communist pressure in the Formosa Straits, resulting in a U.S.-enforced Chinese Nationalist retreat from the strategically important Tachen Islands. Both Communist China and the U.S.S.R. wooed the people of southeast Asia, and worked hard to extend the anti-American "neutralism" of India, Burma, Ceylon, and Indonesia elsewhere. The international Communist movement employed the following tactics and techniques in penetrating southeast Asia:

1) Open political activity,

12. John W. O'Daniel in "Soviet Total War," hearings of the House Committee on Un-American Activities, Sept. 30, 1956, Vol. II, p. 845.

2) Penetration and mobilization of groups and organizations,
3) Cultural work,
4) Diplomatic maneuvers,
5) Economic offensive,
6) Use of armed aggression and subversion.[13]

According to Asian expert Rodger Swearingen, both the Soviets and the Chinese Communists remain convinced that sooner or later their system should and will triumph everywhere. Consequently, all of the present and any future non-Communist governments in south and southeast Asia are regarded by Moscow and Peking as both non-permanent and, in the long run, unacceptable. The immediate tactical objectives of Communism in Asia were (a) removal of United States influence and power, (b) neutralization of the region and (c) destruction of the Western alliance.

Swearingen also analyzes the reasons for Communist influence and expansion in these words:

> While an unhappy colonial background, lack of enlightened social and economic policy, and the absence of a realistic appraisal of Communist intentions and tactics may have a direct relationship to the degree of Communist support in a given area, proximity to Communist China is not necessarily an advantage. The degree of enthusiasm and support for Communist China among the Chinese in Hong Kong, with close and regular contacts across the border, appears, for example, considerably less than in more distant Indonesia or India, with controlled or limited contacts with mainland China. Most observers agree that this can be explained, in large part, by the greater availability in Hong Kong of factual information on Communist China.[14]

KHRUSHCHEV AND THE TWENTIETH PARTY CONGRESS

Soviet and Communist policies in south and east Asia, as of 1956, could boast of the capture of the Indian state of Kerala,

13. Rodger Swearingen in "Soviet Total War," p. 835.
14. Ibid., p. 826.

increased influence in Burma, Ceylon, Laos, and Indonesia, and the continuing pressure on the international diplomatic front to gain recognition for Red China.

Towards the end of 1955 and even more noticeably during 1956, Soviet and Communist activity seemed to swing away from the profitable east Asian theatre, and into that of the Middle East. Here Communist activities were less overtly hostile and military, and it was possible to present a face of "accomodation" to the West. But just as the program of "de-Stalinization" and "smiling diplomacy" went into full gear, a revolt took place in Hungary which shook the Soviet Empire to its foundations and led to the reimposition of Stalinism. Yet the setbacks in central Europe in no way impaired the expansion of Soviet and Communist influence in the Middle East.

Prior to examining the Middle East situation since the fall of 1955, let us consider the role of Khrushchev as successor to Stalin, and the events in Hungary. The thinking of Khrushchev and the new Soviet leadership is perhaps nowhere better exemplified than in the Central Committee Report to the Twentieth Party Congress of the Communist party of the Soviet Union, February 14, 1956:

> True, we recognize the need for the revolutionary transformation of capitalist society into socialist society. It is this that distinguishes the revolutionary Marxists from reformists, the opportunists. There is no doubt that in a number of capitalist countries violent overthrow of the dictatorship of the bourgeoisie and the sharp aggravation of class struggle connected with this are inevitable. But the forms of social revolution vary. And it is not true that we regard violence and civil war as the only way to remake society.

The Report suggested that in some countries, presumably France and Italy, where large Communist parties wield great influence, "socialism" (that is to say a regime controlled by Moscow Communists) might come to power through evolutionary or peaceful means. Theoretically, also, some "capitalist" states might succumb to Communist dictatorship without fighting. But, continues the Report:

Of course, in those countries where capitalism is still strong, where it possesses a tremendous military and police machine, serious resistance by reactionary force is inevitable. The transition to socialism in these countries will take place amid sharp revolutionary class struggle. In all the forms of transition to socialism, an absolute decisive requirement is political leadership of the working class, headed by its vanguard. The transition to socialism is impossible without this. It is necessary to emphasize strongly that the more favorable conditions for the triumph of socialism in other countries have arisen because socialism triumphed in the Soviet Union and is winning in the people's democracies. And our victory would have been impossible if Lenin and the party of the Bolsheviks had not championed revolutionary Marxism against the reformists who broke with Marxism and took the road of opportunism.

Khrushchev also told the Congress:

Leninism teaches us that the ruling classes will not surrender their power voluntarily—and the greater or lesser degree of intensity which the struggle may assume, the use or the non-use of violence in the transition to socialism, depends on the resistance of the exploiters. . . . In the countries where capitalism is still strong . . . the transition to socialism will be attended by a sharp, class, revolutionary struggle.

Thus, the "new line," as it was so well summarized by the late Peter Meyer:

If you yield to us without resistance, we will not use force. If you resist, we will use force. But yield you must. So it is up to you to decide whether there is to be a rape, or a peaceful voluntary yielding.[15]

15. *New Leader*, March 12, 1956.

HUNGARY

During this post-Stalin period the stress was on "peaceful co-existence" and "national Communism," suggesting that the Soviet satellites could have some degree of autonomy. For a short period of time Moscow seemed to have convinced not only some in the satellites, but also some in the free world that Khrushchev's policy towards the West, and towards the satellite states, would be more "liberal" than Stalin's had been.

However, the peoples of eastern and central Europe had not forgotten the east German uprising, nor the bygone days when they were free. Communism, whether "national" or "international," was pretty much the same thing to them; it was a Moscow-directed enslavement of their countries. In June, 1956, workers in Poznan, Poland, launched a bloody strike, coupled with popular demonstrations against the Communist regime, which was ruthlessly put down. Then, in October, 1956, the Hungarian people rose up to strike at their dictatorship. Theirs was the most violent challenge to Communist despotism ever to erupt in eastern Europe:

> On October 22, 1956, as throughout the previous nine years, Hungary was held captive by the Soviet Union. On the next day the Hungarian people began to march toward freedom. One week later Hungary was free. For a period of four days ending in the early hours of November 4, Hungary had emerged from captivity. During this period the Soviet Union even made a semblance of acknowledging the country's new status and pretended to negotiate with it on withdrawing Soviet troops. At the same time the Hungarian regime itself was changing. Within the first 24 hours of the uprising it became clear that the old-style Communist police state was without power to maintain itself . . . The army melted away, and the Moscow-inspired secret police, the AVH, was too deeply hated to be a source of strength. . . . The Hungarian Communist party, with an allegedly reliable membership of nearly 900,000, disappeared overnight. The hated secret police was disbanded, its best known leaders and members killed or forced into hiding. Statues of Stalin, Soviet memorials, and

various outward signs of the country's former status as a colony of Moscow were destroyed by aroused multitudes . . .[16]

An eyewitness account of the situation on October 23 follows:

People pinned the Hungarian national cockade to their clothes, and a really fantastic miracle occurred, for I regard it as a miracle that the whole people became unified. . . . About 100,000 AVH spies, informers and stool pigeons had been planted in the national life of the nation and forced to supply information. On the morning of this day, for the first time, someone dared to say that the Russian troops should leave Hungary. We had reached the point where we dared to say this publicly. This was what gave us unity, and the point at which the chains were broken which had bound us until then; the point at which the net in which the AVH spy system had been holding us was broken. Everyone became convinced. No one asked in the street, "Who are you?," everyone used the familiar form of address even in talking to strangers, everyone was on familiar terms, everyone could be trusted, everyone had a feeling of complete unity, because the entire system based on lies had collapsed in a moment on the morning of 23 October.

The battle-lines were clearly drawn between Hungarians and the Soviets. After some hesitation and fear of Western support for the Freedom Fighters, the Soviets invaded Hungary with Mongol divisions on November 4, seized the Hungarians who had been negotiating with them for removal of Soviet troops, and overthrew the government of Imre Nagy. Nagy was quickly replaced by the Soviet puppet Janos Kadar. The report of the UN Special Committee on the Problem of Hungary (1957) states:

. . . there is no evidence that during the fighting from 4-11 November there were any soldiers or groups of Hungarians,

16. Henry Cabot Lodge in *State Department Bulletin*, Sept. 30, 1957, p. 516.
17. Ibid., p. 517.

whether organized or unorganized, who fought against each other. The evidence supports the conclusion that all fighting occurred exclusively between Hungarian national and Soviet forces. . . . A massive armed intervention by one Power on the territory of another, with the avowed intention of interfering with the internal affairs of the country must, by the Soviet's own definition of aggression, be a matter of international concern.

Soviet terror tactics in Hungary, the subsequent tightening of control in Poland, the so-called "national Communist" Gomulka's approval of Soviet actions in Hungary, and the judicial murder of Imre Nagy and General Malater (who was negotiating with the Soviets when he was kidnapped) suggested that Khrushchev was another Stalin, and that such disarming slogans as "peaceful coexistence" and "national Communism" were in the tradition of comparable Stalinite slogans: tactical maneuvers designed to encourage wishful thinkers in the West that the Soviets had given up their Marxist-Leninist religion.

Chapter 9

NATIONAL LIBERATION WARS 1956–1962

SOVIET PENETRATION OF THE MIDDLE EAST AND AFRICA

Turning now to the Soviet and Communist penetration of the Middle East, we observe a pattern of Soviet support of Arab nationalism against Israel and especially against the West. Egypt was the jumping-off point of Soviet activity in the Middle East as it began to spread in 1955. Until mid-1955, the Soviet and Communist press was highly critical of Egypt's dictator, Nasser. But after the Bandung Conference of that year, which was dominated by neutralist leaders, Nasser was commended by Pravda for having contributed "a great deal to the success of Bandung, supporting the principle of peaceful coexistence."

A similar change took place in Moscow's attitude toward the other Arab countries, with the exception of Iraq, which had joined the Baghdad Pact.[1] The Soviets now argued that the "na-

---

1. 1955 defense pact including Britain, France, Turkey, Iraq, and Pakistan, and supported by the United States.

tional bourgeoisie" (hitherto depicted as the faithful ally of imperialism) was, in effect, fulfilling a progressive role in the liberation movement of most Asiatic countries. Yet these changes

> ... did not affect basic Soviet contentions: that the present
> regimes were only transient stages in the progress toward
> Communism in Asia and the Middle East, and that full vic-
> tory could be achieved only after the leadership had passed
> from the national bourgeoisie into the hands of the working
> class.[2]

The beginning of the Soviet political offensive in the Middle
East can be traced from the visit of Dimitri Shepilov (then editor
of *Pravda,* and for a short time thereafter, Soviet Foreign
Minister) to Cairo in the summer of 1955. A Soviet-Egyptian
arms deal was then concluded, and Soviet advisers and
technicians began to pour into Egypt. During the various crises
of 1956, from the nationalization of the Suez Canal Company to
the Israeli invasion of Egypt, Soviet foreign policy came out
squarely in favor of Egypt's demands. Radio Cairo became
merely an extension of Radio Moscow, and Communist and neutralist agitation in the Middle East and Africa spread rapidly.
Soviet and Egyptian intrigue in Syria during 1957 led to a coup
d'etat, and the establishment of a pro-Egyptian and pro-Soviet
regime in the fall. There was a violent campaign to overthrow the
pro-Western regimes of Jordan, Iraq, and Lebanon, as Soviet
equipment and advisers moved into Syria. At the end of 1957 an
Afro-Asian conference, dominated by Communist representatives, convened in Cairo and established a permanent secretariat
to step up agitation in Africa and the Middle East. Meantime
Communist influence was furthered through cultural exchanges
and economic penetration. There were:

> ... intense Soviet propaganda efforts to present the United
> States as a "neo-colonial" power which wants to "enslave and
> exploit the free Arab nations." Hence also the stress put time
> and again on the allegation that the Soviet Union merely

2. Walter Laqueur in *Problems of Communism* (July/August, 1957), p. 20.

wants a neutral and free Middle East, whereas the West wishes to ensnare it in all kinds of military pacts and alliances ... there can be no doubt that the slogan ("positive neutralism") has been very effective. ...[3]

During 1958 rebel forces in Lebanon, with some support from Egypt, succeeded in overthrowing the pro-Western government of President Chamoun, and in Iraq, citadel of the Baghdad Pact, pro-Nasser and anti-U.S. nationalists brutally assassinated King Faisal and Premier Nuri-es Said. The new Iraqi regime of General Kassem hewed to a "neutralist" line. The revolution in Iraq was cause for rejoicing in the Soviet bloc. It meant a revival of the Communist movement in that country, and the availability of press and radio facilities for leftist groups. On the international level, the upheaval apparently signified the end of the anti-Communist Baghdad Pact. "The Baghdad Pact without Baghdad"—sneered the Soviet press.

By 1958, the Soviet Union had emerged as a significant Mid-Eastern power, with a claim to be the protector of the Arabs, and the dominant influence in Egypt. But the Soviet efforts were not completely successful.

For the short term, many Arabs realized that it was primarily the United States, not the U.S.S.R., which had blocked the 1956 invasion of Egypt. Further, the initial contacts between Soviet advisers and Egyptian civilian and military leaders were not very congenial. And the U.S.S.R. discovered that not all anti-Western Arab nationalists were necessarily pro-Soviet.

According to David Dallin:

> Despite the propitious situation, however, despite the fiasco of London and Paris, and despite the trend in Asia and Africa to minimize the issue of Hungary as compared with the issue of Suez, the Soviet Union did not derive as much influence and prestige from the conflict as it might have.[4]

Possibly because Soviet policy in the Mid-East was not a com-

3. Ibid., p. 25.
4. David Dallin, *Soviet Foreign Policy Since Stalin* (New York, Lippincott, 1961), p. 246.

plete success, Khrushchev dismissed Shepilov as Foreign Minister on January 15, 1957, and replaced him with the veteran Andrei Gromyko. Shepilov then had the misfortune to join the "anti-Party group" of Molotov, Malenkov, and Kaganovich, and all began to suffer a series of downgradings by dictator Khrushchev.

During the period immediately following World War II, the Soviet Union had viewed Africa as part of the "rear of the capitalist system." The freedom movement of the colonial peoples was seen, firstly, as an embarrassment to the capitalist West, and, secondly, as an opportunity for Communist infiltration, particularly under the cover of Communist-front organizations, and Soviet diplomatic, trade, and cultural exchange missions.

Soviet experience with unification movements in the Mid-East (especially Nasser's unsuccessful attempts to retain control of Syria and gain control of Iraq) had evidently provided a lesson, as a warning by Khrushchev against premature and forced unions has been prominently quoted within Communist circles in relation to Africa.

In North Africa, the Soviet government accorded recognition to the Provisional Algerian government, which also received aid from Communist China. Inside France, Communists and leftists agitated during 1961 for a tougher policy against the "Algeria is French" groups. Of the former French colonies south of the Sahara, Soviet influence was greatest in Guinea, and Soviet observers wrote with uniform approval of the social and economic policy of Sekou Toure's Guinean Democratic party.

Of the former British colonies, Communist and Soviet influence was strong in Ghana and Kenya. The Soviet Union benefited from the neutralist line followed by the late President Nkrumah of Ghana. The latter, according to Walter Kolarz, "like Sekou Toure . . . is an Afro-Marxist who lays greater stress than the Guinean president on Marxism, but who in actual fact is much less familiar with Marxist thinking." (in *Problems of Communism*, Nov.–Dec. 1961, p. 23).

Elsewhere in Africa, the Soviet Union supported revolutionary and terrorist activity in Angola against Portugal, and Lumumbist groups in the Congo. Largely through the good offices of the Indian and other neutralist influences within the United Nations Congo Command, political developments in the former Belgian colony became more favorable to the international Communist movement during 1961. First, the central Congolese government was induced to form a coalition with the pro-Communist Gizenga group, and then the UN Congo Command engaged in acts of aggression against the relatively stable, pro-West and anti-Communist government of Katanga. The second UN invasion of Katanga (the first failed) took place in December, 1961. It was supported by the United States, the neutralists, and the Soviet bloc, and opposed by France, Britain, and most of the NATO countries. Meantime the central Congolese regime appointed a pro-Communist Gizenga follower as governor of Katanga, in anticipation of the defeat of the anti-Communist government of President Tshombe. The latter was finally overthrown in the 1963 invasion. In 1964, as Premier of the Congo, Tshombe was attacked by Soviet-supported forces in Stanleyville.[5]

SOVIET AND COMMUNIST ACTIVITIES IN LATIN AMERICA

Until the advent of the Castro regime in Cuba in 1959, Latin America was not a major field of attention for the Soviet Union. However, it was by no means neglected. Moscow was anxious to increase the number of countries extending diplomatic relations to the U.S.S.R., and it has sought to increase trade with the countries of the region. Through cultural exchanges programs, the Soviet bloc has tried to lower psychological resistance to Communist influence.

Communist leaders from Latin America are trained and given refresher indoctrination courses behind the Iron Curtain. Daniel James, of the *New York Times,* describes one of the principal centers of such indoctrination as follows:

> . . . in Prague, Czechoslavakia . . . there exists the so-called Institute for the Study of Latin American Relations. This Institute, which is part of the Faculty of International Relations of the State College for Political and Economic Sciences, trains agitators, spies and saboteurs for work in Latin America. The Institute has an enrollment of 750 students. . . . The purpose in having Communists from Latin America and

5. Anthony Bouscaren, *Tshombe* (New York, Twin Circle, 1967), Chapter 9.

> Europe study together is to train them as teams. Upon
> graduation, the Latin Americans return to their native coun-
> tries and are later joined by European graduates, who may be
> former classmates . . .[6]

One of the principal activities of the local Communist parties
in various Latin American countries is the organization of a wide
variety of front groups. These include organizations of youth,
women, professional people, trade unionists, as well as "peace"
organizations, etc. These national groups are all affiliated with
their international counterparts, which constitute an integral part
of the worldwide Communist *"apparat."*

The Communists have been very successful in winning the
cooperation of non-Communist Latin Americans in these front
organizations. Leading political figures, such as Mexican ex-
President Lazaro Cardenas, and leading intellectuals and labor
leaders have been recruited into these groups. Castro's success in
Cuba, together with increased Soviet and Chinese Communist
diplomatic, economic, and psychological penetration, have led to
an alliance in Latin America between the numerically small
Communist parties and the far larger faction described by
Robert J. Alexander as the "Jacobin Left." This faction is revolutionary although not specifically Communist. It is anti-United
States and has no faith in democracy. A decade ago, Juan Peron
failed to achieve his objective of becoming hemispheric leader of
this faction. But today Castro, with the support of the international Communist movement, is making a far bolder bid for
power.

The Allende Government in Chile, which came to power in
1971, is a Marxist coalition which includes two Communists.
Allende is a great admirer of Castro.

His regime has confiscated many foreign holdings and na-
tionalized most of industry, usually with but minimal compensation. Opposition newspapers have been harassed and opposition leaders threatened. Extreme leftist radicals are
pressuring Allende for even tougher measures against centrist
and rightist groups.

Between 1947 and 1954, Guatemala came under increasing
leftist domination, with the Communist Party leading the way.

6. Daniel James, *Red Design for the Americas* (New York, John Day, 1954), p. 203.

However, in 1954 anti-Communist groups, with covert U.S. aid, overthrew the leftist regime of Jacobo Arbenz. The Communist tactics in that country were described by Victor Alba:

> The essential elements of the Communists' infiltration tactics, as exemplified in Guatemala, are thus: (a) disguising themselves as non-Communist revolutionaries in order to enter and utilize the democratic parties; (b) obtaining government posts by this means, especially in such vital areas as education, propaganda, labor and agriculture; (c) acquiring control of labor unions, teachers' organizations, and other popular bodies so as to translate their support into increased political influence; and, (d) seizing all favorable opportunities to press for pro-Soviet or provocatory anti-U.S. policies when such action suits the current needs of Soviet diplomacy.[7]

At the end of 1961, Fidel Castro boasted that he had fooled Western observers of his revolution, and proclaimed that he had been a Marxist-Leninist all his life. Indeed, as Daniel James of the *New York Times* demonstrates in his book *Cuba, The First Soviet Satellite in the Americas,* Castro had close ties with Communist leaders such as Lazaro Pena (Mexico) and Carlos Rafael Rodriguez (Cuba) from the earliest days, not to mention his closest intimates Che Guevara and Raul Castro. Yet, according to James:

> Not a single American or other foreign journalist, to this writer's knowledge, ever came down from the Sierra with the slightest suspicion that all might not be so well . . . Not one of these reporters . . . found the smallest sign of Communist infiltration in the Sierra. On the contrary, the Latin American experts, chiefly Herbert Mathews and Jules Dubois, found every reason to deny that anything resembling a Communist could be found in the pristine ranks of Fidel Castro's army.

SOVIET DIPLOMACY 1956-1961

From the time of the 1955 Geneva "Summit" conference until

---

7. *Problems of Communism* (Jan/Feb, 1961), p. 26.

the re-imposition of the "hard line" in Hungary and Poland, the Soviets adopted the propaganda line that past errors and misunderstandings had been due to Stalinism. By the beginning of 1957, however, the Soviets had altered their emphasis, adopting the slogan that "There was no alternative to peace," meaning by this that any Western or generally anti-Communist effort to effectively check Communist expansionism would lead to violence, and violence was "unthinkable." Meantime, the Soviets used their alleged lead in missile development to try to blackmail the West into submission.

During 1959 Moscow demanded that the United States withdraw its forces from Germany (and ultimately from all Europe), Korea, Okinawa, and Taiwan. The North Atlantic Treaty Organization and other allied regional groupings must be liquidated, and the United States must stop all testing of nuclear weapons. Various schemes, such as the Rapacki Plan (1958), suggested "disengagement" and demilitarized zones in central Europe. Many pacifists and frightened non-Communists agreed with the Soviets on all or most of these ideas. There are always those in the West who feel that the Soviets cannot be as bad as they seem to be, and that perhaps the world is in a mess because of shortcomings in the West. Geoffrey Hudson of Oxford University has pointed out, however, that:

> Unfortunately it is extremely difficult, because of the actual circumstances of the strategic situation in Europe, to imagine any agreement on limitation of arms which, however fair it might seem on the surface, would not in practice work out to the disadvantage of the West.[8]

The Soviets fully realized that the demand for peace—even at any price—was growing. There was a widespread aversion to the use of nuclear weapons, even for defense, an aversion which found expression in the defeatist declaration of the Bishop of Manchester and others. Hudson aptly summarized the temper of the times as follows:

> All the signs point to a new era of appeasement, which the So-

8. *U. S. News and World Report* (July 19, 1957), p. 98.

viet government will foster by all means. What the collective leaders in Moscow now most need is to be trusted. . . . The confidence trickster can never, of course, count on his victims retaining confidence in him after the trick has been played; all that is necessary is that the faith should last until the spoil has been collected. The question is whether the Soviet leaders can refrain for long enough from clearly hostile and provocative actions to build up the degree of confidence required. They quickly spoiled the effect of the Summit Conference of 1955 by a series of such actions during the next few months, and the hopes aroused by "de-Stalinization" in the following year were soon dashed by the slaughter of Budapest—though it should be noted that there were not a few people in the West who were disposed to put the blame on the Hungarians for having set back Russia's gradual self-reform by their reckless impatience. So it may be that Russia will once again thwart her own quest of confidence by actions too plainly in contradiction of her professions of good will. But if these mistakes can be avoided for a sufficient period of time, we can expect a revival on a large scale in the West of the state of mind which appeased Hitler before 1939 and Stalin from 1943 to 1946.[9]

Having consolidated power at home with the purges of Malenkov, Zhukov, Bulganin, Shepilov, Serov, and others, and having re-established firm control in Hungary and in Poland, Khrushchev sent Deputy Premier Anastas Mikoyan to the United States at the beginning of 1959 to promote "flexibility" in United States foreign policy. In addition he was to encourage greater East-West trade, sound out United States intentions in Berlin, and press for another "summit conference."

Mikoyan was well received by multimillionaire industrialist Cyrus Eaton, as well as by some other prominent Americans, although he was greeted in several cities by Hungarian pickets. Commenting on the reception accorded Mikoyan, former President Harry S. Truman declared:

I am particularly disturbed by the eagerness displayed by some of our leading industrialists and financiers to shower the

9. Ibid., p. 101.

visiting Communist with solicitous attention and social
glamour resulting in pressure on the White House.[10]

The success of Mikoyan's visit was somewhat marred when the
United States made public a tape recording of Soviet pilots
shooting down an unarmed American transport plane which had
strayed across the Soviet border from Turkey (or was lured
across by a "false" Soviet radio beam). It developed that
Mikoyan knew of this wanton attack, but while in the United
States, he denied that it had ever occurred when questioned about
it.

During 1959 the Soviet Union seemed interested in a nuclear-
test-ban agreement which would lead to a permanent American
cessation of nuclear tests, but under which the Soviets could
cheat with tests in outer space and underground up to 25 kilotons
of yield. The Soviets encouraged flexibility in U.S. policy: concessions in Berlin and on Germany, recognition of Communist
China, greater East-West trade, and weakening of NATO and
the Far East alliance system.

Continuing Soviet pressure on Berlin led to prolonged
meetings of the Foreign Ministers of the U.S.S.R., the United
States, Britain, and France in Geneva, during the spring and
summer of 1959. The Soviets succeeded in gaining the admit-
tance of the Communist East German puppet regime as an ob-
server, but the West indicated it would not betray the people of
West Berlin to Communist imperialism.

Late in 1958, as pressure against Quemoy and Matsu failed to
frighten the West, Khrushchev announced that the Soviet occupation of East Berlin was going to be ended, and that the East
Germans would be masters in their own city. But the western
powers and the West Berlin government rejected the Soviet overtures, recognizing the danger to West Berlin if the Western
Powers pulled out. Berlin municipal elections in December, 1958,
demonstrated a firm pro-Western stand by the Berliners, and the
Communists polled less than two percent of the vote.

Following the visits of Mikoyan and Deputy Premier Kozlov
to the United States, Vice-President Nixon visited the Soviet
Union in late July and early August. While Nixon was still in the

10. *Chicago Daily News*, Jan. 19, 1959.

U.S.S.R., the United States government announced that Soviet leader Khrushchev and President Eisenhower would exchange visits in the fall of 1959.

The Soviets seemed bent on regaining lost prestige among East Germans, and on forcing the western powers and the Federal Republic of West Germany to deal directly with the East German regime, thus granting it at least *de facto* recognition.

In spite of much wishful thinking in the United States about Khrushchev's visit in the fall of 1959, the Soviet dictator came not to learn but to teach. In California, after a public meeting at which he was mildly heckled and a fairly stormy private conversation with American labor leaders, he threatened to go home unless he was treated with more respect. Whereupon, instead of replying that America was a free country, in which citizens were able to air their personal opinions openly, jittery State Department officials asked people to please refrain from provoking him further.

President Eisenhower assured Khrushchev that we had no hostile designs on the Soviet Union, and went so far as to state that the situation in Berlin was "abnormal." As a result of the talks at Camp David, Maryland, the Soviet dictator went home to Moscow convinced that the West would come to a Summit conference prepared to make more concessions to the Soviet bloc:

> I would like to tell you, dear comrades, that I have no doubt that the President is prepared to exert his efforts and his will to bring about agreement between our countries to create friendly relations between our people and settle problems in the interests of a durable peace.[11]

But meantime Germany's Adenauer and France's de Gaulle had made clear their opposition to concessions, and President Eisenhower went to the Summit prepared to talk and listen, but not to make concessions of substance. Secretary of State Herter and Undersecretary of State C. Douglas Dillon announced the American position in unmistakable terms.

Instead of calling off a conference from which he could now see

11. Nikita Khruschev, *Face to Face with America* (Moscow, 1960), p. 386.

in advance that he was not going to induce substantial Western concessions, Khrushchev took advantage of a comparatively unimportant American intelligence incident to attack the United States and accuse it of "sabotaging" the conference. This incident was the flight of a U-2 reconnaissance plane over Russia. In self-protection and in response to a long record of Soviet bloc espionage, the United States, in cooperation with its allies, had been engaging in aerial surveillance of the U.S.S.R. to guard against a sneak attack. Khrushchev had known about such operations for at least three years, but he chose this particular U-2 incident as a pretext for breaking off the Summit meeting.

The abortive Paris Summit Conference (May, 1960) was the starting point of a series of new tactics in Soviet foreign policy. Threats and accusations increased; Soviet demands were regularly coupled with threats of retaliation by military means, especially missiles; short-term ultimatums were issued, notably on Berlin.

The new Soviet techniques also found expression in the developments in Latin America. Soviet bloc support for Castro's Cuba increased, and more effort was put into propaganda, agitation, and infiltration of all Latin America. In February, 1960, Anastas Mikoyan visited Cuba, signed a trade agreement with her, and granted her a loan of 100 million dollars. An agreement providing for the delivery of Soviet oil to Cuba and the sale of Cuban sugar to Russia (at prices well below those formerly paid by the United States) was signed in Moscow that month. On July 18, Khrushchev received Raul Castro in a five-hour audience and promised him all necessary help, including arms. On July 9, Khrushchev had declared:

> Figuratively speaking, Soviet artillerists can, in case of necessity, support the Cuban people by rocket fire if the aggressive forces of the Pentagon should dare to start an intervention against Cuba.[12]

In Africa, the Soviet bloc stepped up their infiltration effort, notably through diplomatic, trade, and cultural exchange gambits. When the Congo conflict broke out, the Soviet Union

12. *Pravda*, July 10, 1960.

rushed forward as the most unselfish defender of the Congo's independence from Belgium and the West as a whole. But after the volatile and eccentric Lumumba was ousted, and replaced by the Kasavubu-Mobutu group, Soviet bloc representatives were expelled from the Congo. Thereafter the Soviets recognized and supported Prague-trained Antoine Gizenga and his regime in Stanleyville.

In Laos, the Soviets gave full support to neutralist Prince Souvanna Phouma, together with his Communist supporters led by Captain Kong Le and Prince Souvannavong. In early 1961, the United States accepted Souvanna Phouma as Premier of a coalition government for Laos.

Meantime the U.S.S.R. supported revolutionary and terrorist incursions into Angola, the Indian invasion of Portuguese Goa, and Indonesian claims to Dutch New Guinea.

During 1961, while U.S. and Soviet negotiators continued their talks in Geneva on a possible nuclear test-ban agreement, the Soviets made secret preparations for a series of gigantic atmospheric tests. Then suddenly, in the fall of the year, they exploded a series of at least 60 nuclear detonations, including one sixty megaton shot. This seemed to bother the professional neutralists not at all. Krishna Menon of India declared that three U.S. underground tests with no fallout were a greater threat to humanity than sixty Soviet atmospheric tests with fallout.

The most serious of all Soviet moves, however, was against Berlin. On August 13, 1961, Soviet and Communist forces in Berlin built a wall dividing East and West Berlin, thus blocking further movement of population out of East Germany. From the end of World War II to that date, an average of 200,000 people annually had left the "proletarian paradise" of East Germany to seek freedom in the West. But now Khrushchev built the "wall of shame," and got away with it. After first stating that the Berlin issue was not negotiable, President Kennedy authorized Secretary of State Dean Rusk to initiate negotiations with Soviet Foreign Minister Gromyko. But Chancellor Adenauer of Germany and President de Gaulle of France opposed the concessions that were urged on President Kennedy by Prime Minister Harold Macmillan of Britain.

After President Kennedy met with Khrushchev in Vienna in the Spring of 1961, he seemed to become less hopeful about negotiations with the Soviets, especially after the Communists

violated a cease-fire in Laos. At the end of 1961 Kennedy told
Izvestia editor Aleksei Adzhubei that Soviet efforts to com-
munize the world constituted the chief threat to peace. *Izvestia*
derided the President's statement as a "cock and bull story," but
Red China's official newspaper, *People's Daily,* promptly set the
record straight. The Communist bloc would never stop "supporting the revolutionary struggles of the oppressed nations and
people," said the *People's Daily,* and anyone who thinks
otherwise is living "an idiot's day-dream."

THE 22nd CONGRESS

The highlights of the 22nd Congress of the Communist Party
of the Soviet Union held during November and December of
1960 were the open airing of Sino-Soviet differences over the
treatment of the Albanian Worker's party and the full-scale attack on Stalin and the anti-party group. This was in spite of the
fact that the Congress was supposed to be primarily concerned
with illuminating the future road to Communism through a new
party program and revision of party rules.

The Congress opened and closed without really resolving
differences between the Chinese and Soviet Communist
leadership. The compromise declaration patched together at the
Moscow meeting of eighty-one Communist parties in
November–December, 1960, provided a surface show of unity,
but the subsequent exacerbation of relations between Moscow
and Albania and the Chinese adoption of the Albanians as a
client party gave their protestations of amity an increasingly
hollow ring.

The first sign of impending trouble was the failure of a delegation from the Albanian Workers Party to appear at the
Congress. Then followed Khrushchev's attack on Albanian party
leaders, in which he accused them of departing from "the
generally agreed line of the whole Communist movement on the
most important questions of modern times," reviving Stalinist
methods in Albania, and "coming out against the course of the
20th Party Congress." (*Pravda,* Oct. 18, 1961). And yet the door
still seemed to be open for the Albanians to "abandon their mis-
taken views," and to return "to the path of unity" and "friendship with the C.P.S.U."

Two days later Chou En-lai of China brought the greetings of the Chinese party to the Congress. But after some polite words praising Soviet achievements, he proceeded to take a view of Albania, Yugoslavia, and relations with the Free World somewhat at variance with that of Khrushchev. Whereas Khrushchev had suggested that the West could be beaten without war, Chou insisted that "all the activities of American imperialism show that we are still confronted with the danger of war and that the people of all countries must heighten their vigilance." Whereas Khrushchev had taken a soft line on Tito (possibly to woo him back into the fold in connection with the attack on Albania), Chou coupled "the Yugoslav revisionist clique" and "American imperialism" together as the main enemies. But Chou's most significant remarks were reserved for Khrushchev's attack on the Albanians:

> We hold that if a dispute or difference unfortunately arises between fraternal countries, it should be resolved patiently in the spirit of proletarian internationalism. . . . Any public, onesided censure of any fraternal party does not help unity and is not helpful in resolving problems. To lay bare a dispute between fraternal parties or fraternal countries openly in the face of the enemy cannot be regarded as a serious Marxist-Leninist attitude. Such an attitude will only grieve those near and dear to us and gladden our enemies. The CCP sincerely hopes that fraternal parties which have disputes or differences will unite afresh on the basis of Marxism-Leninism and on the basis of mutual respect, independence, and equality. This, in my opinion, is the position which we Communists ought to take on this question.[13]

All subsequent speakers supported Khrushchev's denunciations of Albania except the North Koreans and Vietnamese. There was no direct reference to the Chinese delegation (which meantime had returned to China) until Khrushchev, in his concluding remarks, declared:

> The leader of the delegation of the Communist party of China, Comrade Chou En-lai, in his speech expressed anxiety

13. *Pravda*, October 20, 1961.

over the matter of openly raising at our Congress the question
of Albanian-Soviet relations . . . We share the anxiety of our
Chinese friends and appreciate their concern for the
strengthening of unity. If the Chinese comrades desire to ap-
ply their efforts to normalization of relations on the part of
the Albanian Workers party with the fraternal parties, then
hardly anyone can make a better contribution to the solution
of this problem than the Communist party of China. This
would really benefit the Albanian Workers party and would
correspond to the interest of the whole commonwealth of socialist countries.[14]

Why did Khrushchev use the forum of the 22nd Party Congress
to re-open the subject of Stalin's crimes, and to crown his attack
with that last act of total repudiation by the removal of Stalin's
body from the mausoleum? Khrushchev's own official answer in
his concluding speech is that he would have gone much further in
exposing Stalin's abuses of power at the 20th Party Congress had
he not been hampered by the leaders of the anti-party group
(Molotov, Malenkov, Kaganovich, and Voroshilov). According
to him they continued after the 20th Congress to sabotage his
efforts, "fearing lest their part as accessories to mass repressions
be brought to light." With the rout of the anti-party group, presumably the obstacle was removed. "Our party is doing this,"
Khrushchev said, "so that similar phenomena will never be
repeated."

In assailing Stalin, Khrushchev was also attacking and
seeking to denigrate the remnants of the anti-party opposition
within his own party as well as the opposition outside. The
elaborate documentation of the involvement of Molotov,
Malenkov, Kaganovich, and Voroshilov in Stalinist
repressions and the assault on the Stalinism of the Albanian
partly leaders (and by implication also the Chinese)
represented an effort to tar all these opposition elements with
the same brush, to discredit and cauterize the past, present or
future opposition which might seek to rally under the Stalinist
flag which his most formidable rivals, the Chinese, still held
high.[15]

14. *Pravda*, October 29, 1961.
15. Merle Fainsod, *Problems of Communism* (Nov/Dec., 1961) p. vi.

Thus Khrushchev emerged from the Congress in complete control of the Communist party of the Soviet Union; his control over the international Communist movement was, however, somewhat less than clear. In his attitude toward the major issues of international politics, Khrushchev displayed a strong, yet partially justified optimism about the prospects of Communist victories in Asia, Africa, and Latin America. Toward the West and Japan, and particularly the United States, he exhibited the same unyielding illusions and the same arrogance, notably on the Berlin situation, that led to the increasingly dangerous confrontation of this time.

Chapter 10

FROM KHRUSHCHEV TO BREZHNEV

Nikita Khrushchev dominated Soviet policies for a decade, most of it as absolute dictator. It was a period of profound change, at the end of which there was no longer a single "Communist world" but several worlds, full of conflicts and sharpening rivalries. The movement of events changed all the relationships of the world's Communist governments—to each other, to their own peoples, to Communist parties outside the bloc, and to the whole non-Communist world.

At first some Westerners, encouraged by Khrushchev's merciless denunciation of Stalin, hoped for some lessening of communism's determination that its system would prevail throughout the world. It soon became clear that the changes in this regard were confined mainly to tactics. Khrushchev proved himself an even bolder antagonist than Stalin, and willing to take bigger chances. Stalin had confined his probes to the Soviet Union's own borders. Khrushchev did not hesitate to charge into Egypt, to make a stab at the distant Congo, and even to penetrate the Western Hemisphere through Cuba.

Time and again, Khrushchev proved himself the master of the

"rolling crisis" technique through which he turned tension on or off like a faucet. Using this technique, he managed to keep the West vacillating between peaks of optimism and anxiety. Thus, he ran a warming bath of "spirit of Geneva" optimism in 1955, followed by a cold shower of rocket threats during the Suez Canal crisis of 1956. At Vienna in 1961, Khrushchev told President Kennedy that he would force the West out of Berlin. This threat evaporated in the face of American firmness. But in 1962 Khrushchev set up missile bases in Cuba, and the world came to the edge of nuclear war. Only a strong hand by the United States forced Khrushchev to back off. And then followed a period of relatively relaxed tensions, culminating in the nuclear test ban treaty.

On balance, the Soviet Union during these years seemed to have embarked on a program of trying to make its Communist system prevail—in Khrushchev's words, "to bury the West"—by peaceful rather than warlike means. It is now clear that this policy of giving at least lip service to peace was the basic cause of what history will undoubtedly record as the greatest event of the Khrushchev era: the cataclysmic split between the two giants of communism—China and the U.S.S.R.

Communist China had its own firmly-implanted Stalin in the person of party boss Mao Tse-tung, and he had no intention of changing either himself or his system, whatever the Soviet leaders might do. In fact, at the very moment that Khrushchev started tearing down Stalin's pictures and monuments in the U.S.S.R., Mao began giving them even greater prominence in China.

The Chinese distrusted the "red-haired devils" from the West—the Russians—who in the past had taken from them a land mass in Siberia and northern Asia almost as big as Europe. The Soviets, while saying they opposed annexation, had virtually absorbed Outer Mongolia, and since World War II had menaced China's westernmost province of Sinkiang. At the war's end, Stalin seized Manchuria's factories and dominated its railways and the Port Arthur naval base, abandoning all this quite reluctantly when Mao came to power in 1949. Mao also resented Stalin for letting China's Communist party almost be destroyed in 1927 and for rejecting Mao's theory that the peasants rather than the workers would make China's revolution. Mao felt he had succeeded in spite of Stalin, and clearly regarded himself—

after Stalin died—as the world's number one Marxist-Leninist. Mao regarded Khrushchev as an upstart, but tolerated him until his 1956 speech denouncing Stalin disrupted the whole Communist bloc.

The breach widened after the Soviets beat the United States to the successful testing of an intercontinental missile and, later, to the orbiting of a satellite in 1957. The Chinese then assumed the balance of power had shifted against the West, and they expected the Soviets to embark on more aggressive steps toward world revolution. Specifically, Peking wanted a share in Russia's atomic bomb and wanted Moscow to back up the Chinese Communists in their continuing threats against the nationalist government on Formosa. The Chinese bombarded the offshore islands opposite Formosa—Quemoy and Matsu—in 1958, but got no real help from Moscow. And no help in atomic development was offered. Instead, in 1959 Khrushchev made his tour of the United States, visiting President Eisenhower and preaching the line of "peaceful coexistence."

Mao regarded all this as a betrayal of Lenin's admonition that communism must "destroy" capitalism or be destroyed by it. He also began charging that Russia had broken its promises to China and was making deals with the United States. Mao took the extreme position that if nuclear war came, China could lose half its people and still have more than 300 million left—enough to rule what was left of the world. The name-calling was soon out in the open for all to see. In answer to charges of broken promises, Khrushchev began talking about "lunatics and maniacs who wanted war."

There were other sources of friction. In the economic field, Mao resented Moscow's withdrawal of help for China's industrial development, particularly since the Soviets were giving massive aid to a non-Communist regime by helping President Nasser of Egypt build the Aswan High Dam. Also, when the Chinese staged their invasion of India's Himalayan borders in late 1962, Russia infuriated the Chinese by going ahead with plans to deliver warplanes to India.

Even Khrushchev's greatest aggressive move, the attempt to place missile bases in Cuba, failed to appease the Chinese. They termed this "adventurous" and branded his decision to remove the bases as "cowardice." The Soviets later charged that in the Cuban crisis, Peking had offered what the Soviets called "inflammatory" advice, which, if followed, "would have plunged the world into thermonuclear war."

At first many suspected that both sides might be using the break as a smokescreen in a purely naked power struggle. Mao certainly did set out to try to displace Khrushchev as the number one Communist leader. He sent emissaries to other countries, particularly to the neutralist Asian and African nations, selling Peking's brand of communism with considerable success. Mao was well aware that 69 percent of the world's people are nonwhite and that racial as well as ideological arguments were advanced in these areas. In Cuba considerable headway was made with the charge that Moscow had abandoned the Cubans when the missile bases were pulled out.

But beyond these moves, and behind the millions of propaganda words, there was the ideological split between the Chinese and Soviet leaders, a cleavage far deeper than the personal ambitions of a Mao or a Khrushchev, and one that seemed destined to outlast them both.

Each side claims to be the only true interpreter of Marx and Lenin. To the Chinese, the Russians are "revisionists" seeking to discourage revolutions in order to protect their "have" nation. To the Soviets, the Chinese leaders are "dogmatists" willing to risk nuclear war in order to promote small wars and revolutions to benefit the "have-not" nations.

Khrushchev made a national policy of blowing hot and cold in his relations with the United States. But he was always careful to leave himself a graceful exit—except once—and that reminds one of the great mysteries of the Khrushchev era. Why, in 1962, did the Soviets take such a gamble as placing missiles in Cuba, on the doorstep of the United States?

There is still no clear answer to this question, but several possible reasons present themselves. It is now known that if the Soviets had embarked on a crash program in 1957 to mass-produce intercontinental ballistic missiles (ICBMs), they could have gained a clear military superiority over the United States. For whatever reason, they failed to do this. They made large quantities of short-range missiles, but left the United States with superiority in long-range missiles. By deciding to place short-range missiles in Cuba, the Soviets may have hoped to create the same advantage they would have held with more ICBMs, and thus perhaps to soften the hard United States stand on such pressure points as Berlin.

Also, those continuing Chinese charges of "softness" toward the West may have exerted pressure on Moscow to take bolder steps. And the disastrous American-backed Bay of Pigs invasion in 1961 may have caused Khrushchev to doubt the firmness of U.S. leadership. Whatever the reason, in 1962 Khrushchev decided to take the risk of sending missiles to Cuba. He also swiftly landed some 22,000 Soviet troops, equivalent to two combat divisions. Communism had made its first armed penetration of the Americas. The Soviets evidently were not prepared for the American response. At best, they may have hoped to alter the world's balance of power without a real challenge. At worst, they may have been prepared to see the bases destroyed by an air attack. This would have given them an enormous propaganda advantage: to portray the United States as an "imperialist aggressor."

They evidently were not prepared for President Kennedy's policy of limited, gradually increased pressure. Instead of bombings, they confronted a mighty United States naval cordon and a firm warning that Soviet ships carrying missile supplies would have to turn back. And they faced, as well, the careful marshalling of world opinion by the American delegate to the United Nations.

In the end, all this combined pressure forced Khrushchev to abandon the venture. He agreed to dismantle and remove the missiles under U.N. inspection in return for an American pledge not to invade Cuba. As it turned out, since the Cuban leader Fidel Castro refused to allow U.N. inspection, the United States pledge was never required. But President Kennedy continued to pursue a restrained policy toward Castro, and Khrushchev, in turn, began removing his Soviet troops in stages throughout 1963.

On the afternoon of October 15, 1964, many Americans were in front of television sets watching the seventh game of an exciting world series. News bulletins interrupted the game, bulletins they could scarcely believe. Nikita Khrushchev had been relieved of power.

There had been no hint of such a development to the outside world, yet it turned out to be true. But how? And why? No one, inside or outside the Soviet Union, believed the official explanation carried by the Russian news agency Tass: that Khrushchev, who was seventy, had requested that he be replaced because of his age and health. It developed that not even the

Russians believed this, for two days later *Pravda* carried editorials indirectly attacking Khrushchev for "hare-brained schemes" and for seeking to establish a "cult of personality," indicating clearly that his ouster was far from voluntary.

As to what had happened to the deposed leader himself, there was not a word. For a time, in fact, it was as though Khrushchev had never existed. His pictures suddenly disappeared from public places. Books and official histories recounting his accomplishments vanished from stores and library shelves (many would be reissued later after suitable editing).

Five months later Khrushchev was to make his first public appearance—to vote—but so strict was party discipline that neither then, nor the few later times when he was seen, did this once so articulate man say anything. He was permitted to live in comfort, which was an improvement over the days of Stalin. But, he was politically dead. As far as the people are concerned, Khrushchev vanished just as swiftly and just as effectively as did those who physically died in the earlier, more bloody purges. The former Soviet leader died Sept. 11, 1971.

As to how the ouster was accomplished, the outlines of the story came out slowly. The first hint, if one had been wise enough to see it, had come three months before. It was announced then that the president of the Soviet Union, Leonid Brezhnev, had given up that largely ceremonial post to become a full-time deputy in the Communist party, chief assistant to his friend and mentor Khrushchev. From this strategic post, Brezhnev with other of Khrushchev's "friends," including the first vice-premier, Aleksi N. Kosygin, and the man who had succeeded Brezhnev in the presidency, Anastas Mikoyan, began their work in great secrecy.

Khrushchev's big mistake, which he must later have ruefully realized, was in spending so much time traveling and speech-making, while leaving these trusted associates to run the government back in Moscow. In 1957, the majority of the Politburo, or Party Presidium, had voted to oust Khrushchev, only to be overruled by the full Central Committee. But in 1964 the dissidents made sure that they had lined up a majority of the committees as well as the Presidium.

On September 30, 1964, Khrushchev left for a vacation on the Black Sea coast. On October 12 he spoke by radio to three Russian cosmonauts orbiting the earth, saying he would greet them back in Moscow. It was an appointment he was not to keep. For that same day, the Presidium met in Moscow and made its grave decision.

Khrushchev was called home. He was allowed to plead his case before the stony-faced members of the Central Committee, but on October 14 they voted his removal as first secretary of the party. The next day the Presidium removed him as premier. Then at last they told their people—and the world—that for the first time in Soviet history a supreme leader who had held power for a considerable length of time had been dethroned before his death.

Unlike previous purges, only a few others in high places fell with Khrushchev. The chief one was his son-in-law, Aleksi Adzhubei, who lost his job as editor of *Izvestia*. Most of his other former close associates stayed on, and two of them assumed the top posts. For, as in the early Khrushchev days, the jobs of party chief, or first secretary, and premier, or chairman of the Council of Ministers, were again going to be separated.

The Chinese press had jubilantly hailed the downfall of Khrushchev. In fact, the event seemed to rank in importance with China's first explosion of an atomic device, which came just one day later, on October 16, 1964. Things, indeed, seemed to be looking up for the Peking faction of the party, and China's Premier Chou En-lai hurried off to Moscow to reap the advantages. He was destined for disappointment.

It was the first top level Sino-Soviet meeting in a year and a half. Chou arrived with fanfare, spent six days in the Russian capital in long conferences with the new Soviet leaders, and departed in silence. It was evident there had been no healing of the split. Soon the recriminations, increasingly bitter, began to flow from Peking. And soon the new, now silent, Soviet leadership was working quietly among Communists in other countries to stem the Chinese tide.

A climax to the Sino-Soviet split came after the Chinese tried again to foment trouble with India. While Peking was encouraging Pakistan in her war against India in 1965, who should step in and settle things but that alleged mother of revolutions, Russia. The new Soviet premier, Kosygin, brought the Indian and Pakistani heads of state together in the ancient city of Tashkent, and on January 10, 1966, succeeded in getting them both to agree to a settlement.

Now, indeed, the cleavage between the U.S.S.R. and China

appeared to have reached the point of no return. At the very time that Peking was calling for wars of liberation and revolutions almost everywhere, the Soviet Union had actually stepped in to settle a war between two non-Communist nations.

The United States reacted cautiously to the Khrushchev ouster. Three days after the event, on October 18, 1964, President Johnson discussed it in a nation-wide television address. He had guarded praise for Khrushchev, who, he said, had been guilty of "dangerous adventures" but had "learned from his mistakes." He paid tribute to Khrushchev for agreeing to the test ban treaty, for keeping outer space free of nuclear weapons, and for establishing the "hot line" between Washington and Moscow.

The President said he did not think Khrushchev had been deposed because of these peaceful gestures and added that he had been assured by the Russian ambassador that the new Soviet rulers planned no basic change in foreign policy. The Soviet leaders themselves, as a matter of fact, were already publicly and privately assuring the West of just this continuity of policy. Specifically, they announced they would adhere to the test ban treaty and other arrangements, and in July 1965 they agreed to a resumption of disarmament talks. Kosygin and Brezhnev also began seeking increased trade with the West and welcomed all visitors from the West, particularly spreading out the red carpet for France's President De Gaulle when he toured the Soviet Union in the summer of 1966.

But a new factor entered the picture insofar as relations between the U.S.S.R. and the United States were concerned. In their statements immediately after Khrushchev's ouster, the new leadership had pledged to carry on with the program of "peaceful coexistence." But at the same time they were careful to say they would also support what the Communists call "people's wars of liberation." To them, the fighting in Vietnam was just such a war, and Russia had long been aiding the North Vietnamese. So in February 1965, when increasing North Vietnam aggression caused the United States to start bombing North Vietnam and to build up its land forces in the south, the cold war thaw with Russia that had set in after the Cuban crisis was threatened with a new freeze. At first little was said, but on March 4, 1965, Russian police stood aside and allowed some 2,000 students, mostly Asians, to attack the United States embassy in Moscow. And in subsequent public statements, the Soviet leaders have stuck to the line that, much as they wish to improve relations with the United States, no such improvement is possible until the end of what they call "American aggression" in Vietnam. To many neutral observers all of this has seemed rather restrained. Certainly it was restrained enough to further infuriate the Chinese.

When the Soviets staged their big twenty-third Congress of the Communist party in March 1966, the Chinese refused to attend. Instead, Peking issued a propaganda blast charging Moscow with "working hand in glove with the United States in a whole series of dirty deals" aimed at selling out North Vietnam. The Chinese went on to charge that the Soviets and the Americans were threatening her with "encirclement," a charge reminiscent of the fears Stalin used to raise, for propaganda purposes, against the West.

To none of this did Moscow reply publicly. It continued to criticize "American aggression" and continued to send supplies to North Vietnam. China continued to attack both the United States and the U.S.S.R., sometimes the latter more fiercely than the former. On July 12, 1966, for example, Peking declared that Russian aid to North Vietnam was "sugarcoated poison designed to give (the Soviets) a free hand in sabotaging the revolutionary struggle." All of which seems to indicate that if Moscow-Washington relations were getting no better, Moscow-Peking relations were getting steadily worse.

Although there had been rumors in the spring of 1970, when the 24th Congress of the Soviet Communist Party was postponed a year, that he was in trouble, Leonid Brezhnev not only got top billing when the show finally opened March 30, but he was handed almost enough flowery compliments by comrade-delegates to take one nostalgically back to the days of the genial Stalin. Brezhnev lived up to the tradition of his predecessors by running his keynote speech flat out to a full six hours. And this one, for a first, was televised.

A Communist Party congress is so boring that it is tempting to let it go with the headlines and turn to the day's sport pages. But sprinkled here and there in the bog-bound official prose are occasional sentences that point the current direction of the writhing Party line.

Did the 24th Congress carry forward the "liberalization of the economy" that our Kremlinologists are so fond of discovering every six months? The full answer to that one is found in Section X ("Improvement of Control and Planning") of the new Five-Year Plan adopted, unanimously it is needless to add, on the recommendation of Brezhnev and Kosygin. Stalin's ghost has no occasion to turn after reading Section X. It explicitly repudiates all notions of decentralization, consumerism, and response to market forces. The coming five years will "again [yes, again] demonstrate the superiority of the planned socialist system of management." In all cases, the top echelon controlling the economy is to be "ministries"—i.e., the economy will be run by political bodies composed of Party members. The training of managers must be improved "first and foremost in the sphere of Marxist-Leninist economic theory." The Party will "strive for the strictest observance of state discipline."

How about a liberalizing tendency in domestic political life? Brezhnev reported that steps were being taken "to strengthen legality and law and order, to educate citizens to observe the laws and rules of socialist community relations." And, lest any delegate should have had any doubt about what that meant, the government annotated Brezhnev's point by choosing the day before the 24th Congress opened as the suitable moment for revealing the new arrest and forthcoming trial, with a prospective seven-year prison sentence, of Vladimir Bukovsky, one of the best-known members of Moscow's tiny and much shrunken band of "dissident intellectuals," for "anti-Soviet agitation and propaganda." The 28-year-old Bukovsky's previous crimes include presentation of a small showing of nonsocialist realist paintings by friends of his, and a protest against the procedures used in the trial of the well-known Soviet dissident writers, Sinyavsky and Daniel.

Is Moscow, then, liberalizing its relations with the other nations in the Camp of Peace? Brezhnev cleared up all doubts on that matter by his detailed analysis of the 1968 Czechoslovak episode. "It was quite clear to us that [the Czechoslovak events were] not only an attempt on the part of imperialism and its accomplices to overthrow the socialist system in Czechoslovakia. It was an attempt to strike in this way at the position of socialism in Europe as a whole and to create favorable conditions for a subsequent onslaught against the socialist world.

. . . In view of the appeals by party and state leaders, Communists and working people of Czechoslovakia, and considering the danger posed to the socialist gains in that country, we and the fraternal socialist countries then jointly took the decision to render internationalist assistance to Czechoslovakia in defense of socialism. In the extraordinary conditions created by the forces of imperialism and counterrevolution, we were bound to do so by our class duty, loyalty to socialist internationalism, and the concern for the interests of our states and the future of socialism and peace in Europe." It will be seen that Brezhnev fully qualifies, also, as an historian in the Stalinist tradition.

But surely Brezhnev, as the sober pragmatist we all know him to be, seeks reasonable understanding and detente with the United States? His speech did not lack abundant expression of his feelings for the United States. "The continuing U.S. aggression against the peoples of Vietnam, Cambodia and Laos is the main atrocity committed by the modern colonialists; it is the stamp of ignominy on the United States. It is hard to keep a calm tone when speaking about the atrocities committed by the interventionists." "The victory of the popular-unity forces in Chile . . . has incensed domestic reaction and Yankee imperialism, which seek to deprive the Chilean people of their gains. . . . The governments of Peru and Bolivia are fighting against enslavement by the U.S. monopolies." "So-called 'Vietnamization'— that is, the plan to have Vietnamese kill Vietnamese in Washington's interests—and the extension of the aggression to Cambodia and Laos—none of this will get the U.S.A. out of the bog of its dirty war in Indochina or wash away the shame." "We cannot pass over the aggressive U.S. actions in various parts of the world."

A promising foundation, surely, for what Brezhnev, like Stalin, terms "peaceful coexistence."

The 24th Congress of the Communist Party, Soviet Union, reflected confidence in Soviet foreign policy achievements: 1) the Soviet strategic build-up (surpassing the U.S. not only in deliverable megatonage but in numbers of launchers), 2) the Soviet-Indian success against East Pakistan, 3) Soviet consolidation in eastern Europe—notably Czechoslovakia and Poland, 4) continued Communist pressures in the Middle and Far East, 5) Communist successes in Chile, and 6) the growth of anti-Americanism in America.

In attendance at the 1971 meeting in Moscow were not only Communist leaders from most of the world (excepting China and its allies) but also leftist leaders from countries of the "Third World." Foreign Minister Gromyko struck the right note when he declared: ". . . there is not a single question of any importance which could at present be solved without the Soviet Union or against its will."

The Congress, and Brezhnev in particular, evidenced satisfaction over the state of affairs in the European sector of the Communist interstate system. As Brezhnev made clear, the Soviet feeling of greater security in this chronicly unstable area stemmed from three major factors: 1) more effective use of the Warsaw Pact organization as a vehicle to enforce military-political cohesion in the area, 2) the harsh lesson Moscow feels it has effectively taught the world with the 1968 invasion of Czechoslovakia, and 3) Soviet detente in central Europe which Moscow feels has resulted in Western acquiescence to the status quo, especially the dividing lines between the two sides along the Iron Curtain. Even the violence in Poland in 1971 was optimistically viewed as merely an unpleasant episode which was now well in hand.

With regard to Sino-Soviet relations, the Congress views reflected the seriousness of the situation. Brezhnev declared that the USSR would never compromise its national interests in seeking rapport with Peking, implying perhaps that troubles between the two states were rooted in basic national divergencies rather than transient phenomena such as personalities or ideological disagreements. The Soviet position vis a vis China and in Asian affairs generally was the main area of foreign relations in which the posture of confidence and optimism adopted at the Congress appeared a bit strained. To maintain the overall cheerfulness, the erosion of Soviet influence among certain Asian Communists had to be either minimized or ignored.

The harshest anti-U.S. rhetoric was contained in two separate statements adopted by the Congress regarding the Middle East and Vietnam. The usual language about "national liberation wars" and "imperialistic aggression" was used. Both Gromyko and Brezhnev expressed reservations about the possibility of conducting fruitful negotiations with the United States. But the relatively mild tone was hardly based on any new friendship for the U.S. Rather it reflected increasing Soviet concern about China, the Middle East and Southern Asia.

The Congress broke no new ground in the development of Communist ideology, and it retained the same order of foreign priorities as the previous Congress had: 1) strengthen the international Communist system, 2) national liberation wars, and 3) "peaceful coexistence." Congress resolutions in 1971, as in 1966, made no mention whatsoever of disarmament.

What was probably the major new development in Soviet foreign policy since the 1966 Congress—Moscow's military involvement in the Middle East—was given only routine treatment. Brezhnev noted measures to restore the Egyptian arsenal destroyed in 1967, and the Congressional resolution spoke of continuing to render the "utmost support" to the Arab peoples. At the same time the tone of his speech suggested that the Soviets were aware of the dangers of giving carte blanche to Sadat of Egypt.

Moscow certainly sees new opportunities in Latin America, and a recognition of these opportunities was highlighted both in Brezhnev's speech and the Party resolution.

> The triumph of the revolution in Cuba dispelled the myth of the omnipotent power of American imperialism in Latin America. It showed that the U.S.A. . . . cannot undertake armed intervention with her former ease. The Cuban revolution demonstrated that even a small country has the possibility of overthrowing a dictatorial regime that relies on U.S. support . . .[1]

Brezhnev spoke at length on the problem of relations with Peking. He declared that Peking and Moscow must work together against the common enemy in Indochina regardless of other differences. At the same time he stated that "we will never forsake the national interests of the Soviet state." The Congress resolution reaffirmed Brezhnev's words with respect to relations with China, including a veiled threat of future action against Peking.

Brezhnev spoke of the difficulties caused not only by Trots-

---

1. As quoted in Alvin Z. Rubenstein, *The Foreign Policy of the Soviet Union* (New York, Random House, 1972), p. 435.

kyites but also by China's efforts to establish splinter parties in various countries as a counterweight to the international communist movement. Brezhnev described the "special ideological-political platform" of the Chinese leaders as "incompatible with Leninism."

As for eastern Europe, Brezhnev felt compelled to defend again the Soviet invasion of Czechoslovakia, justifying it in the name of "class duty to socialist internationalism." He also referred to the riots in Poland, underscoring Soviet support of the Warsaw Government's actions in dealing with that situation. Brezhnev noted that Soviet friendship with Poland was "unflinching," thus placing that country on a level higher than the other Communist regimes of eastern Europe. No other Warsaw Pact country was so honored, although East Germany's claim to international recognition was endorsed.

While the general attitude toward the United States at the Congress was more or less restrained, remarks by Brezhnev and Gromyko clearly indicated skepticism about the future. Brezhnev asserted that the U.S. position on certain issues which touch upon the interests of the USSR had hardened, and he professed to see "zig-zags" in U.S. policy apparently due to domestic political developments. Gromyko cited such issues as Vietnam, the Middle East, Berlin and the SALT talks as problems between the two countries.

The Soviet leaders praised the flexibility of the Federal Republic of Germany, and especially the agreements softening the western position on Berlin and recognition of the "sovereign rights of the German Democratic Republic as an independent specialist state."

Brezhnev mentioned arms limitations, but the Congress Resolution said nothing about it. The United Nations received only sporadic attention, mostly in connection with the discussion of other issues.

Special attention was paid by the Congress to the so-called "Third World." The resolution gave a somewhat more prominent place to those countries said to be on the "non-capitalist path" than Brezhnev had done. These countries were said to be in the "front ranks" of the national liberation struggle. The resolution notably advanced Latin America's role in this struggle by ascribing "revolutionary-democratic" changes to current developments there.

In regard to priorities, Brezhnev gave the Third World exactly the same order of precedence as in the last congress: he placed support for national liberation struggles in second place after the cardinal priority of strengthening the communist world, but before peaceful coexistence with the West.

Chapter 11

PROBLEMS OF INTERNATIONAL COMMUNISM

DIVERSITY IN THE POSTWAR ERA

What made the crucial difference between world communism before 1945 and in the two and one-half decades after 1945, was the fact that before 1945 Moscow could command revolutionary, conspiratorial parties which had no state responsibility. But after 1945 when those parties assumed state power, they took on a system of national values and priorities that often conflicted with the demands of Moscow's proletarian internationalism.

Out of this conflict between Communist internationalism and the claims of the modern nation-state, a loyalty crisis developed among the parties in the postwar era. In Eastern Europe, the crisis was manifested in Tito's break with Stalin in 1948; in the spreading "infection" of nationalism; in revolution in Hungary and political upheaval in Poland during 1956; in Rumania's drive for national independence and Czechoslovakia's thrust toward reformism in the 60's, and in the general diffusion of power that produced a loosening of Stalinist controls and the emergence of a more traditional form of an alliance system. What did not change, however, was the predominance of Soviet power and influence in the area.

By far the most serious loyalty crisis in world communism was Russia's dispute with China; it ruptured normal party relations, strained state relations, and adversely affected the entire international Communist movement. Elements in the dispute were nationalism, the subliminal issue of racism, and the more visible issue of conflicting great power interests. Powerful and deep-rooted, these elements combined and conflict surfaced as open contention developed on such basic matters as the concept of peaceful coexistence with capitalism as a viable policy in the thermonuclear age; the competing Chinese theory of aggressive revolutionism; practical relations with the United States and the capitalist West; "united action" against alleged American imperialism in Vietnam; and the convening of an international Communist conference, the implied Soviet purpose of which was to "excommunicate" China from the world brotherhood of Communists and in general to mobilize the world Communist movement against "American imperialism."

Other forms of diversity arose within the movement, rooted in nationalism, that combined to weaken Moscow's centralized control and threaten unity. Polycentrism among the non-ruling parties, a Communist variation of the principle of self-determination, had a serious, enervating effect. Castroism, another disruptive ideological diversity, constituted a competing theory of revolution that caused much mischief for Moscow in Latin America; it challenged Russia's traditionally accepted authority and control over the area.

By the end of 1966, the forces of diversity within world communism seemed to have become more deeply entrenched and more all-pervasive than ever before. A process of crystallization seemed to set in, insuring a degree of permanence wholly unexpected 15 years before. Nationalism has become a vital factor in the politics of Eastern Europe, generating forces that conflicted with Moscow's aggressive designs of universalism. The Sino-Soviet dispute, unresolved and seemingly unresolvable, proved to have far-reaching effects: it polarized the movement into competing factions and became the fulcrum used by those parties with room to maneuver to achieve some degree of diversity.

Polycentrism had succeeded in reconstituting the attitude toward Moscow among the non-ruling parties, particularly those of Western Europe. Castroism continued to make progress in creating an alternative to Moscow's peaceful coexistence.

The Soviets hoped to regain some control over these forces of diversity, and as their organizational and political problems magnified, they seemed to become increasingly convinced that an international conference of fraternal parties would somehow create a new and improving situation for world communism. It was towards this goal that much of their political energy was directed for the three years following 1966.

Russia's first concrete opportunity to pursue the goal of unity along the conference route opened up early in 1967 with the conference of European Communist parties at Karlovy Vary, Czechoslovakia. Preliminary preparations for the conference were undertaken amid a renewal of tensions in Sino-Soviet relations; the particular occasion was the unleashing of the Red Guards and the clash between Soviet police and Chinese students during a student demonstration on Red Square in Moscow in January; relations had very nearly reached the breaking point. This specific incident and the general virulent anti-Sovietism of the Chinese Cultural Revolution had the effect of winning greater sympathy for Moscow among the European Communist parties. This, combined with the Russians' disavowals that they were calling a conference to "excommunicate" China, increased the margin of support for the Soviet point of view.

But this margin of support in early 1967 would not be sufficient to achieve Soviet purposes in convening a summit conference. European communism was in a state of disarray. Among the ruling parties, Rumania and Yugoslavia were suspicious of Moscow's centralist tendencies; Albania was still openly hostile. Nor was unity much in evidence among the non-ruling parties of Western Europe which shared Yugoslav and Rumanian suspicions of Russia's hegemonic tendencies.

The conference convened at Karlovy Vary on April 24, 1967 and lasted until the 26th. Delegations from 25 of Europe's 31 parties attended. Among those absent were representatives from Yugoslavia, Rumania, and Albania among the ruling parties; Norway, Netherlands, and Iceland among the non-ruling parties. European security, that is, German "revanchism," was the main focus of the conference, and only by inference did it seem to have relevance to the larger problems besetting world communism. In an opening speech Brezhnev surveyed the broad scene of international relations but significantly placed greatest emphasis on the issue of unity. Sensitive to the views of the delegates on the China question, he touched on Peking's lack of cooperation, but only in passing. The conference approved documents relating only in a general way to internal organizational and political problems of world communism; the main thrust was in the broad area of international relations, notably East-West relations in the Cold War.

However much the conference documents and proceedings appealed to organizational unity, the fact remained that Karlovy Vary exposed to public view the true state of diversity and disarray within world communism, particularly within European communism. The retreat to generalities in the final conference declaration gave further evidence of the compelling force of nationalism within the ranks of European communism. And the willingness of the Russians to forego criticism of China at the conference, a stipulation insisted upon by the Italians and others, demonstrated the inability of the Soviets to impose their *diktat* over the West European parties.

But Karlovy Vary was not without its positive aspects for the Soviets. The fact that the conference was convened at all testified to Russia's primacy and power within European communism. The conference also demonstrated a new kind of solidarity which acknowledged diversity, a positive mark for Russia. And the Soviets might have gained some foreign policy benefits by the expressed agreement on broadening contracts with various groups in European society. Finally, the conference might have had the effect of strengthening the Soviet hold over their more reliable East European allies.

For the remainder of 1967, the Russians seemed to concentrate their main political efforts within world communism on arrangements for commemorating the 50th anniversary of the Bolshevik Revolution. They tried to make this golden anniversary an occasion for reminding the world of Soviet achievements as the first Communist nation-state and for reaffirming the doctrines of communism as an infallible guide to national greatness for the benefit of the Communist parties throughout the world. The conclusion to be drawn here by all member parties of international communism had an obvious connection with the Soviet campaign for unity and recognition of Soviet predominance within the movement. In brief, the anniversary was used, at least in part, as an instrumentality for rallying the forces of unity with world communism.

But divergencies within the movement continued unabated after Karlovy Vary, rendering highly improbable any measurable Soviet success in their November unity effort. Disturbing events included the reaffirmation in May by Rumanian party leader Nicolae Ceausescu of Rumania's intention of pursuing its independent course; the splitting effect of the Arab-Israel June war arising from Soviet support for the Arabs and dissident supporters of Israel within the movement, and Castro's sharp criticism of Soviet policy at the meeting of the Latin American Solidarity Organization in July–August. All these factors contributed to accelerating the forces of diversity within this already much divided international political community.

Faced with a groundswell of spreading diversity during the spring and summer of 1967, the Soviets seized upon the golden anniversary of the Bolshevik Revolution to somehow rally the forces of unity within the movement. For months they had been preparing for this jubilee, and all efforts were bent toward making the celebration pleasing to the Soviet population, impressive to the outside world, and, no doubt, convincing to the fraternal parties. Stability, compromise, and calm were the watchwords for the occasion as the leaders of world communism assembled in Moscow during November to pay homage to the U.S.S.R.

But still there were rumblings of dissent in the wings. China and Albania boycotted the commemoration; Castro showed his displeasure by sending a low-level representation from Cuba; attending parties would not unanimously endorse Moscow's conference plea; and Brezhnev's opening speech at the Kremlin's Palace of Congresses gave little evidence of compromise and calm within the movement. In one part of his address, Brezhnev reiterated Moscow's demand for unity and insistence on a world conference, though he did make some conciliatory gestures toward parties having polycentric tendencies. But he also sharply criticized Peking.

Listening to Brezhnev's keynote speech was the largest gathering of high-ranking Communist officials ever to be assembled in the history of world communism. In many respects the reaction of the fraternal parties to Brezhnev's call for an international conference and sharp criticism of China was somewhat less than predictable. Generally, the numerous speakers commented respectfully and approvingly of Soviet achievements in the past 50 years, but they were largely silent on Brezhnev's appeal for a conference and his condemnation of Mao. Even some of Moscow's previous supporters failed to mention these two vital points at issue. In general, the conclave provided still more convincing evidence of a global political system in a state of disarray.

Having gathered representatives in Moscow from many of the world Communist parties for the jubilee celebration, the Soviets were not likely to let this opportunity for pressuring the Communist leaders into a commitment for an international conference pass by. At the beginning of the celebration it was estimated that at least 18 parties of more than 90 attending opposed the Soviets on this matter. However, the Soviets succeeded in their efforts, and on November 25 it was formally announced that 18 parties (though not the same 18) would sponsor a "consultative" meeting to be held in Budapest in February 1968 to plan a world conference. A majority went along with this meeting and no serious opposition emerged.

For the Russians, the road to Budapest was not a particularly smooth one: world communism remained a many-splintered thing; the forces of diversity and diffusion of power continued to proliferate at a disturbing pace; something of a climax seemed to be reached in August when the Czechoslovaks asserted the right to determine their own style of socialism.

Compared with the preceding year, relations between China and Russia in 1968 were to be somewhat calmer, but the rift between the two powers remained deep and apparently irreparable.

It was Eastern Europe, particularly Czechoslovakia, which was to hold the center of attention in 1968. By the end of 1967, dissent in Czechoslovakia had reached near revolutionary proportions. Finally, in January 1968, as a consequence of total failure, the Soviet-committed Novotny regime was replaced by the reform-minded Alexander Dubcek. Within a few months long pent-up forces were unleashed that brought the country a long way toward liberalization.

Castroism further complicated Moscow's search for Communist unity. At the end of 1967, Castro had energized extremists and dissident Communists in several Latin American countries into attacking national party leaders (Monzon in Guatemala and Mora in Costa Rica) for failing to adopt the Cuban strategy of revolutionary communism. As a result, fractionalism spread among some parties; serious strains developed in others.

Perhaps nothing better illustrated the extent of diversity and fractionalism within international communism at this time than the spectrum of positions held by the diverse groups during the period preceding the Budapest conference. They could be categorized as the polycentrists, the centralists, and the outsiders.

The Italian party epitomized the polycentric view; it sought maximum organizational independence and diversity and proposed a conference that would be broadly based in representation, permissive and tolerant of dissent, and loosely structured organizationally. The polycentrists sought a flexible approach to the problem of unity. Among the ruling parties Rumania was identified with this view; the Czechoslovaks were rapidly moving into that category.

At the other end of the political spectrum were the centralists, led by the Russians and followed close behind by the Poles, East Germans, and Bulgarians. The leaders adhering to this view sought to re-establish tight, centralized control over the movement and construct unity along old organizational forms.

The outsiders represented a sizeable configuration of power and influence within the movement, and, accordingly, would deny Moscow substantial support. China was the most formidable party in this category; Yugoslavia also held a place of prominence.

The consultative conference opened in Budapest on February 26, 1968; it closed on March 5. Eighty-one invitations were sent out; 67 parties attended. All told, the representation accounted for scarcely more than 60 percent of the total world party membership. Numerical representation was, however, a deceptive, inaccurate measure of Russia's drawing power: many of the most powerful ruling and non-ruling parties were absent, and among those present were several mini-parties, which had little or no power base and a membership numbering in the few hundreds or, at best, thousands.

The conference was fairly unstructured; there was no established agenda at the opening session, and provisions were made for publishing reports on conference developments. Unstructured though the conference may have seemed at the outset, this situation did not last for very long. The Russians moved quickly to give it direction and focus, the principal agent for this purpose being Soviet theoretician Mihail Suslov. By upstaging the dissenters the Soviets and their supporters were able to seize the initiative, establish their preferences and goals for the guidance of the attending parties, and put the opposition on the defensive.

In his speech Suslov spelled out in a very general way the Soviet terms for unity. Among the points he stressed were: the utility of bilateral and regional conferences for establishing international ties, but the necessity of international conferences as the preferred instrumentality for solving problems and creating unity; the importance of convening such an international conference in November–December 1968; recognition of the autonomy and independence of the fraternal parties, but within the larger framework of proletarian internationalism. Suslov kept the door open for the Yugoslavs and Chinese. In many respects his speech was a compromise effort, designed to attract all dissident forces. Still, the essential core of Soviet policy was never sacrificed.

The Russians were able to get their way—but not completely. Sources of contention existed here and there, and in varying degrees of intensity. Some, like the Italians, had deep reservations but, nonetheless, went along with Moscow. Others expressed moderately dissenting views but, when the roll was called, adhered strictly to the Soviet line. Alone among the dissenters and polycentrists stood the Rumanians who bolted the conference in open defiance of Moscow's *diktat*. The Rumanians reiterated their now familiar position on the independence and autonomy of parties within the structure of world communism and took issue with the centralist point of view. In a matter that impinged upon the honor and integrity of the Rumanian party and state, the Rumanian delegate bolted the conference and returned to Bucharest. But the real purpose ran much deeper: this action was an insistence upon recognition of and respect for Rumanian independence.

In a formal sense Budapest was a notable achievement for the Soviets: they got what they had been striving for since November 1966, namely, agreement on calling an international Communist conference. Moreover, they got a vague declaration of unity.

Hence, they were able to maintain, at least formally, the ideological purity of Marxism-Leninism, for they firmly laid down the ideological conditions for loyalty to the movement and ambiguously advanced their historic claim of Moscow as the international center for guiding the Communist movement. Finally, they won a tactical victory by outmaneuvering the opposition and suppressing both real and potential dissenters.

But the Russians paid a price for this strictly organizational victory; what they had achieved was more formal than substantive, more institutional than political. No agreed political settlement was reached; no genuine compromise was hammered out. In reality, Budapest was a one-party show, staged and managed by the Communist Party of the Soviet Union. At best, Budapest was, therefore, a hollow victory for the Soviets; it was an illusion, remarkably symbolized by the cautious Soviet attempt to resurrect the old international organizational forms of the Stalinist past, the Communist International.

During the post-conference period in the Spring and early Summer of 1968 two main forces seemed to be operating: one, the surge toward liberalization in Czechoslovakia that appeared to crest on the eve of the Soviet-led invasion on August 20; the other, the Soviet effort to counteract, contain, and destroy the trend toward political diversity.

Liberalization in Czechoslovakia acted as a general chemical agent, catalyzing the forces of political independence within European communism and polarizing those forces against the growing counterforces of conservatism and reaction. Rumania and Yugoslavia responded with sympathy toward developments in Prague and began to consider a special relationship among all three revisionist powers. The parties of Western Europe, encouraged by changes in Czechoslovakia, perceived growing possibilities for developing a type of communism more acceptable to a West European constituency.

But this force of liberalization and diversity was counteracted by the Soviet determination to impose doctrinal rigidity on world communism and, more importantly, to arrest the momentum toward independence in Czechoslovakia, for "socialist democratization" in Czechoslovakia represented a direct challenge to the ascending Soviet mood of defensive conservatism. To Moscow, liberalization in Czechoslovakia meant a further weakening of the bloc and a threat of ideological subversion.

Within this environment of accelerating centrifugal forces and countervailing forces of conservative reaction, the Soviets continued their search for unity. A preparatory meeting opened in Budapest on April 24 with the task of establishing the organizational machinery to plan for the Moscow conference and to set a firm conference date. Perhaps the only real surprise at this otherwise uneventful meeting was the accumulating evidence of growing independent behavior by the Czechoslovaks. The meeting succeeded in establishing the date for the conference (November) and setting up a working group to hammer out the conference details. From the Soviet view, the meeting was a success, but like the Consultative Conference it again exposed to public view the deep fissures of disunity within world communism.

Problems aside from those arising from preparations for the Moscow conference also emerged in the Spring of 1968 to plague the efforts of international communism in the pursuit of its political goals. Most important was the threat from student radicalism and the New Left. The source of this threat lay in the principle of competition, for this new force, representing a combination of utopian anarchism and revolutionary romanticism, was a political and ideological competitor to communism in the cause of world revolution. In Western Europe and to a lesser extent in the United States, the problem of student radicalism was particularly troublesome to the Communist parties.

To add to Communist problems, some non-ruling parties suffered serious setbacks at the polls in the Spring of 1968, and there were still other setbacks, notably the spread of factionalism throughout the movement.

It was, however, the Soviet-led invasion of Czechoslovakia that created international communism's gravest problem: its implications were as troubling as they were far-reaching; for in this act of aggression, the Russians tried to accomplish by force what they had failed to achieve through political negotiation. As a result, they split the movement wide open, generated widespread dissension and distrust, and arrested whatever momentum they had built up for an international conference.

SOVIET INTERVENTION IN CZECHOSLOVAKIA

Liberalization had gone apace in Czechoslovakia during the

Spring and early Summer. But concern within the Soviet bloc, especially within the Soviet Union and the northern tier states of Poland and East Germany, heightened as the reformers pressed forward with their organizational changes and ideological innovations within the party and government. Against a background of threat and intimidation, the Czechoslovak leaders conferred with the Soviet Politburo at Cierna and Bratislava during August 1–3. A tentative compromise was reached; but the Soviets, concerned about the ideological and strategic threat that Czechoslovak innovations posed, intervened on August 20 and proceeded to establish a military occupation, destroy the reformist movement, and return Czechoslovakia to its pre-January path.

As in the case of the Hungarian intervention of 1956, the Czechoslovak crisis shook the foundations of the movement, but, unlike the Hungarian case, it failed to generate widespread defection. On the other hand, the general negative impact was, perhaps, more far-reaching.

Among the ruling parties the reaction was fairly predictable. The Poles and East Germans, as participants in the invasion and having shared interests with Moscow, supported the Soviets; the Hungarians, also a participant, seemed to be more reluctant supporters, probably owing to their own independent aspirations; the Bulgarians, also loyalists and partners in the invasion, wholeheartedly supported Moscow, but with a minor quali-fication—they were less critical ofthe Rumanians; Cuba gave only qualified support; the North Koreans, North Vietnamese, and Mongolians supported and justified the invasion. Among the critics were Rumania, Yugoslavia, Albania, and China.

Among the nonruling parties, the divisions were sharpest in Western Europe. In some instances open factionalism erupted, but in the course of time the Soviets succeeded in pressuring dissident groups into line. The Communist Party, U.S.A., supported Moscow but against sharp opposition from a dissenting faction.

The effects of the Soviet intervention on world communism were serious and far-reaching. Most serious was the fact that existing breaches in the movement were widened and new ones opened. This and other negative effects dominated inter-party relations for the remainder of the year, brought the Soviets into serious and open conflict for the first time with some of their most reliable defenders in the movement, and added new fuel to the Sino-Soviet dispute. The main source of concern among critics of the invasion was the violation of Czechoslovakia's sovereignty: the Rumanians and Yugoslavs saw this as a potential threat to their futures. The nonruling parties, especially in Western Europe, saw it as a setback for their attempts to enter the mainstream of their nation's lives as "national" parties and not bear the stigma of being instrumentalities of the Soviet Union.

The effects of intervention on Soviet policy, at least momentarily, were twofold: it led to a regeneration of Stalinism in the Soviet approach to international communism; it revived the spirit of the Cold War in East-West relations. Intervention had to be justified, morally and theoretically: moral justification could only come from Prague's admission that the reform movement was counterrevolutionary, which was a difficult admission for the Soviets to obtain credibly. Theoretical justification could come more easily, by merely adjusting the rubrics of communism to cover the present situation, and this was done in the Brezhnev Doctrine. According to this Doctrine, the Soviet Union had the right to intervene in the affairs of another socialist state to protect what it deemed to be the integrity and security of the socialist commonwealth. It was a self-ordained, self-defined pledge for "mutual security."

The repressive spirit of the Brezhnev Doctrine permeated the entire Soviet world outlook, and in the aftermath of intervention the Soviets initiated a series of practical actions designed to tighten their control and consolidate their power and authority over the socialist community in Eastern Europe and over international communism, particularly in Western Europe. This policy of constriction was evident across the board, in the field of military relations; in political and economic affairs; and even in the cultural area.

Consolidation of power and authority over European communism was, therefore, a first Soviet priority in the aftermath of the Czechoslovak crisis; the next priority was to get agreement on holding the long-planned, but now postponed, international Communist conference.

At Budapest, (late in 1968) the date for the world Communist Summit conference was set for April or May, 1969; provisions were made for interim meetings of the Preparatory Commission during February and March to work out details. Perhaps the most important result of this Budapest meeting was that the Russians finally succeeded in reenergizing their drive for a world conference, a drive that had been stalled since the invasion of Czechoslovakia.

By the year's end the Soviets seemed to be well in command, at least of their wing of world communism. Before Czechoslovakia, they had been somewhat tolerant of diversity, and permissive within limits toward dissenters. Now a certain toughness characterized their relationships with the fraternal parties: a spirit of neo-Stalinism, generated in the form of the Brezhnev Doctrine, permeated their attitudes and behavior; an insistence upon enforced conformity and strict obedience became a clearly observable *modus operandi.*

Thus the Russians seemed to be visibly progressing toward achieving their goal of a world conference. The Czechoslovak issue, the most significant and most disruptive development in world communism during 1968, was rapidly fading away as a viable political question; only embittered recollections of its implications seemed to remain, especially with Western European Communist leaders, and the Yugoslavs and Rumanians. But other more durable and perplexing realities were to appear in view that could neither be wished away nor pressured away.

For the Soviets the year 1969 was expected to be a time of fulfillment: momentum towards the Moscow conference was once again gathering force; pressure against dissident groups, especially in Western Europe, was paying off and expectations that a world conference would be convened sometime in 1969 seemed justified.

How successful such a conference might be, however, remained an open question, for no fundamental changes were visible in world communism that might portend a successful meeting. On the contrary, trouble loomed on the horizon for Moscow, trouble that was to further exacerbate intra-bloc tensions.

International communism as a world movement continued to be in disarray, fractionalized into four major power groupings, each adhering to varying forms of communism, namely, Sovietism, Maoism, Castroism, and polycentric reformism. And each generally pursued distinct policy goals and separate means for achieving their particular ends—even the binding cement of ideology seemed increasingly to be giving way under pressure of changing political realities.

Viewing world communism in the large, little had changed: the forces of diffusion and erosion were still generating disunity, notwithstanding Moscow's revival of a form of neo-Stalinism within and beyond Russia in the aftermath of the Czechoslovak crisis. Indeed, Russia's adversaries added to the political burden of the Kremlin leadership by unleashing a series of sharp thrusts in the preconference period that quickened the forces of disarray: armed clashes broke out along the Sino-Soviet border, stirring up anew latent feelings and hostile attitudes within the movement; Rumania and Yugoslavia, emboldened by the dissolving Soviet threat to their security in the aftermath of the Czechoslovak crisis, once again directed new criticism at Moscow's centralist pretensions within the movement; the self-immolation of Jan Palach, a young Czech student, seemed to stir up a renewed awareness of the anomaly of a Soviet military presence in the country of a socialist ally; dissension was voiced again among non-ruling parties in Western Europe whose polycentric tendencies surfaced again with renewed vigor and abrasiveness. All of these developments had the effect of loosening the bonds of unity and reducing the scope of Soviet control over the movement.

Though faced with this upsurge of hostile presures, the Russians nonetheless vigorously pursued their unifying efforts begun in earnest during the aftermath of the Czechoslovak crisis: they sought to tighten controls over the Warsaw Pact, integrate Comecon, and pressure nonruling parties into line. Commemoration of the Comintern's founding 50 years before provided a suitable occasion for restating many of the orthodox-flavored Soviet goals for world communism. In this entire preconference period, as before, the Soviets directed all their energies within the movement towards one goal: the convening of the Moscow conference.

Among the most significant manifestations of continuing disarray within international communism was the eruption of new and far more serious armed clashes along the Sino-Soviet border in March, 1969. The effect of this new crisis was to cast an ominous shadow over Soviet preparations for the Moscow conference: the crisis widened still further the breach in Sino-

Soviet relations, bringing to the surface again in hostile confrontation the old divisive attitudes among the world Communist parties and generating renewed polycentric forces within the movement. In the weeks after this so-called Damansky incident, Brezhnev became obsessed with the Chinese threat and strenuously sought support for the Soviet side. But Moscow met resistance in its efforts to initiate military preparations within the Warsaw Pact (notably from Rumania) and to obtain agreement on condemnation of the Chinese aggression (notably from the Italian party). On the other hand, Moscow could depend upon a long list of pro-Soviet parties for their accustomed reliable support. For example, the East German party, among the ruling parties, and the CPUSA, among the nonruling parties, joined Moscow in the condemnation of Peking.

The centrifugal forces of power diffusion and political diversity were given a further thrust forward as Rumania, now emboldened by the dissolving Soviet threat inherent in the Czechoslovak crisis and spurred on by the renewed opportunities arising from the Sino-Soviet dispute, voiced again its long-standing dissenting views. The profound implications of the Brezhnev Doctrine deeply disturbed the Rumanians, and they went to great lengths in public declarations to insist upon respect for the sovereign rights of independent states and to deny either the doctrinal or practical relevancy of the doctrine to the socialist system. With equal vigor the Rumanians resisted Soviet pressure to restructure the Warsaw Pact command system along supranational lines that would enhance Russian power and control over the organization while reducing that of the other pact members. At the same time the Rumanians successfully resisted Soviet pressure to stage Soviet military maneuvers on Rumanian soil in the spring, obviously having in mind the Czechoslovak experience. But this was not all. The Rumanians sent a greeting to the Ninth Chinese Party Congress, the only Soviet bloc state to do so, and, moreover, resumed close political and military relations with revisionist Yugoslavia as a counterforce to Moscow's integrating efforts in Eastern Europe.

Within their own Eastern European bloc, the Soviets continued their integrating efforts, having as their goal the assertion of unrestricted Soviet hegemony over the area. But the eruption of the border strife with China introduced a complicating issue, as noted above. Faced with opposition at the mid-March Budapest conference of Warsaw Pact powers, the Soviets were forced again to postpone their attempts to restructure the organization along supranational lines and bring it more securely under Moscow's control. They also continued their pressures to integrate the East European bloc economically, again without much success. Moreover, they continued to pressure the non-ruling parties of Western Europe with equal persistence and apparently with even less favorable results. Their objective was to reduce the influence of party leaders who were still unreconciled to the invasion of Czechoslovakia and the Brezhnev Doctrine. Attempts were made to intervene in party activities and turn the rank-and-file against their leaders. Pressures were also placed on recalcitrant parties who were financially dependent on Moscow for support.

Soviet unifying efforts also took another form, which attempted to transcend this crass resort to political pressure. Commemoration of the 50th anniversary of the Comintern provided a unique opportunity for appealing to a past filled with nostalgia and reminiscences of bygone revolutionary days, and for relating it to the requirements of the present and future. Here was an occasion to rekindle the old revolutionary spirit within a new generation. The golden anniversary of the Comintern was for the Russians a unique moment: It was a time for all to pay their collective homage to this revolutionary institution and the role it had played; it was a time to take stock of the revolutionary requirements of the present in the light of the past; it was a time to contemplate the unity of communism in new organizational forms and adapted to the demands of a new and challenging era.

As spokesmen for Moscow, Suslov and B. N. Ponomarev, Secretary of the CPSU's Central Committee, eulogized the success of the Comintern, called attention to the lessons it held for the present generation, reasserted the primacy of Leninist principles, rejected the idea of unifying world communism along lines of the old Comintern, and voiced their approval of new organizational forms, those of conference diplomacy, as mechanisms of unity. Theirs was a "soft-sell" approach seemingly intended to mollify the dissenters and win adherence to the Soviet point of view through persuasion.

American Communist leaders also eulogized the Comintern and voiced approval of Moscow's unifying efforts and its vigorously pursued centralizing policies. The convening of the

19th National Convention of the Communist Party, USA in April provided another opportunity for the American leadership to endorse the general Soviet position.

To hold a world conference of Communist parties in Moscow continued to be the prime Soviet target within the politics of the international Communist movement. The year 1969 was to be the climax of a 3-year effort to stage this conference.

Tension and uncertainty seemed best to describe the state of world communism as delegations from all over the world converged on Moscow for their first international conference in nearly a decade. Recurring violence along the Sino-Soviet border in the spring and summer sent powerful and disturbing shockwaves of tension and concern throughout the entire Communist bloc. Other problems made their unwanted presence felt in Moscow during June. The implications of the Czech crisis were still fresh in the minds of many Communist parties whose leadership perceived in the neo-Stalinist Brezhnev Doctrine a potential threat to their autonomy and independence. And those parties with polycentric tendencies were prepared to meet the Russians head-on. The preparatory conferences had already given evidence of their mood and their intent.

The world conference opened in Moscow on June 5, 1969. Brezhnev greeted the delegates with a carefully worded 10-minute speech that avoided any mention of the two most divisive issues in international communism: the problem of China, and the invasion of Czechoslovakia. The conference agenda cited two main tasks, the struggle against imperialism, and commemoration of Lenin's anniversary. Seventy-five parties sent delegates to the conference, but this representation, though numerically strong, was substantively weak. Five of the 14 ruling parties boycotted the conference, the Chinese, North Korean, North Vietnamese, Yugoslav and Albanian parties. In all, 16 Asian parties, both ruling and nonruling, failed to attend. The collective effect of these absences was to underscore the *de facto* split in the movement and to show that the movement was fast becoming European centered.

Numerical representation was, therefore, deceptive as a true measure of Soviet strength at the conference. As in the case of the Budapest Consultative Conference of February 1968, there were many parties represented that were extremely weak and ineffective. The inadequacy of numerical representation as a measure of real strength was further revealed by the complex of dissenters of all shades and descriptions among the participating parties. To a great extent, therefore, this numerical representation of 75 parties was something of a Soviet-induced illusion. But illusion or not, the Soviets wanted this conference and possibly for the following reasons: to create organizational unity within the movement; to create unity on a general Soviet political line (i.e., against Peking); to check the divisive forces of polycentrism; to reassert Soviet claims to ideological legitimacy, and to fulfill a political goal in which they had invested much prestige. Whether the conference would succeed was at the outset believed to be doubtful.

Brezhnev's brief remarks on June 5 opening the conference stressed one principal theme, unity; this was the slogan of the conference. On June 7, Brezhnev elaborated on the Soviet position in a main report of over 20,000 words. The speech, divided into three parts, was intended to present the Soviet position on the "tasks of the anti-imperialist struggle"; Communist unity against imperialism and other problems besetting international communism, and the role of the CPSU in the present epoch.

Essentially, the first part of Brezhnev's speech amounted to a general restatement of traditional Communist theory and a wide-ranging projection of the Soviet worldview. Insistence upon unity was the major thrust of the second part of Brezhnev's speech, and this problem was placed mainly within the context of the Sino-Soviet dispute. In fact, nearly one-third of this section, comprising over some 6,700 words, dealt with China in the form of a vigorous attack on the Peking regime, an elaborate justification for the Soviet view of the dispute, and an earnest plea for support from the conference delegates. In his prescription for unity Brezhnev cited the importance of "joint actions" against imperialism, "all-round" expansion of ties and contacts among the fraternal parties through bilateral and multilateral conferences (presumably with the world conference as a grand collective), and finally the need to achieve unity by energizing interest in the study of theory. Part III of Brezhnev's speech presented to the delegates an assessment of Soviet power and also a reaffirmation of well-known Soviet commitments in foreign policy.

On June 17, 1969, the conference adopted its main document entitled *"Tasks at the Present Stage of the Struggle Against*

Imperialism and United Action of the Communist and Workers' Parties and All Anti-imperialist Forces." Divided into four parts, the document presented a generalized overview of the state of world communism and the tasks it faced in the struggle against imperialism. It was at once a commentary on Marxism-Leninism as applied to the present era and an analysis of current problems in world politics and international communism. The principal theme of the document was a call to "united action" of all Communist and anti-imperialist forces, the purpose: to maximize the use of all energies for mounting an offensive against the forces of imperialism and reaction, that is, against the United States, its allies both East and West, and all anti-Communist forces.

An assessment of the power, strength and contradictions of the imperialist forces constituted part I of the document. Part II dealt with the strength of the world socialist system and its role as a "decisive" force in the present epoch. Part III laid out a program of "united action" by all anti-imperialist forces and fighters for "peace, freedom, and progress" under the leadership of the Communist parties. The imperatives of unity and the selection of instrumentalities for achieving it were the main points discussed in the fourth and final part of the document.

The main document was a compromise document; this seemed to be its dominating characteristic. It reflected more the politics of coalition than the *diktat* of authoritarianism. Failure to mention China by name indicated the strength of resistance among dissidents; conversely, the absence of any direct criticism of the Czechoslovakia invasion revealed the limitations on their pressures. Elements of realism were reflected in the document by the recognition that no organizational center of international communism existed as in the Comintern days and that unity was to be achieved through the politics of conference diplomacy. The document also revealed the parallel, if not identical, interests between the goals of international communism and those of Soviet foreign policy. Finally, the document exuded the spirit of "triumphalism" in sketching out the certainty of Communist victory. In some respects, therefore, the document reflected the realities of life, as in acknowledging political diversity within the international Communist system, but in others it was a utopian declaration of great expectations, the fulfillment of which was assured by a self-fulfilling philosophy of life.

Support for the main document, even though it was a

compromise of competing views, was far from unanimous. Of the total 75 parties attending, 61 signed the main document without reservation. Opposition and reservations were voiced by the remaining 14: 5 refused to sign (the Cuban and Swedish parties sent only observers; the British and Norwegian wished to consult their Central Committees; the Dominican rejected it outright); 3 would sign only part (Italian, Australian, and San Marino parties), and 6 signed but with reservations (Rumanian, Spanish, Swiss, Reunion, Moroccan and Sudanese parties).

Thus, unanimity could not be achieved, and agreement, such as it was, could be reached only on the basis of the least common denominator—a document so bland that only the most extreme would find it wholly offensive.

On the whole the conference produced no great results. None of the controversial problems dividing world communism—the dispute with China, the invasion of Czechoslovakia, and so forth—was settled and none was shelved. They remained in a state of suspended animation to bedevil the Soviets and divide the movement. In large measure, the conference appeared to be neither a success nor a setback for Moscow, but a "show" without any great consequence. At best, the conference marked the climax of a 3-year Soviet effort in the search for unity and new organizational forms. But "anti-climax" might be a better choice of words since the failure of the conference, at least on Soviet terms, seemed virtually predetermined by the powerful disruptive forces of contemporary history. And perhaps at worst the conference marked a new stage in the disintegration of world Communist unity.

However much the Soviet claims to universalism contradict reality, it would be a mistake to press this point too far and ignore the powerful forces of cohesion that operate to Russia's advantage. These forces of cohesion are derived from the reality of Soviet power and prestige, and the appeals of tradition and ideology.

At the present time the unity of world communism is obviously an unachieved Soviet goal. Powerful forces of disunity have disrupted the movement, yet powerful counterforces of cohesion exist within its dismembered parts that might bring about at least some form of structural unity, although probably not on the Soviet principles of unshared power, authority, and leadership.

"As for the future trends and tendencies in the development of international communism," according to Joseph G. Whelan, "perhaps the most that can be safely conjectured is the possible extension into the future of what already exists today. How long this international Communist order will prevail in its present form, none can accurately predict. But as a world system it contains two preserving elements: one is the reality of power that the combined strength of Russia and China represents; the other is the preserving quality of ideology."[1]

1. *World Communism, 1967–1969; Soviet Efforts to Re-Establish Control,* Internal Security Subcommittee, Senate Judiciary Committee, 1970, p. 22.

Chapter 12

THE CHINESE COMMUNISTS

Students in the English class at Peking No. 26 secondary school had their books open to lesson no. one titled, "A Long Life to Chairman Mao." The teacher led the students, ages 14 through 16, by rote through each line of the lesson: "Chairman Mao! You are the red sun in our hearts. We are sunflowers. Sunflowers always face the red sun. We think of you day and night. We wish you a long life."

The teacher then raised a shade over the blackboard revealing a picture of Chairman Mao, and asked: "Whom do you see?" In unison the class sang out, "Our beloved leader, Chairman Mao."

Thus the glories of education in the so-called Peoples' Republic of China. The chairman of the revolutionary committee running this school explained to Peter Lisagor: "Education must serve proletarian politics and be combined with productive labor. " Chinese society is rapidly becoming a society of human ants, harnessed in the service of their present day Stalin, Chairman Mao.

In his study *The Human Cost of Communism in China,* Professor Richard L. Walker writes: "It is my considered judgment that the cost of progress achieved under Communist rule is too high for the conscience of the world to absolve its perpetrators. In terms of human life and human suffering and in terms of destruction of moral and cultural values this cost cannot be condoned by any rationalization. The high Chinese Communist Party leaders who sit down at convivial banquets with visiting Americans may be guilty of as great crimes against humanity and their own people as were Hitler and Stalin and their followers."[1]

That charming host of the Nixons during the 1972 visit, Chou En-lai, did not hesitate to supervise personally the extermination of the family of Ku Shun-chang in Shanghai. This is but one of many incidents detailed in the autobiographical series published in *Ming Pao* (Hong Kong, No. 41, May 1969, p. 94) by Chang Kuo-t'ao, a former Communist colleague of the Chinese Premier.

Shortly after the establishment of the Peking regime in October, 1949, Chairman Mao declared: "The right of reactionaries to voice their opinions must be abolished." He wasted no time in eliminating "class enemies." With the passage of the Land Reform Act in 1950, even small property owners, as well as landless peasants, were killed as "enemies of the people."

By the end of the first five year plan in 1957, despite the report that over-all agricultural goals had been over-fulfilled, "agriculture was falling behind the country's consumption needs, the demands of an expanding industry and the servicing of the external debt."[2]

In 1956–57, during the Hundred Flowers movement, the Peking regime invited liberal criticism, "only to be confronted with clear evidence that the party and its leadership were by no means held in the esteem that had been assumed."[3] More heads rolled.

During the second five year plan, which started in 1958, the land that had been distributed to the peasants was taken back by the State. The "Great Leap Forward" mobilized tens of millions of Chinese to smelt iron in primitive and ineffective backyard furnaces (a testament to the Chairman's ignorance of modern science) and sought to push the Chinese peasants into militaristic communes, thus breaking up family life. The human cost of this

1. Subcommittee on Internal Security, Senate Judiciary Committee, 1971, p. 7.
2. O. Edmund Clubb, *New York Times,* February 23, 1972, p. 16.
3. Ibid.

scheme in terms of wasted energy and resources, suffering and death was staggering. To put it mildly, in the words of a writer not known for his hostility to Mao, the "Great Leap" was a "disastrous failure." (*Loc. cit.*) Mass repressions took place in "labor re-education camps," and during 1960 alone, Mao's regime may well have exterminated more Chinese than were killed in the war against Japan. An editorial in the *New York Times* (June 2, 1959) stated that Mao's regime had exterminated thirty million people in ten years.

Because of the political and economic fiascos of the first two five year plans, Liu Shao-chi succeeded Mao as chief of state in the spring of 1959. The regime publicly acknowledged that the amazing production figures issued late in 1958 (and swallowed whole by Peking apologist Edgar Snow) had been grossly inflated.

After the Central Committee meeting of September, 1962, Mao resumed his "class struggle" in a drive on domestic "revisionism." In July, 1964, "The Great Proletarian Cultural Revolution" was launched to purge the universities of impure thoughts, professors and students. Spear-headed by Marshal Lin Piao, students were mobilized into roving bands of Red Guards, and massive purges took place inside and outside the party. The chief aim "was the destruction of Mao's opposition within the party and his restoration to full leadership of the Chinese Revolution."[4] Things got so out of hand that in the summer of 1968 the army was turned loose on the Red Guards. Liu Shao-chi and other leaders were purged by the Central Committee in violation of the constitution which states that only the National People's Congress has the authority to select or dismiss the head of state.

In his recently published book, *The Revenge of Heaven* (Putnam, 1972), former Red Guard Ken Ling relates the terror of the times. Waving their red Mao-bibles, packs of youths, girls as savage as boys, masking their barbarism as righteousness, smashed, looted, tortured and murdered, beginning first with their own teachers and local officials, then fanning out from the cities into the countryside. They were urged on by Mao himself, who felt the need to eliminate certain individuals and classes, bringing uncounted others down with them as incidental casualties. Many bodies that floated down the river from Canton were picked up in Hong Kong . . .

4. Ibid.

During 1971 the Peking regime was scheduled to convene its long overdue fourth National People's Congress to draw up a new constitution and sanction Mao's actions since the last Congress sat in 1964–5. But the Congress did not convene, and mysterious events in September, 1971 suggested that a new crisis had arisen in the party, leading to the purge of Lin Piao and his allies.

In foreign policy, Mao has succeeded in antagonizing everyone but Albania. He invaded Korea in December, 1950, Tibet in 1951 and India. The Peking regime attacked Quemoy and Matsu in 1949, 1954, and 1958, and seized the Tachen Islands in 1955. It supports so-called "wars of national liberation" in Southeast Asia, has antagonized Japan, the Soviet Union and even neutralist Burma. Even sympathetic writer O. Edmund Clubb cites Peking's "rash and unprofitable adventures in the field of foreign affairs."

The United Nations, whose membership is open only to "peace loving states," was apparently so impressed with Peking's track record as to clasp it to its bosom in the fall of 1971.

Obviously, solving the problems of China is a formidable and vexing task, and the temptation to go for the grandiose scheme as a solution is great. But there are other paths, far more peaceful and far less destructive, through which the Chinese civilization can find its proper role in the modern world. Three specifically Chinese alternatives come to mind.

There is, first of all, the wonder of Hong Kong which has in large part been made possible by the talents of the Chinese people, and which is far more a Chinese phenomenon than it is a British phenomenon. The rule of the British Crown may be deemed "undemocratic" by some, but under standards of British law and justice and normalized expectation in stability and commerce, the Chinese have shown a remarkable capacity for democratic community, social and professional organizations. The Chinese in Hong Kong have successfully handled one of the greatest refugee problems in the world and have had remarkably good results in their efforts to raise living standards in Asia in a meaningful way.

Singapore is yet another essentially Chinese example which indicates that problems of poverty, development, and education are better solved without violence, class struggle or subordination to totalitarian dogma.

Taiwan, too, is another dramatically successful Chinese alternative to the Communist approach to the problems of the Asian peoples. Though one may criticize the Nationalist government for certain authoritarian aspects of its rule, it is a very long way from the most rigid authoritarianism to the merciless and all-pervasive totalitarianism of a Stalin or a Mao Tse-tung. Certainly, it would be impossible to argue that there has been in Taiwan in the past two decades the kind of human cost which China's Leninist-Stalinist, Mao Tse-tung, has deemed necessary and indeed desirable.

The announcement of President Nixon's trip produced shock waves across the Asian continent. It caused the declaration of an emergency in South Korea and the military take-over of the government of Thailand. The Japanese Liberal Democratic Party, long pro-Western, is in serious trouble, and Japan is now making overtures not only to Communist China but to North Korea as well. Asians did not view the President's initiative to Peking as anything but a sign of weakness, since it came at the very moment of American withdrawal from Vietnam, as well as at the time when Soviet strategic weapons seemed to be moving ahead of those of the United States, a fact of which Asians are very much aware.

What the new policies may produce is not a "generation of peace," but a generation of instability which can lead only to testing and probing by those Communist countries which maintain their aggressive policies. During 1971 Asian economic progress was offset by political anxieties over the emerging realities of the Nixon Doctrine. The prospect became clear to many that the essence of Vietnamization was an American acceptance of considerable Asian instability and uncertainty.

It is clear that American domestic politics is playing a larger part in determining U. S. strategic policies in Asia than is a clear understanding of what is necessary to provide for stability and, as a result, peace in that area. But, even within this context, the U. S. has acted in a way which appears to Asians to have slighted them. In a continent where symbols and "face" are as important as substance, the United States has trod heavily and harshly. Professor Zbigniew Brzezinski, writing in *Foreign Affairs,* comments that ". . . we must pay more careful attention to atmospherics and symbols. It is most unfortunate that President Nixon chose to announce his planned visit to Peking before going to Tokyo." He notes that "There is . . . a potential for a demonstratively anti-American leadership even within the Liberal Democratic Party, and American clumsiness and insensitivity could easily have the effect of bringing it to the surface."

Beyond the question of what any failure to fulfill its commitment to Taiwan would do to America's credibility elsewhere in the world, lies the tragedy——morally, militarily, politically, and economically——which would be brought about by any failure to preserve the integrity of the Government on Taiwan.

If Taiwan were ever abandoned, the United States would be turning over to Communist China Free Asia's No. 2 economic power. After a decade of growth averaging 10 per cent annually, Taiwan has become, in the words of *Fortune* magazine, "a resilient industrial mini-state." Taiwan is that rare developing country which exports principally industrial goods (which constitute 78 percent of foreign sales), rather than raw materials.

In 1971, for instance, Taiwan matched the estimated $4.3 billion total trade of the Communist mainland: the per capita gross national product, $400 per annum, is already about four times as large as in Communist China. The island's exports rose 40.6 percent during 1971 to $1.6 billion. Taiwan amassed a $34 million trade surplus.

Those businessmen who short-sightedly foresee huge markets on the Communist mainland should consider the fact that if Taiwan were to fall, far more would be lost to American industry and investment than it could ever hope to recover in a decade or more from the Communists. For example, there is little market for consumer goods on the mainland, and little prospect of doing business on any basis other than long-term credits.

More important than this is the fact that in Taiwan the ancient Chinese culture, literature, and religious traditions continue to live and to thrive, while on the mainland those traditions have been ruthlessly crushed. The cultural revolution of Mao Tse-tung was a massive and deliberate assault against the very core of Chinese culture, and it went even further than similar assaults in the Soviet Union since it attempted to destroy the authority of parents and teachers.

A danger America faces, and one of which its allies both in Asia and Europe are very much aware, is that of an emerging isolationism in America. A generalized sentiment in favor of isolation has followed every war, and it is only natural that it would follow Vietnam. It is essential, however, that responsible political leaders avoid the easy path of going along with this erroneous and potentially disastrous feeling.

The time is at hand to break away from the kind of double entry moral bookkeeping which has characterized the approach of all too many Western intellectuals to the facts of the rule in mainland China under Mao Tse-tung. The cost in human terms—whether related to social improvements which communist insurgency prevented during Mao's drive for power or to the grandiose schemes of the "Great Helmsman" during his more than two decades of rule—stands as a formidable indictment of a half century of communist experience in China. There can be no rationalization for the attack upon those qualities which have made the Chinese among the world's most civilized humans. Their civilization has a long memory, and this is a period which will be remembered as a blot on their approach to the human condition.

There is a general agreement that in America's quest for peace and security it must perforce, deal with the Chinese Communists. But in doing so, it is important that America not allow a temporary tactic to obscure its understanding that the top leaders of the Chinese Communist Party remain committed to their faith and to their past record.

In a dinner party with American correspondents in Peking on June 21, 1971, Chou En-lai argued that the American protective shield should be withdrawn from Taiwan so that the Taiwan problem could be solved as a strictly internal matter. He assured his guests that no revenge would be inflicted on the mainlanders in Taiwan, who would be permitted to return to their homes. He was quoted as saying, "Far from exacting revenge on them, we will reward them."[5]

Such words may sound convincing to those Americans who are anxious to disengage from responsibilities in the Western Pacific, and who have short memories. But these were just the terms which Chou En-lai and Mao Tse-tung promised to the former Nationalists and third-party intellectuals who joined the Communists on their accession to power in 1949, yet they were

5. Seymour Topping, *New York Times*, June 23, 1971.

among the first victims who are now statistics in the sobering table of recorded casualties. These, too, were the terms which Mao offered in the "Hundred Flowers" period of 1957, yet in the anti-rightist campaign which followed, a vindictive revenge was exacted. Would this same Chinese Communist leadership, whose record is so bad, be likely to behave in any different manner once they had, by their current soft line, won the very concession from the United States which they have sought for over two decades by a hard line? It seems well nigh incredible that certain leaders of the American scholarly community urged that we accept Chou En-lai's word and abandon the firm commitment of the United States government to the security of the people in Taiwan.

If the outside world cannot learn that the Chinese Communist leaders are indeed a remarkable group of "true believers" in their doctrines, if we are prone to forget or ignore their history and their past actions, if we do not exercise the wisdom which can point toward the day when the Chinese people can abandon class struggle and revolutionary world violence as the path to their modernization, then the human cost of Communism in China will, in all probability, mount very much higher.

Chapter 13

THE AMERICAN RESPONSE TO COMMUNISM

On November 23, 1970, a Lithuanian seaman aboard the trawler *Sovetskaya Litva* jumped from his ship to the U.S. Coast Guard cutter *Vigilant,* seeking asylum. The Soviets demanded that he be returned. The *Vigilant's* skipper, Cmdr. Ralph Eustis, called Boston Coast Guard District Admiral William B. Ellis for instructions. Eustis was told to hand the seaman, Simas Kudirka, back. When Eustis replied that he was afraid the Russians would hurt Kudirka, Admiral Ellis declared: "I don't think that will happen. They are not barbarians." The Russians came to get Kudirka, beat him repeatedly, and with Coast Guard co-operation, returned him to the Soviet ship.

In mid-1941, when President Franklin Roosevelt had made up his mind to help the Soviet Union following the German invasion, his foreign policy advisor William Bullitt recalled Stalin's crimes against humanity and the Soviet record of treaty violations. Bullitt recommended some *quid pro quo* to insure that the Soviets not replace the Nazis as overlords for eastern and central Europe. Roosevelt replied: "Bill, I just have a hunch that Stalin is not that kind of man, and that if we give him everything he asks for, *noblesse oblige,* and demand nothing in return, that he will work with us for a world of peace and democracy."

Maybe Stalin and his successors are not barbarians, and maybe Hitler wasn't either, but they make good substitutes. Even Khrushchev admitted Stalin's crimes, and the Soviet record in the Katyn Forest massacre, the rape of Poland, Czechoslovakia and Hungary, and the Cuban missile crisis is there for all to see. Perhaps history is not Admiral Ellis' strong point. And Roosevelt admitted he knew little about Communism or the Soviet Union. Our civilian and military leaders, more often than not, have failed to do their homework. General Eisenhower, for example, failed to see anything wrong in letting the Russians take Berlin in the Spring of 1945, even though the Allies could easily have gotten there first.

It has been argued by Herbert Feis and others that had Roosevelt lived longer, he would have dealt more realistically with the Soviets than did Truman (who agreed to forcible repatriation of refugees and escapees from the Communist world in Germany). I am inclined to accept this thesis, as the evidence is clear that Roosevelt, a week before his death, realized he had been taken in the Yalta agreement about Poland. But this is small consolation for the Poles, who trusted in the Anglo-American commitments made in the Atlantic Charter.

It was not until 1947 that President Truman came to recognize the stark fact that the Soviets were not only not reciprocating America's concessions and effusively emotional good will, but that Stalin was deliberately expanding the areas of Soviet domination as part of a new conflict, euphemistically called by some "the Cold War." Truman resolved a crisis in his administration by firing Henry Wallace (who favored more concessions to Stalin), and by supporting Secretary of State James Byrnes (whose experiences with the Soviets in Germany led him to recognize the stark realities of the situation). The upshot was the Truman Doctrine and the beginning of containment, a bipartisan foreign policy which remains in effect today (although not always successful, as witness the take-over of Cuba in 1958).

The United States did not seek conflict with the Soviet Union, as the concessions made at Teheran, Yalta and Potsdam demonstrate. After the war, the U.S. withdrew its forces from Europe and China in hopes of a return to peace, convinced that with the defeat of Germany and Japan no serious obstacle lay in the path of peace. It was not until the communists threatened Greece, Turkey and Berlin, and took over in Prague in 1948 (not content with a coalition government) that the United States even began to react. The take-over in China did not elicit the same response that Japan's earlier invasion of China did. Indeed Truman and Marshall sought to force a coalition government on Chiang Kai-shek, and even went to the lengths of placing an embargo on all arms shipments to Nationalist China (June 1946 to June 1947) in a vain attempt to twist Chiang's arm.

Revisionist historians have tried to suggest that somehow the Americans, not the Soviets, started the cold war. Their arguments are about as valid as those of certain earlier historians who insinuated that the Americans and the British were more responsible for starting World War II than the Japanese and the Germans. I remember a political scientist at Yale seriously telling my class that Finland, not Russia, was guilty of threats to the peace in 1939 and 1940.

There are more revisionists now than then, because of the leftist bias which social scientists have exhibited over the years. Late in 1969, the Carnegie Commission on Higher Education released the tabulations of a survey of 60,447 faculty members in American universities. 58 percent of the political scientists described themselves as "liberal," 13.8 percent "left," and 16.2 percent "middle of the road." Only 8.4 percent considered themselves "moderately conservative" and a mere 0.7 percent "strongly conservative." 68.7 percent of the historians were either liberal or leftist.

The above may help to explain why, at this late date in history, educated Americans like Coast Guard Admiral Ellis still do not regard the Soviets as being anywhere near in the same category as the Nazis. As one who has been active in Captive Nations work in this country, I can testify that there are many steelworkers, miners, janitors and other humble folk of central and Eastern European extraction who have a far better understanding of what we are up against than most Ph.ds in the social sciences. There is much wisdom in William F. Buckley's observation to a Syracuse, New York audience in 1961 that he would rather have the country run by the first 800 people in the Syracuse phone book than by 800 professors at Harvard.

But the prospects are not all bleak. There are many liberals today who, through bitter experience, recognize the reality of the

Communist challenge. They include Dean Acheson, Walt Rostow, Sidney Hook, Dean Rusk and George Meany, among others. Unreconstructed liberals at M.I.T. refused to take Rostow back after government service, and it was a long time before Dean Rusk found a job.

Indeed, in many ways, the internal dialogue (to use the current polite word) on foreign policy is no longer between liberals and conservatives; rather it is between leftists, on the one side, and liberals and conservatives on the other. Strongly anti-Communist liberal Democrats in the Senate like Henry Jackson of Washington and Gale McGee of Wyoming have received as many brickbats from the Left as have conservative Republicans, perhaps even more. During the 1968 presidential campaign, Hubert Humphrey and his supporters were often heckled unmercifully, and were even the targets of physical violence. Toward the end of the Johnson-Rusk administration, our leaders were afraid to accept speaking engagements due to the demonstrated hooliganism of the Left.

Many liberals and most conservatives support Israel against the Egyptian-Soviet build-up following the seven-day war of 1967. Somewhat the same coalition supports collective security in Europe (NATO), in Asia (SEATO) and in the Caribbean (Cuba, 1962 and Dominican Republic, 1965). In a more general way, and noting the decline which set in during the Kennedy Administration (in a vain effort to induce the Soviets to reciprocate our restraint), a coalition of liberals and conservatives has supported the concept of deterring the Soviets from adventurism through a nuclear power that is both formidable and credible. On each of these issues the Left is implacably hostile to U.S. foreign policy; indeed some of its shrillest voices favor enemy victory on one or several fronts.

For better or worse, most Liberals and now many conservatives accept, as a matter of practical politics, the "no-win" policy of containment, from Truman through Nixon. Eisenhower endorsed it in Korea, as did Kennedy during the 1962 missile confrontation, when the U.S. agreed not to invade the island if Russia withdrew its missiles. Although the U.S. did, before the Chinese intervention in Korea, at one time liberate north Korea, it has refused to liberate North Vietnam, under three administrations. Indeed, there was no bombing of North Vietnam for ten years after the Communists crossed the 17th parallel in 1955, and then only of secondary targets. U.S. foreign policy is gradually becoming more and more restrained, more and more defensive. A 1969 paper produced by R. G. Shreffer and W. S. Bennett of the Los Angeles Scientific Laboratory states categorically: "Military victory, like concepts of 'unconditional surrender,' has been recognized as obsolete since World War II. We must structure our policies accordingly. . . . Our military goals should not be victory but deliberate stalemate. . . . The role of our military services must be to support a national strategy of diplomatic deterrence; failing that, they must merely seek an early stalemate, not defeat of enemy forces."

On the surface this sounds like an exceedingly mature and restrained approach, but it is enormously handicapped in international relationships by the fact that our adversaries refuse to limit their own strategy. Both Hanoi and Peking are formally and openly committed to the idea of victory, not standoff, in Vietnam. *The Peking Review* commends "the 34 million (Communist) Vietnamese people who have the firm resolve to fight and win." We were accustomed to such exhortations and were inclined to shrug them off, while analyzing deeds, not words, in order to produce the basis for American withdrawal and a *de facto* settlement in Vietnam. But we have not become accustomed at all to the idea that powerful forces in Soviet Communism are equally unwilling to tolerate the thought of compromise, whether in the Middle East, Hungary or Czechoslovakia.

In October, 1970, there appeared in the Czech military journal *Lidova Armada* an article by Lt. Col. Josef Sedlar, entitled "Education in Hatred of the Enemy." Sedlar is close to high ranking Soviet officers, whose views he reflects: "Concepts like struggle, hostility, hatred of the enemy have, in the terminology of the Communist movement, a just and humane meaning. . . . Those who wage this struggle (for Communism) have a truly historical right to. . . . preach hatred against a social system (capitalism). . . . Education in hatred of the enemy therefore has an important place in the theory of Communist education."

"Hatred of the enemy," writes Sedlar, "is a high moral-political goal. . . . Education in hatred of the enemy must be an indivisible part of socialist education in patriotism and internationalism. The need for education in hatred of the enemy is greater in the armed forces than in any other social organism."

Thus in the case of Soviet Communism, instruction is advocated in hating an ideological opponent with whom there isn't any war and with whom vital negotiations such as the SALT talks are proceeding. The gap between an increasing moderation of thought in the West (together with its concrete application) and the revival of extreme military chauvinism in the East is increasingly evident. It is hard to conceive of the possibility of any enduring accord between the two in areas of vital interest so long as one side develops a strategy postulated on compromise while the other side pursues a strategy of victory fanned deliberately by inculcated hatred.

Having established our frame of reference, we can proceed to examine the application of United States foreign policy in the indicated major areas: the Middle East, Europe and NATO, East Asia, the Caribbean, and the overall strategic confrontation. With the partial exception of the Middle East (the period 1947–1955), these areas must be considered within the framework of The War which the Soviets thrust upon us (which many have called the Cold War, and which others describe as the third World War), beginning with the threat to Greece and Turkey. The battles of this war have included: Greece (1944 and 1947–1949), Berlin (1948 and 1961), Czechoslovakia (1948 and 1968), Hungary (1956), Iran (1946), Lebanon and Iraq (1958), the seven-day Middle East conflict (June 1967), the China war (1945–1949), Quemoy-Matsu (1958), Tibet (1951), Korea (1950–1953), Indo-China (1955–present), Philippine Hukbalahap insurgency (1947–1957), Malaya (1947–1957), The Congo (Belgium) (1960–1964), Cuba (1958, 1961, 1962), Guatemala (1947–1954) and Dominican Republican (1965).

The East Asia battles largely stem from the Yalta decisions which strengthened the USSR in the Far East (as well as in Poland), the continuing Soviet assistance to the Chinese Communists (notably 1945–1949), and the refusal of the U.S. to render similar aid to the Chinese Nationalists. The Communist take-over of mainland China led to the Korean war, the conquest of Tibet, and the Communist challenge to southeast Asia. U.S. liberal policy toward Syngman Rhee of Korea was similar to the U.S. policy *vis à vis* Chiang Kai-shek. Briefly, this policy is characterized by the attempt to disengage the U.S. from a firm commitment to hard-line anti-Communist conservatives· based on alleged fear of confrontation with the USSR.

We have already examined the Korean War from the perspective of the Communists. Let us look at it again from the perspective of the United States, in order to delineate the different goals which the two sides sought.

In January, 1950, Secretary of State Acheson, speaking for President Truman, announced that henceforth Taiwan and South Korea would be excluded from the U.S. defensive perimeter in the Pacific. Shortly thereafter Soviet Marshal Malinovsky began to train North Koreans and Chinese for the invasion of South Korea. Using the liberal argument that Communism was primarily an economic question (people "go" Communist because they are hungry), the Truman Administration embarked on a program of economic aid to South Korea, while withholding military aid beyond what was required for a constabulary force. The Communist invasion of June 25, 1950 pitted T-34 tanks against .45 caliber automatic pistols and carbines.

Once the Communists crossed the 38th parallel, the U.S. Government (together with token UN forces) decided to help defend South Korea. For the first time in history a fairly sizeable element of American society vigorously opposed the efforts of Presidents Truman and Eisenhower to save South Korea. This leftist fall-out from the Wallace-Communist crusade of 1948 organized into "peace councils" which made contact with Communist authorities in Pyongyang to exploit American prisoners of war and their families (by inducing them to sign "peace petitions"). This same phenomenon occurred, on a much larger scale, during the war in Vietnam.

After the retreat to the Pusan perimeter, General McArthur landed behind the enemy lines at Inchon, liberated Seoul, and in accord with the UN General Assembly resolution of October 7, 1950, liberated North Korea. This was rather significant, considering the inhibitions of containment; no similar venture was undertaken in the Vietnam war. The Chinese Communist invasion of Korea in December, 1950, coming on the heels of the liberation of North Korea, led the U.S. policy-makers to back down. First, the Truman Administration refused to retaliate against the enemy base on Manchuria, and even severely restricted bombing the Yalu river bridges (while ruling out attacks against the Korean rail center at Racin—40 miles from the Soviet frontier); secondly, the U.S. abandoned the liberation of North Korea. Refusal to bomb the enemy effectively led to severe

Allied casualties during the Allied retreat to east coast evacuation ports, and to the second Communist capture of Seoul.

Although the UN Charter specifically calls for sanctions, including naval blockade in cases of aggression, there were no military sanctions applied against the territory of Red China or the seas bordering that country. Chapter 7, articles 41 and 42 of the Charter remain unenforced to this day. Following the firing of General McArthur, a limited Allied offensive led by General Van Fleet liberated Seoul and pushed into North Korea again (although not with the intent of liberating the entire north). The enemy forces were in full flight, when Soviet diplomat Jacob Malik, on the first anniversary of the Communist invasion, called for negotiations. The Truman administration stopped the successful offensive, and there followed two years of talks first at Kaesong, then Panmunjom, while men died on the stalemated battlefield.

As chief negotiator Admiral C. Turner Joy recounts in his book *How Communists Negotiate,* the United States made the major concessions on truce supervision and inspection, and the prisoner of war issues. The Panmunjom settlement of July, 1953, was hardly America's finest hour; General Mark Clark later said he was ashamed to sign the agreement which allowed the Communists (named by the UN as the aggressor) to remain in North Korea, undefeated and unpunished. The Chinese Communists began, with some justification, to refer to the United States as a "paper tiger," and the Pyongyang regime has, since 1953, engaged in a series of provocations, including the Pueblo incident in 1968 and a 1972 attempt to murder President Chung Hee Park of the Republic of Korea.

Clearly, the differences in ideology dictated different strategies in Korea. With "containment" as a goal, the U.S. adopted a defensive posture despite superior strength. Since the Communists actively sought expansion, they were able to make gains despite a shaky position.

Although the Communist World was weak and divided during 1953 (partially due to Stalin's death and evidenced elsewhere by the uprising in East Berlin), the West did nothing to take advantage of the opportunities that existed. We, not the Communists, were in a position to negotiate from a position of strength in 1953. Taking advantage of the timid policy of defensive containment, the Peking regime began to demand the

Chinese Nationalist offshore islands, beginning with the Tachens. After much clamor, the Eisenhower Administration forced the Chinese Nationalists to evacuate the Tachens to the consternation of the authorities in Taipei. Following a visit to the Far East by Secretary of State Dulles, Congress passed the Defend Formosa resolution, which provided for the U.S. defense of Formosa (Taiwan) and such offshore island positions as were considered vital to that defense. In 1958, when the Communists attacked Quemoy and Matsu, the Eisenhower Administration (after some hesitation and ambiguity) supported the successful Chinese Nationalist defense of the strategic islands.

The involvement of the United States in Southeast Asia, as in northeast Asia and China, stems from prior Communist action. After World War II, Communist elements in the Philippines, Dutch East Indies (later Indonesia), Malaya, Indo-China, Thailand, and Burma engaged in acts of violence against the governments of these countries. In most cases (except Burma and Malaya which were in the British sphere of influence), the U.S. Government came to the assistance of the threatened governments. Previously the U.S. government had pressured the Netherlands and France to grant self government to Indonesia, Vietnam, Laos and Cambodia. The Southeast Asia Treaty of 1954 included Thailand and the Philippines, together with Vietnam, Laos, and Cambodia as protocol states. After the 1954 Geneva Conference on Indo-China and the French withdrawal, the United States became more involved, in response to the Vietminh threat to the State of Vietnam (shortly thereafter the Republic of Vietnam), Laos, and later (1970) Cambodia.

Both the United States and the State of Vietnam (South Vietnam) refused to sign the Geneva Agreement because the French and the British made too many concessions to the Communist Vietminh (notably, handing over Hanoi and Haiphong), and because the Communists rejected the U.S.-South Vietnamese insistence on free elections for all Vietnam under UN supervision. The Eisenhower Administration, together with leading Democrats like Senators Kennedy and Mansfield, were pleased with the accession to power of the Vietnamese nationalist leader Ngo Dinh Diem in Saigon and extended military and economic aid to his government.

Diem, with U.S. support, defeated the rebel armies of the Cao Dai and Hoa Hao religious sects and resettled almost one million refugees from North Vietnam, while seeking to make South Vietnam more secure from the Vietminh attacks. He was reasonably successful until 1962. That was the year that the Kennedy Administration tried to compromise the crisis in Laos by forcing the resignation of the anti-Communist leader Phoumi Nosavan, while bringing to power a coalition government including the Communists. This more or less legalized the Communist control of one-third of Laos, including land adjacent to South Vietnam along which the Vietminh soon built the Ho Chi Minh trail. The changed situation in Laos made the defense of South Vietnam more difficult. Then Sihanouk, in Cambodia, having lost confidence in the United States, decided to accommodate himself with the Communists, who soon began using his country as a privileged sanctuary from which to attack South Vietnam.

To compound Diem's problems, a neutralist and pro-Vietminh Buddhist clique, led by Thich Tri Quang, began to engage in acts of violence against the Diem Government. Half of Diem's cabinet members were Buddhists, and there was no truly religious problem. From Diem's point of view there *did* exist a treasonous clique hell-bent on accommodation with Hanoi. But when he moved against Thich Tri Quang, his enemies (in Vietnam and in the United States) accused him of repressing Buddhism. Averill Harriman and Roger Hilsman, in the Kennedy Administration, persuaded the President to encourage anti-Diem forces in Vietnam. This led to the uprising of November 1, 1963, and to the death of Diem and two of his brothers (some members of the Kennedy Administration accused Diem of "government by family!"). The immediate post-Diem period was characterized by coups and counter-coups, all set in motion by the original anti-Diem uprising. It was not until the advent of Thieu-Ky Government, based on the elections of 1966, that relative stability returned to South Vietnam.

In the wake of the Tonkin Gulf incident in 1965 and the general escalation of the ground war by the Communists, the Johnson Administration decided at long last to engage in air strikes against secondary targets in North Vietnam. But the airfield at Hanoi was never touched, nor was there any interdiction of the supplies coming into Hanoi (in 1943 the U.S. Government mined that port to deny its use to the Japanese). The bombing, limited as it was, took some of the pressure off the U.S.

and South Vietnamese forces, and certainly complicated for the Communists the problem of transporting supplies from north to South Vietnam. However, in response to much clamor by leftist groups in the United States, President Johnson unilaterally stopped the bombing in 1968. Senate "doves" assured us that this would lead to fruitful negotiations with Hanoi.

The Nixon Administration decided to turn over more responsibility to the South Vietnamese armed forces (ARVN) and began a unilateral withdrawal of U.S. forces from South Vietnam. This was further facilitated by the successful though limited operation of May, 1970, which cleaned out the privileged sanctuary of the North Vietnamese Army in Cambodia. The 1970 elections in the United States retired such vociferous opponents of collective security as Senators Goodell, Gore and Tydings, and Congressman Lowenstein, which seemed to indicate public acceptance of the Nixon policies in Southeast Asia.

Early in 1972, a massive Soviet-supplied North Vietnamese force crossed the DMZ to invade South Vietnam. The Nixon Administration, while not using U.S. ground troops (most of whom had already withdrawn) fully supported the South Vietnamese defenders with helicopters and, later, air strikes into North Vietnam, and the mining of North Vietnamese harbors, including Haiphong. The Communist attack was blunted and in January, 1973, after months of negotiations, a cease fire was signed. But the agreement did not provide for withdrawal of all North Vietnamese invaders from the South.

THE MIDDLE EAST

The U.S. commitment to Israel, beginning in 1947, led to a gradually increasing U.S. involvement in Middle East Affairs. In 195? the United States acted to shore up governments in Iran and Lebanon which were threatened by the U.S.S.R. and/or internal leftist forces. In 1955 the Eisenhower Administration abandoned plans to help finance the Aswan High Dam project in Egypt, when it learned that Nasser had concluded a secret arms deal with the U.S.S.R. The Soviets, taking advantage of the U.S. pro-Israel position, decided in 1955 to espouse the cause of the Arabs, notably in Egypt. In 1956 the United States helped to block a joint Israeli-French-British invasion of Egypt (which was triggered by Nasser's blocking of the Suez Canal and seizing of the

International Suez Company which operated the Canal). The reasoning was that the U.S. could not condone this invasion, any more than it could condone the Soviet invasion of Hungary. The difference was that the United States government did nothing at all to stop or even deter the Soviets from acting in Hungary. The U.S. didn't even recognize the regime of Imre Nagy.

By the Spring of 1967 the Soviet arms build-up in Egypt and Syria had reached alarming proportions, with Israel calling for help from the United States, Britain and France to counter it. Fortunately for the West, Israel was able to gain a complete and convincing victory in the June war of 1967 by engaging in a devastating preemptive air strike against the Soviet tanks and planes employed by Egypt and Syria. But neither Nasser nor Brezhnev accepted their defeat as final, and soon the flow of Soviet military aid to Egypt resumed, while Cairo called for a war of revenge.

The United States sought to encourage negotiations which might cool off the combatants, negotiations which might induce the Soviets to stop aiding Egypt, so that it might be able to slow down or stop aid to Israel. But neither Egypt nor the U.S.S.R. seem to be much interested in ceasing or desisting.

The Middle East conflict has led to some most interesting domestic political ramifications. Many Vietnam "doves" become "hawks" when the question of defending Israel comes up. Senators who advocated withdrawal and negotiations in Southeast Asia demanded blockade of Egyptian ports and, if necessary, U.S. military involvement to defend Israel. Generally speaking, liberals and conservatives have supported collective security in the Middle East, whereas the more extreme elements of the American Left have taken a pro-Soviet and anti-Israeli position.

The Middle East problem has, since 1955, become "Sovietized," thus leading to a greater U.S. involvement. This involvement has also been occasioned by the Soviet naval build-up in the Mediterranean, and the change of government in Libya (now pro-Egyptian). The United States has gradually assumed Britain's role of guardian of the eastern Mediterranean after World War II. The commitment grew with the Baghdad Pact in 1956 and then, in 1958 (when the enemy took Baghdad), the Central Treaty Organization. The long-standing commitment to Israel took on new proportions when the Soviet Union became a Middle East power and egged Cairo on to greater adventurism.

WESTERN EUROPE

Many Americans believed that with the defeat of Germany in 1945, the U.S. could withdraw its influence from Western Europe and return to business as usual. But postwar economic problems in Europe plus Soviet belligerency and the crises of 1948 in Czechoslovakia and Berlin forced the U.S. to become involved, first with the Marshall Plan, and then, a year later (1949) with the North Atlantic Treaty Organization. NATO, reinforced by the nuclear deterrent, was supposed to cool off the Soviets. It succeeded, with respect to western Europe, but not with respect to Berlin, Hungary or Czechoslovakia. And as the Soviets developed their own nuclear capability, they felt free to engage in adventures as far abroad as Vietnam, Laos and Cuba.

In 1961 the Kennedy Administration decided to soften the nuclear deterrent first by a slowdown in its development (don't build "offensive" weapons which might antagonize the Soviets), and finally by a complete cessation of the construction of ICBMs and nuclear submarines. More than this, President Kennedy announced that in the event of a Soviet attack on western Europe or the United States, there would be a "pause" rather than an automatic nuclear response. This was hardly reassuring to our Western European allies; France, especially was unwilling to consign its fate to the whims and fancies of an American president. Under De Gaulle's leadership, France then proceeded to develop its own *force de frappe.* The defection of France from NATO weakened the organization and forced the moving of headquarters to Belgium.

It was Kennedy's hope that if the United States unilaterally limited its own strategic arms program, the Soviets might reciprocate. Kennedy's gamble did not pay off, and the Western world is less safe today as a result. First the Soviets caught up to the United States in deliverable megatonnage, then they caught up in total numbers of ICBMs. In addition they developed an Anti-Ballistic Missile (ABM) system.

Berlin has been subjected to a series of Soviet pressures, largely due to the fact that the Truman Administration in 1945 did not insist on firm Western control of a strip of land connecting West Berlin and West Germany, or iron-clad guarantees of access to the city. The American response to the 1948 blockade was the immensely costly airlift, instead of sending in a tank column (the U.S. still possessed a monopoly of nuclear weapons at the time). In 1953 we stood by and did nothing during the East Berlin uprising. Indeed the Eisenhower Administration shut off the RIAS Radio so as not to spread the news of the uprising to East Germany. And in 1961 the Soviets began to build the ugly wall right through the city, in flagrant violation of the Occupation Statute, while we did nothing.

CUBA

There has been speculation that Khrushchev put the missiles in Cuba in order to be able to blackmail us in Berlin. Whether or not this is true, the Soviet and Communist success in Cuba in 1958 marked a turning point of great portent—the breaching of the Monroe Doctrine for the first time in history. The advent of Castro to power reflects credit not only to his friends in Moscow but also to some Americans who were so obsessed with the evil of Batista as to conclude that any change would be for the better. Herbert Matthews of the New York Times, in particular, portrayed Castro as a sort of modern Robin Hood. Castro's PR men could scarcely have improved on Matthews' "news" stories.

By early Spring, 1961, leading liberals, as well as conservatives, recognized the threat which Castro and his sponsors presented not only to the Americas, but to the Cuban people. President Kennedy decided to go ahead with the plan, originally launched by the Eisenhower Administration, to help Cuban exiles overthrow Castro. Unfortunately for the Cuban people, however, timidity and what can be most easily interpreted as a guilt complex so enveloped advisers like Adlai Stevenson that key elements in the liberation attempt were eliminated, notably the final air strike against Castro's air force. Had this strike been carried out, it is likely that the landing at the Bay of Pigs could have been effected without interdiction by Castro's war planes. The defeat of the Cuban exiles was even more a U.S. defeat, and a defeat for the Cuban people.

During the summer of 1962, Cuban exiles warned the Kennedy Administration that offensive Soviet missiles were being installed in Cuba. It was not until October 14, 1962, that the Administration believed the warnings. On that day a U-2 plane took photographs of several MRBM and IRBM sites under construction. The purpose of the Cuban installations was revealed to

President Kennedy on October 18th, when Soviet Foreign Minister Gromyko informed him that the Soviet Union would conclude a separate peace treaty with East Germany, immediately after the Congressional elections of November 6th, 1962. This was approximately the date by which the Cuban missile bases would become operational. At a critical point in urgent negotiations on Berlin, Khrushchev would then be able to disclose that he now had a formidable fire-power deployed on America's very door-step.

The U.S. response to the Soviet build-up was a show of naval strength (but not a blockade). There ensued secret negotiations resulting in an agreement whereby the Soviets promised to withdraw the missiles if the U.S. would promise to block Cuban exile efforts to overthrow Castro. In addition, the U.S. dismantled missiles in Turkey and Italy. It was quite a price to pay.

Castro remains as a thorn in the side of the Americas, repressing his own people as they were never repressed even under Batista, exporting revolution to the Americas (including the United States), and threatening the security of the Caribbean with Soviet submarine activity centered at Cienfuegos (Bouscaren, "Soviet Global Naval Strategy," *Washington Report,* Dec. 7, 1970).

In 1965 leftists forces inside and outside the Dominican Republic sought to overthrow the government of that country. One of the ringleaders was Juan Bosch, former Dominican President and the darling of many American liberals and leftists. U.S. troops were sent to the area when President Johnson disclosed that the threat of another Castro takeover existed. The Organization of American States (OAS) then established an inter-American military force to protect an interim government until elections could be held, and U.S. forces withdrew. The interim government was the result of U.S. pressures to force the resignation of General Wessin y Wessin and other conservatives considered distasteful in liberal circles. Subsequent elections brought to power moderate conservative President Balaguer, and the situation became stabilized.

The bipartisan policy of containment has more or less succeeded in East Asia (once it was applied *after* the Communist success on mainland China) and in western Europe. In the Middle East however, Soviet influence has expanded into Egypt, Syria, Yemen, Libya and Algeria. In eastern Europe Soviet control has been reestablished in Poland, Hungary and Czechoslovakia, as "national Communism" seems to have gone up in smoke (Yugoslavia excepted). In the Caribbean, and Latin America generally, Soviet and Communist influence are on the rise. These situations pinpoint a difficulty of the policy of containment when there is no clear agreement on just where the borders within which Communism is to be contained are. In the revolutionary protracted conflict there are no clear fronts, as there are in classical military wars. The policy of containment has difficulty dealing with this situation. It is in the nature of the dynamics of the Western-Communist confrontation that the defender refuses to cross the fifty yard line. Only the attacker can score.

As suggested above, most conservatives and many liberals support containment. The policy was in fact launched by liberals, George Kennan, the U.S. Ambassador to the USSR, among them. The major alternative to containment is general withdrawal, based on certain isolationist assumptions of the past. This alternative is presented in its radical form by the leftists, and in its moderate form by an element of the liberal movement which for the most part has no governmental experience (in the Executive Branch) and appears to be motivated at least in part by the political objective of overthrowing the Establishment of the Democratic Party.

I submit, however, that some conservatives and even a few liberals believe that containment can be improved on. Several years ago there appeared a learned treatise entitled *A Forward Strategy for America,* written by Robert Strausz-Hupe and William Kintner of the University of Pennsylvania, and Stefan Possony of Stanford. It contains many suggestions for the improvement of U.S. foreign policy which would not leave all the initiative to the other side.

We have, of course, undertaken some initiatives, as in Guatemala (1954), Iran (1951), Dominican Republic (1965), Cambodia (1970) and perhaps some others of which I am unaware. (I do not include initiatives against allies, like President Diem of South Vietnam.) Yet even in these cases our action was precipitated by prior Soviet action. Only in the case of Guatemala was there a bona fide recovery of territory previously controlled by the other side. There have been other "successes" of sorts: the change of governments in Indonesia (Suharto replacing Sukarno), in

Cambodia (Lon Nol replacing Sihanouk) and in Ghana (the overthrow of Nkrumah). But many students of strategy believe that the Free World performance can be improved, utilizing something of the "active defense" concept employed by Israel, extending even, as it did in 1967, to preemptive strikes. Possibly our Cambodian venture and the mining of Haiphong in 1972 could be compared to this example.

A forward strategy for America and its allies would be based on the proposition that if the Soviets, the Red Chinese and their proxies persist in their efforts to extend Communist tyranny outside the boundaries of the USSR and Red China, then the Free World can (as it did during World War II and part of the Korea war) react by, in selected cases, liberating territories taken by the Communists. We are not talking now of countries like Bulgaria or Rumania, but rather of peripheral areas such as North Vietnam, Albania and Cuba. The emphasis, practically speaking would be on eroding away pockets of Communist power, through a comprehensive strategy of political, economic and psychological warfare, combined with counter-guerrilla operations. Wherever possible, indigenous rather than U.S. forces would be utilized.

In the case of Cuba, U.S. naval power can prevent any future Soviet attempt to re-install missiles. Meantime the U.S. government and citizenry could quietly encourage and even assist the efforts of Cuban exiles to harass Castro in every possible way. Such a new program would offer some hope to the Cuban people. A forward strategy would also further impede if not stop altogether Castro's training of leftists from other countries in the Americas (including U.S. citizens).

The concept indicated would tie our cause to that of the nations captive under Communist rule—would identify the United States with the hopes and aspirations of the 95 percent of the population of these countries which are non-Communist. Captive Nations Week would become Captive Nations year; exiles, refugees and escapees from Communist rule would be given the opportunity to serve in NATO, SEATO and other allied units under their own colors. We would actively encourage defections, and make more clear than we have to date that the United States welcomes those who seek to escape tyranny, whether it be Nazi, Fascist or Communist.

Because of the realities of today's nuclear age, there are many situations which greatly inhibit our freedom of action. Unfortunately, thus far, we have limited our own freedom of action far more than the other side has. In the case of the Hungarian uprising of 1956, for example, we could easily have recognized the Imre Nagy Government; our Ambassador in Vienna, together with other allied ambassadors, could have gone to Budapest after Nagy came to power to demonstrate our solidarity with his cause, thus constituting a sort of international presence which might well have deterred the Soviets from re-invasion.

Our entire cultural exchange and trade relationships with Communist countries should be re-examined to ascertain their worth within the framework of the proposed forward strategy. The idea of the "pause" after an initial Soviet attack would be abandoned. We would make it very clear that any such attack would result in automatic counterattack either against Soviet missile and air bases or, if too late, against Soviet cities. We would proceed with a full ABM program, never again to engage in unilateral limitation of arms program, research and development.

In the case of Vietnam, we would fully support our allies in Indo-China (including if necessary the reintroduction of U.S. air and naval power until all North Vietnam's forces are permanently withdrawn from Laos and Cambodia).

I cannot say whether such a program would be politically feasible in the United States. But it could be sold, as President Roosevelt sold the policy of internationalism after his famous Quarantine Speech of 1937. Emphasis would be on protective reaction, as practiced by Israel. It could be sold not necessarily as a new policy, but as an extension and improvement of present policy—in order to *more effectively* secure threatened areas of the Free World, and to save lives. We would no longer, in short, wait every time until the other side attacked.

In his remarkable book *The War of the Innocents,* Charles Bacelen Flood notes that most of his writer, publisher and professor friends oppose the defense of southeast Asia (although not of Israel). "They wanted the entire effort liquidated, but to this desire they added a corollary . . . If they could not have it cease altogether, they wanted it limited, held to a minimum of provocative activity. . . . I thought of the face of that dead boy when they carried him past at Polei Djereng. What were we supposed to say to him? Sorry, son, that weapon that killed you might have been destroyed some six hundred miles north of here, but there were policy considerations? The policy considerations, the untested notion that bombing a port in North Vietnam would substantially widen the war, was not going to do that boy any good—he was as dead as he was ever going to be, and we went on letting his brother draftees be attacked from a sanctuary in Cambodia that outflanked South Vietnam."

The spirit of a forward strategy is also reflected in these words of Flood: "The inescapable fact was that if we were not going to do more to put North Vietnam out of action, then we were allowing ourselves to be confronted by a situation in which the struggle between a mighty and indecisive nation and a small and determined one came down to small groups of armed men hunting each other in the jungle. The least we could do was to put in more hunting parties than the other side had, which it was certainly clear that we could do on a population basis alone; but we were not doing it. When we were not trying to hit a mosquito with a hammer . . . we were playing six-man touch against an eleven-man tackle team on the ground."

Chapter 14

CONCLUSIONS

In the topical lexicon of abuse, "cold warrior" is a new vogue term. It denotes a man who is extinct but does not know it, like an Indian Army colonel babbling tales of the Khyber Pass. Yet such use of the term should not be casually accepted, since it involves theses and assumptions that have not been clinically examined.

The central assumption is that "the cold war is ended"—whatever that may mean—though just when such a terminal event occurred is in dispute. Some relate it to the Cuban missile crisis in October 1962; others, such as M. Andre Fontaine of *Le Monde,* tie it to the signature of the test-ban treaty in August 1963. Along with this assumption goes a second: that "the era of the superpowers is over." The world, it is said, is no longer polarized between the United States and the Soviet Union, but has become "multi-polar" or "polycentered," depending on whether one prefers Latin or Greek to garnish his neologisms. Meanwhile, so the thesis runs, we should abandon our efforts to "contain" Soviet power and search for means to "relax tensions" and conjure up a "detente."

The impulse of men to proclaim the ending of eras is an ancient story—particularly when those eras have been neither safe nor pleasant. But before we erect a policy on the assumption of fundamental change, should we not look cautiously to see just how much change has actually occurred? Most important, should we not carefully distinguish between the alteration of material facts and mere shifts in manner or mood. Granted that Moscow and Washington now speak more politely to one another than they once did, is that a firm basis for mutual confidence?

The weight of the evidence falls clearly on the negative side. What is the basis for concluding that the Soviet leaders have abandoned their longtime ambitions? Have they not merely chosen to seek them within the limits of the possible? Only the naive have faith that the Kremlin would refrain from exploiting every possible power advantage were Western Europe to grow flabby. Nor dare we ignore Russia's growing influence in the Middle East, the expansion of her naval power in the Mediterranean or her longer-term ambitions in both the Indian Ocean and the Persian Gulf.

I see no definitive change in Soviet society to suggest a reversal of her strategic intentions. Though the firing squad is now sparingly used, Siberia still threatens the intellectuals. Anti-Semitism in the Soviet Union again rears its obscene head. Stalin's rehabilitation may be imminent. The Berlin wall is built higher, while the Iron Curtain continues to encage 300 million people; and Eastern Europe still lives under a harsh Soviet *diktat,* writ larger by the tanks that destroyed the brief Prague Spring.

These are not words of despair or defeat. Progress should yet be possible in specific areas, such as the SALT talks—if we are only sensible enough—while, over the decades ahead, we can prayerfully hope for the slow convergence of policies and attitudes that could make for a less hazardous world. But the millennium is far distant, and it would be reckless to confuse the wish with the fact.

Thus, I wonder what it means to say "the cold war is over," since, if one should no longer be a "cold warrior," what should he be? A "warm warrior?" A "cool pacifist?" A "frantic detentist?" It is a subject that transcends nomenclature—and, played as more than a parlor game, it could prove dangerous.

Throughout our history, bright tags and slogans have too often led to complacency and the blurring of issues. A half century ago Wilson pronounced a requiem on such "outmoded" concepts as the balance of power and spheres of interest, and a quarter century later Roosevelt repeated the same litany. Yet, incantation cannot alter the fact that the Soviet leaders have all been reared in the Communist faith, that Soviet ambitions remain an inescapable reality of world politics and that faltering or fragmentation on the side of the West would certainly be exploited to Moscow's advantage.

This is the old orthodoxy; if it becomes today's heresy, we may court not only deception but disaster.

On the whole, if one looks back to what has happened over the past quarter-century, and notably since the death of Stalin, those who expected major changes have been wrong more often than the more conservatively-minded interpreters of the Soviet scene. This was as true of a Marxist, like the late Isaac Deutscher who thought that Stalinism was a sort of excrescence on the system and that Khrushchev's "liberalization" was irreversible, as of the American exponents of the "convergence" theory.

Communist ideology itself—which is the Russian rulers' only source of legitimacy—demands that no opportunity be lost to extend its area of control. World revolution cannot be abandoned as a basic commitment, whatever the immediate situation may dictate in the way of restraint.

The turmoil in the "Third World," which seems likely to persist in the '70s, will continue to give opportunities for Soviet penetration and perhaps for the establishment of new areas of control. But one should not proceed from this argument, as is too often done, to assume that such activities will always proceed from a Soviet initiative. On the contrary, the Soviet government has shown (for instance in the Middle East) a strong preference for dealing with and through other governments where possible. The Soviet government's interest in disorder lies in the possibility that the destruction of some existing order can be exploited for the purpose of replacing it by its own.

Nor is this, one may add, a tactic which can be applied only to Third World. If the "New Left" in its various guises succeeds in bringing about chaos in West Berlin, as a sequel to the already almost accomplished destruction of the Free University, the German Communist Party, as an agent of Soviet power, is the most likely beneficiary. And there are other parts of Europe where political instability in the '70s may redound to the ultimate benefit of the Soviet Union without the necessity of direct Soviet intervention or the likelihood of a direct confrontation with the United States.

The other major change in a non-political sense is the acquisition by the Soviet Union of an important naval capacity. It has always been possible to say previously that whatever might differentiate the Soviet Union from the Russian Empire of which it was the heir, both were essentially land powers and were necessarily confined in their possibilities of expansion to areas contiguous to their own frontiers. The failure of the Soviet government to make good a claim to any of the ex-Italian territories in Africa, Khrushchev's inability to hold his advanced military position in Cuba, the extrusion of Soviet influence from the Congo and Ghana—all these could be seen to exemplify the inherently land-locked nature of Soviet power. No one can be certain that this is any longer the case.

The changes in naval armaments, the longer range of nuclear-powered submarines, the possibilities of refueling and servicing at sea with a corresponding decline in the importance of fixed bases such as those which served the once dominant British naval power—all these have helped the Soviet Union to escape from its geographical limitations. It is a naval power in the Mediterranean—though here politics has played its part in making North African ports available—and also in the Red Sea and the Indian Ocean. One must assume that there is no ocean space where Soviet naval power cannot act. Complete freedom of movement has not yet been achieved; the closure of the Suez Canal has been a particular inconvenience; indeed, in trying to fathom Soviet policy in the Middle East one must not forget, as a principal clue, the fact that the Soviet Union is the only important power that seriously suffers from the Canal's continued closure.

It is too early to say what the consequences of this new situation will be. One can only make two general points. First, Soviet naval power is essentially offensive in nature. External sea-borne trade remains and is likely to remain marginal to the Soviet economy; it does not need naval power to safeguard its trade routes. Second, naval power has historically been more flexible and more easily available to pursue particular objectives than land-based strength. We talk as though "gunboat diplomacy" was something as outdated as horse cavalry. But that depends on the purposes and determination of those who have the gunboats. On the other hand, to use naval power effectively and to understand both its possibilities and its limitations demands an expertise of its own which cannot be guaranteed by the mere possession of seagoing vessels. We cannot know whether or how soon this expertise will be acquired. But anyone trying to think about Soviet foreign policy in the '70s must include some assessment of this new element.

The Soviet interventions in East Germany, Hungary and Czechoslovakia have given ample proof of the inability of the Soviet Union to tolerate serious departures from the patterns it has prescribed and of its unwillingness to let the possibility of unpopularity in the West or discontent within Western Communist parties divert it from doing what it has believed to be necessary.

Three conclusions would seem to follow. First, the Soviet Union will not take a different line in the '70s from that which it has taken in the past two decades because there are no new considerations that it has to take into account. We must therefore expect that there will be very severe limitations on what Hungary or Rumania, for instance, can do in the direction of greater independence. We may not have seen the last "intervention."

Second, and more sinister, is the fact that relations with Yugoslavia must be regarded as coming under the heading of "unfinished business." It is impossible that the Soviet leaders should regard the "non-aligned" situation of Yugoslavia and its encouragement of a more humane and decentralized form of socialism as tolerable in the long run. Since, in the order of nature, Marshall Tito can hardly survive the '70s, one of the safest bets to make is that we shall have a Yugoslav crisis on our hands before very long. But because its resolution will depend upon unpredictable attitudes on the part of the United States and its allies, one can hardly say more than that.

Third, the Soviet government may be rather more unwilling than it was in Eastern Europe immediately after the German defeat to rush those countries in which it has influence into full Sovietization. Once it does this, it acquires commitments which, as Cuba has shown for instance, may be awkward and expensive. If existing regimes can be made so dependent militarily or economically that they can be manipulated to suit the Soviet government's purposes, as would seem true of Egypt today, they may for the time being seem a good deal more useful than outright Communist regimes. Such conduct will of course be denounced by the Chinese as showing an unworthy "opportunism," and a determination to put narrow Russian interests before those of the world revolutionary movement, however there is nothing to suggest that the Chinese will not behave in the same manner where it suits them to do so.

The test-case here is of course India. It is in India that Soviet foreign policy has achieved its most considerable successes in the past decade. Despite the long American sympathy for Indian nationalism and the Indian Congress Party, despite the importance to India of American aid, India has clearly been slipping out of non-alignment and into an alignment with Soviet policy on most major issues. That it has so far stood out against the non-proliferation idea is an exception, but not one that appears to worry the Russians overmuch in view of the reasons for India's anxieties. The Chinese pressure to create definite areas of Communist control in parts of India is likely to arouse latent Indian national sentiment and could be counter-productive; the Russian willingness to work through the center, to treat Mrs. Gandhi as another Colonel Nasser, would seem the shrewder course.

Even more important for the '70s must be relations with China itself. China presents peculiar difficulties because it is a dissident Communist country, the particular advantages that it has a non-white poor country in competing with the Soviet Union for influence in the "Third World," and even more important, the fact that unless forcibly prevented it is on the way to becoming a third Superpower by adding a powerful nuclear armory to its existing abundant resources in manpower. The more one reflects upon this threefold threat, local and general, the easier it is to see why relations with China should loom as large as they obviously do with the Soviet leadership, and why there should be so much evidence of divided counsel and vacillation in respect of the policy to be adopted.

What Russia is doing at present to reduce tensions in the West, thereby freeing itself to concentrate increasing power on its eastern borders, is thus natural enough; even its Middle East policy must be understood in relation to this priority of China. However one must add that its opportunities in the Middle East are so considerable that it may well manage to entrench itself further without too many adverse repercussions on its Far Eastern position.

Soviet support of expansionism in Southeast Asia was evidenced by the massive Soviet aid to North Vietnam in the invasion of the South across the DMZ in April, 1972. The USSR and North Vietnam counted on a combination of military superiority and anti-U.S. demonstrations by "peace" groups to achieve their objectives. The Nixon Administration countered with massive airstrikes and the mining of the harbors in North Vietnam. Many feared some new Soviet move in response, but it seemed that Moscow was so desirous of an arms limitation agreement with the United States which would lock in Soviet superiority in ICBMs that it went through with the Brezhnev-Nixon Summit meeting of May, 1972. Out of this came the agreement on arms limitation, which also favored the Soviets in terms of ABMs and nuclear submarines.

If one looks back on international developments over the past decade, it is impossible to avoid the conclusion that Soviet policy has registered impressive gains.

To be sure, since the Cuban confrontation and its blow to Moscow's prestige, there have been other negative developments for the Kremlin. Tension between China and the U.S.S.R. has worsened, causing the Russians to increase their expensive military forces in Asia.

Likewise, the last ten years have seen the Soviets lose more than they have gained in the Arab world. They suffered vast material losses in the Six-Day War. Anti-Russian feeling in Libya waxes. And the blow to Russian influence following expulsion of Moscow's large Egyptian garrison was only fractionally compensated afterward.

But such defeats have been over-balanced by the current Soviet leadership. The Soviet Navy is now the world's second most effective. The Soviet Army is unequaled in a conventional sense. The Soviet nuclear-missile establishment is approximately on a par with America's, and this parity is being ratified in the SALT negotiations.

Soviet diplomacy has managed to secure foreign economic help—notably from the U.S.A., Japan and Western Europe—to compensate for shortfalls, especially in the case of American grain. And Moscow has consolidated its position as a super-capital. It out-maneuvered Washington in the 1971 Bangladesh war and has attained major influence on the Indian subcontinent. Its position in truculent Hanoi is at least as respected as that of Peking.

Finally, the Kremlin has realized a dream to which all Soviet regimes since Stalin's have aspired: formal acceptance of the political *status quo* in Europe. This has not been easy. Throughout the Truman, Eisenhower and Kennedy Administrations the idea was vigorously opposed in Washington.

There have indeed been temporary setbacks: the 1956 Polish upheaval and Hungarian uprising; the Czechoslovakian occupation of 1968; the troubles with heretical Yugoslavia and independent-minded Rumania. But Yugoslavia is now showing dangerous signs of internal discord and potential crisis when President Tito dies. And Rumania is fully aware that its freedom of attitude on foreign matters has rigid limitations.

The courtship of Moscow by France, Germany and America is wholly endorsed in the West but has split political unity in the North Atlantic area. Today there is distinct under-the-table rivalry for advantages in the Soviet market and a distinct undercurrent of mutual suspicions between Europe and the U.S.A.

Chancellor Brandt's victory in the 1972 West German elections, based on an Ostpolitik accepting a divided Germany and the Berlin Wall, was widely hailed everywhere. Yet it was plainly a gain for Moscow since it formalized Europe's *de facto* split.

For Moscow the moment was therefore propitious when preliminary talks on a European security conference opened in Helsinki in 1973. The idea of this conference was first proposed by Moscow in 1954 and was pushed (with Soviet prodding) by Poland and then by Finland. In 1966 Moscow souped up the project. In 1969–70 NATO first responded with serious counterproposals.

The Helsinki meeting was followed by talks on mutual and balanced force reductions (MBFR). The Soviet position was perceptibly enhanced just as these vital negotiations were launched.

Communist rule in East Europe is now implicitly acknowledged by American policy and explicitly confirmed by Bonn. The West also set out along the road to unilateral arms reduction even before MBFR discussions began.

Are all these examples of situations working to Moscow's advantage simply the result of historical accident or extraordinary luck? I think not. I hope I have demonstrated that, while luck and accident have played a part, the most important determinant has been Moscow's steady adherence to Marxist-Leninist ideology in formulating foreign policy.

Communist leaders, through countless temporary setbacks,

have kept their eyes on the ultimate goal of world domination. There is very little hard evidence that they have changed their goals. If this book has contributed in some small measure to understanding the role of ideology in Communist foreign policy, the author will be pleased.

BULLETINS FROM THE DETENTE FRONT

by James Burnham

The policy *of peaceful coexistence . . . is a form of intense economic, political, and ideological struggle of the proletariat against the aggressive forces of imperialism.* (N. Khrushchev, 1961.)

In the view of'the Communists, peaceful coexistence is . . . an active and intense struggle, in the course of which socialism irresistibly attacks, while capitalism suffers one defeat after another. (Sovetskaya Estoniya, 1963.)

The policy of peaceful coexistence . . . has never been a policy based on the acceptance of the status quo in world relations. It has been and it remains a weapon of struggle—a struggle in which both hands are used. With one hand, the aggressive forces of world imperialism are held back; with the other, full support is given to the forces fighting for national independence, and to the peoples moving toward a socialist goal. (World Marxist Review, Moscow, 1965.)

The main direction of the world revolutionary process is de-

termined by the struggle between the two opposite social systems.... Since it is a question of two essentially irreconcilable lines of world development, all countries, classes, social strata, and political currents become involved in the struggle.... Our foreign political measures are restricting further and further the aggressive imperialist circles.... They contribute tò the creation of ever better international circumstances for the expansion of the struggle of the revolutionary forces the world over. (B. Ponomarev, general secretary of the Central Committee of the Soviet CP, 1971.)

Relations with the capitalist nations will remain the relations of struggle, however successful normalization and detente may be.... The essential question is what form that struggle will take. (G. Arbatov, director of the Soviet Institute for American Studies, March 1973.)

Only naive people can expect that recognition of the principles of coexistence by the capitalists can weaken the main contradiction of our times between capitalism and socialism, or that the ideological struggle will be weakened. (Pravda, May 1973.)

Santiago. The Chilean CP, largest in the Americas and the most closely tied to Moscow, pushes Allende toward expropriation of all remaining foreign holdings, beginning with those of U.S. corporations and banks, and toward a total anti-U.S. stand in foreign policy.

Haiphong. A steady parade of Communist-bloc ships brings military equipment sufficient to replace all losses in the 1972 offensive and to beef up forces in Laos, Cambodia, and South Vietnam.

Aden. With Soviet equipment and training, forces in South Yemen move toward strategic goal of overthrowing pro-American government of Saudi Arabia and depriving U.S. of access to its principal foreign source of petroleum.

Oman. Soviet-supported and -equipped Popular Front for the Liberation of Oman and the Arab Gulf (PFLOAG) fights in Dhofar province, aiming at control of Oman and the other oil-rich sheikhdoms along Persian Gulf and southern coast of Arabian Peninsula.

Kuwait City. With Soviet arms and encouragement, Iraqi troops occupy northern strip of Kuwait, enlarging Iraq's access to Gulf. Cadres allied with PFLOAG recruit in Kuwait City and establish guerrilla bases in mountains.

Port Louis, Mauritius. Moscow given access for servicing of Soviet merchant and naval vessels in Indian Ocean.

Mogadishu, Somalia. Soviet technicians, supplies, and money support buildup of harbor as key African control point for Red Sea passage. Moscow arms and supports guerrilla operations against U.S. ally, Ethiopia.

Havana. Soviet KGB completes takeover of Cuban secret police and political subordination of Fidel Castro to Soviet direction.

Belgrade. Soviet Union maneuvers to reintegrate Yugoslavia within Soviet bloc on death of Tito.

Reykjavik. Icelandic Communists, in close liaison with Kremlin, maneuver as part of government coalition to use Cod War as lever for prying Iceland away from NATO and closing down NATO's Keflavik base.

Kiev. KGB carries out new purges of Ukrainian intellectuals and nationalists, paralleling similar purges in Georgia and Baltic states.

Paris. French CP, most closely tied of European CPs to Moscow, presses to increase French aloofness from NATO and to aggravate disputes with U.S.

Moscow. Preparing to welcome larger number of Western businessmen and tourists under detente banner, the Kremlin steps up action to send dissidents to labor camps and KGB mental hospitals, and issues directives warning citizens against close relations with visitors.

Moscow. Preparing for future "mutual balanced force reductions," the Kremlin orders additional heavy equipment and troops into the zones subject to the negotiations.

Moscow. Jamming of VOA broadcasts, prohibition of Western journals and books, and travel restrictions continue in force.

Geneva. Soviet representatives continue to reject "on site" inspection to verify nuclear accords.

Moscow. Deployment of new giant SS-9 missiles continues. A new class of nuclear submarines called "Delta," comparable to advanced U.S. Trident class, is put into production. □

Reprinted by permission from National Review, July 20, 1973.

Index